The Origins of Teapot Dome

UNIVERSITY OF ILLINOIS PRESS, URBANA, 1963

J. Leonard Bates

# THE
# ORIGINS
# OF
# TEAPOT
# DOME

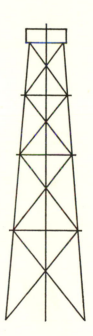

*Progressives, Parties, and Petroleum, 1909-1921*

SECOND PRINTING, 1964

To My Father and to the Memory of My Mother

# Preface

The Teapot Dome scandal first gained national notoriety in 1924. A Senate investigating committee, led by Thomas J. Walsh (Democrat, Montana), was able finally to show that a scandal had indeed occurred and was in some respects without parallel in United States history. The Secretary of the Interior, Albert B. Fall, had accepted "loans" from oil men, to whom he gave leases of United States naval oil reserves. Two other Cabinet members were involved, one of them rather innocently. All three, however, left the Cabinet, and two were really driven from it. Fall eventually went to jail for his part in the affair. Since this was a Republican era, Republican leaders became alarmed, for the revelations of corruption seriously threatened the Grand Old Party. Nevertheless, Republicans swept the election of 1924 and continued apparently to have the confidence of the country until the depression of 1929.

Such is a bare outline of the scandal, with customary emphasis on the 1920's. In this book, what was originally intended to be an over-all study of Teapot Dome has turned out to be a study of origins. The reasons are twofold. First, I became convinced that the background of this affair is important, although no one but John Ise has written at length about it (*The United States Oil Policy*, 1926). Second, I was fortunate enough to gain access to sources unavailable to earlier writers. Personal manuscripts and archival manuscripts are rich and varied. As a result it is possible to trace this oil question from Taft to Harding, with considerable awareness of the many points of view, the maneuvering among disputants, and conflicts that occurred.

The question is essentially one of conservation policy. But people disagree over the meaning of conservation, and policy is shaped by government officials subject to manifold pressures. Teapot Dome, it seems clear, cannot be understood without reference to many things: the Navy's need for fuel oil, the petroleum industry and attitudes of its leaders, the reform urge in both political parties, economic sectionalism (the West versus the East), organization politics, the effects of World War I, and so on.

The story is hardly a simple one. It has been for the writer one of considerable fascination, starting some years ago with work on Senator Thomas J. Walsh.

This book has been a cooperative project. I have benefited immensely from the work and financial support of others. The University of Illinois has given grants for research purposes and its library staff has helped in innumerable ways. Above all, the University has provided research assistants: Robert M. Albert, Harold F. Cahalan, Ralph A. Stone, and Richard A. Swanson—to each of whom my debt is great. "Harry" Cahalan not only helped in the beginning, he came back to rescue me at the end. Travel and additional research were made possible by grants from the Social Science Research Council.

In far less space than they deserve, thanks should be given to the following libraries and their staffs: the Library of Congress, and especially the Manuscripts Division; the National Archives, especially the Justice Department section, Navy section, and Interior Department section; the Duke University Library; the University of Wyoming Library, with especial gratitude to Gene Gressley; the Bancroft Library of the University of California at Berkeley; the Henry E. Huntington Library, San Marino, California.

Then there are those who have helped in other ways, who have read the manuscript or portions of it, and who have generously shared some of their findings. It is impossible to list them all. Frederick C. Dietz and J. Rogers Hollingsworth have recently read the manuscript and given excellent suggestions. Arthur E. Bestor, Jr., E. James Ferguson, Herbert H. Kaplan, Clark C. Spence, Ralph A. Stone, Robert M. Sutton, and Richard A. Swanson at one stage or another have read portions of the manuscript. Others have shared with me some of their notes. Wesley M. Bagby, E. David Cronon, and Richard Lowitt are among them. Conversations with Fola La Follette in Washington, D.C., were quite rewarding, as was a talk with the late Walter Lee Summers of the University of Illinois Law School. Jack De Long of the Sun Oil Company was kind enough to give me a guided tour of Teapot Dome and the Salt Creek oil field. On countless occasions, Dorothy Pettit Bates, my wife, has contributed sound advice or criticism. Finally, I assume responsibility for the manuscript in its present form.

# Contents

# Perspectives

**CHAPTER I**

---

*But, gentlemen, the difficulties here presented, arise from a difference in point of view. The mind and opinion of the West is one way; the mind and opinion of the East and the South is another.*

Isidore B. Dockweiler, Democratic national committeeman from Los Angeles, February 26, 1918

---

1

The long fight over public oil lands, which culminated in the Teapot Dome scandal, was the result of several contemporaneous occurrences: discoveries of petroleum in the western United States, a rising demand for petroleum products, and a rising conservation movement. Those who wished to "develop" oil lands ran head on into those who wished to "conserve," or regulate, the United States Navy aligning itself with the forces of conservation. The struggle was bitter. It swirled through the Taft, Wilson, Harding, and Coolidge administrations, and was much affected by the varying fortunes of political leaders and by great events—notably World War I. In a general way, the differences were sectional. Western oil men and politicians resented interference from Washington, D.C., and fought for local and sectional interests as best they could. In many respects, however, the times were against them.

The oil question was entangled with politics. Both oil and politics in the early twentieth century were affected by "progressivism," for men came to believe in government as a positive instrument. They wished to retain special virtues of the American way and to regain some virtues that appeared lost. Evils associated with big business, monopoly, special privilege, and corruption must be rooted out. Government must be brought closer to the people. Economic opportunities should be enlarged partly through government intervention, trying to assure fair play. There was a widespread reaction against the materialism of the "Gilded Age."

Progressives also believed in executive leadership, or stewardship. This quality was dramatized by Theodore Roosevelt and Woodrow Wilson and by powerful figures in public life like Gifford Pinchot. Where public land policy was concerned, executive leadership had a unique importance. Recommendations for withdrawal of oil lands from private sale or acquisition came from the executive departments. Likewise they called for the establishment of special petroleum reserves for the Navy. Opposition was centered in the Congress, primarily among representatives and senators from public land states.

Progressivism was never quite the same after 1914, when war came to Europe. The new emphasis was nationalism, patriotism, industrial production, preparedness. Nevertheless, the spirit of progressivism was not lost. Fighting reformers like Gifford Pinchot, Robert M. La Follette, and Josephus Daniels had an influence far out of proportion to their numbers. They benefited to some extent from the militancy of wartime. Government controls over business were tightened. Special interests often were sacrificed. The Navy in its struggle with a powerful oil lobby benefited because of a growing demand for a Navy second to none, which could be obtained only by conceding to the Navy many of its wishes in the matter of fuel oil and petroleum reserves.

Progressive-conservationist leaders were constantly in the fight over public oil lands. Without the conservation movement, there would have been no naval oil reserves. Without a determination to carry forward this movement, the naval reserves would have disappeared before 1920. Therefore, conservation is the framework within which Teapot Dome, and its origins, may be understood.

## 2

Conservation as it developed under Theodore Roosevelt and Gifford Pinchot was a coordinated program. There was never any doubt that petroleum lands, forest lands, and other resources must be treated on a specialized basis. Yet behind the diverse policies lay a common purpose: to use intelligently, justly, and democratically the nation's natural resources. All of conservation, therefore, had meaning for the petroleum lands.

Organized conservationists grew increasingly concerned with economic justice and democracy. One aspect of the matter was the price and income situation, the actual monetary rewards from the marvelous wealth of this land. Conservationists believed that somehow the common heritage, the socially created resources and institutions, had passed into the hands of vested interests and that the benefits were being siphoned into the hands of a few. There were several ways in which this situation might be remedied, as they saw it: first, through land withdrawals, to hold on to the remaining public lands at least temporarily, in order to prevent further monopolization; second, to attempt to give the people a fuller share of opportunities and profits; and finally, in that period of low income, to keep prices proportionately low.

The monopolists who maintained prices were anathema, even though their methods might contribute to conservation by reducing consumption. Conservation through penalizing the public was something which democratically motivated leaders were not prepared to accept. In dealing with the petroleum industry antimonopoly feelings ran unusually strong.

The conservationists' approach was broad. They believed in government studies and safeguards for the preservation of irreplaceable resources such as petroleum. They recognized and struggled with problems which remain today only partially solved. They understood the need for federal leadership in an organic structure based on the unity of nature itself. They made mistakes, of course. Like most progressives, they concluded too easily that the opposition on a particular issue consisted of "robber barons," conspirators, and frauds. Yet at times they were capable of a surprising detachment. A key conservationist, for example, referred admiringly to a "very scholarly and fine" argument that the public domain should be turned over to the states.[1]

---

[1] Harry Slattery to Gifford Pinchot, October 7, 1919, Gifford Pinchot Papers, Box 1842, Library of Congress. There can be no doubt that fighting conservationists, such as those described above, played a major part in the story of Teapot Dome. The entire, broad conservation movement is more

In a sense the conservation movement was a nonpartisan, statesmanlike cause, winning support from scientists, politicians, and others all over the country. But a fact of long-range significance was its Republican origins as an organized effort. Many Republicans were proud of their work and almost fanatically devoted to Roosevelt. They did not easily dissociate the Republican party or the "Republican Roosevelt," who had first given them their chance, from the body of their accomplishments.

The career of Gifford Pinchot seemed to touch upon everything relating to conservation. As head of the Forest Service from 1905 to 1910 he fought for principles of unified resource management: for a sustained yield in the national forest lands; for grazing within the forest areas on payment of a fee; for leasing of water power sites, rather than giving them up permanently to private control. In other ways as well the activities of the Forest Service were expanded. Not the least influential was a skillful, vigorously conducted publicity campaign.

Pinchot had boundless energy and enthusiasm, and possessed unusual qualities of intellect, character, and leadership; he was an aristocrat devoting himself to public service. By 1916—as a private citizen and conservation leader—he was directly involved in the fight over public oil lands.[2]

Many of the leaders associated with Pinchot after 1908 were lawyers. Conservation was entering a phase by 1910 in which legal minds grappled over words and phrases, or over decisions of almost appalling magnitude. Opponents of the movement had

difficult to interpret. See the following valuable studies: Samuel P. Hays, *Conservation and the Gospel of Efficiency: The Progressive Conservation Movement, 1890–1920*, Cambridge, Mass., 1959; M. Nelson McGeary, *Gifford Pinchot: Forester-Politician*, Princeton, N.J., 1960; Harold T. Pinkett, "Gifford Pinchot and the Early Conservation Movement in the United States," unpublished Ph.D. dissertation, American University, Washington, D.C., 1953; Erich W. Zimmermann, *Conservation in the Production of Petroleum: A Study in Industrial Control*, New Haven, Conn., 1957. See also the author's "Fulfilling American Democracy: The Conservation Movement, 1907–1921," *Mississippi Valley Historical Review*, XLIV (June, 1957), 29–57.

[2] See Pinchot, "How Conservation Began," *Agricultural History*, XI (October, 1937), 255–265; Roy M. Robbins, *Our Landed Heritage*, Princeton, N.J., 1942, p. 337; Theodore Roosevelt, *An Autobiography*, New York, 1926, chap. xi; Amos R. E. Pinchot, *History of the Progressive Party, 1912–1916*, edited by Helene M. Hooker, New York, 1958, editor's Biographical Introduction, especially pp. 7–20.

been able in the past to retain the finest advice. Expert lawyers now stood ready to defend the new policies of resource management. James R. Garfield, son of the former President, and Walter L. Fisher of Chicago were figures of importance. Garfield served the Roosevelt administration first in the Department of Commerce and Labor and in 1907 became Secretary of the Interior. Fisher succeeded Richard A. Ballinger as Secretary of the Interior during the Taft administration and moved within the inner circle of conservationists.

Other lawyers were Philip P. Wells, George W. Woodruff, and Harry A. Slattery. These three in particular were experts in their understanding of knotty legal problems that arose from land withdrawals and impending legislation. Wells and Woodruff, like Pinchot, were graduated in the Yale class of 1889. Wells went ahead to do graduate work at Yale in economics and history, and in 1900 he received his Ph.D. He also studied law, was librarian of the Yale Law School, and found time for research and writing. In 1906 Pinchot brought Wells to Washington. He served first as chief law officer with the Forest Service and later in the same capacity with the Reclamation Service. Both in and out of government he acted as a special adviser to Pinchot. Woodruff was a former Yale football great and a genial and able friend whom Pinchot brought into the Forest Service as his first law officer. He served later in the Interior Department and after leaving government service was one of Pinchot's trusted advisers. Slattery came later into the Pinchot circle. Good friends and brilliant lawyers, these men worked effectively for the principles of the conservation program.[3]

After 1909 the rallying point for conservationists became the National Conservation Association, with headquarters in Washington, D.C. This organization was in part a reaction against standpatters in Congress but also against President Taft, whose leadership was considered weak. The forces of Pinchot and Roosevelt decided that action was demanded. They formed the Association, a private body, with Charles W. Eliot, former president of Harvard, serving briefly as president. Pinchot succeeded him, with Harry Slattery as secretary, and with Philip Wells as one

---

[3] Pinchot, *Breaking New Ground*, New York, 1947, pp. 302–305.

of its counsels. Among the directors were Jane Addams, Carrie Chapman Catt, Samuel Gompers, Judge Ben Lindsey of Denver, and Irvine L. Lenroot of the House of Representatives.

The Association's effectiveness stemmed in large part from the abilities of Harry Slattery as executive secretary, with headquarters near the Capitol. According to Roosevelt, the Association had first to prevent bad legislation in order to protect public resources from monopoly; second, it had to guide through Congress the best of conservation measures. In the opinion of W J McGee, a pioneering conservationist, the Association had become the "legitimate repository and exponent of conservation doctrine, and the accepted leader of the Conservation Movement, more especially in its moral aspect." Charles R. Van Hise saw it as the propaganda agent of the movement.

With understandable prejudice, Pinchot reviewed its work in 1921 and concluded that "no other Association has exerted anything like so large an influence in proportion to its membership and expenditures. It has overcome, not once, but many times, the efforts of the greatest lobbies ever assembled in Washington." [4] He gave Slattery much of the credit.

A native of South Carolina, Slattery completed his education at Georgetown University and George Washington University and remained in the capital. In 1909, still in his early twenties, he became secretary to Pinchot. A short time later he took over the job with the National Conservation Association. Slattery was an informal and amiable person, folksy in his speech but sharp of mind. People liked him and relied upon him. He was informed on history, law, and economics, but most especially on politics and personalities—the Washington scene. Liberal if not radical, he conceived of himself and the Association as the "watchdog" of conservation.[5]

Slattery and also Philip Wells, as hard-working, little-known specialists, were to figure importantly and perhaps decisively in the petroleum fight.

[4] Pinchot to Howard B. Gill (quoting Roosevelt), September 19, 1921, Pinchot Papers, Box 1846; W J McGee, "The Conservation of Natural Resources," Mississippi Valley Historical Association, *Proceedings for the Year 1909–1910,* III (1911), 375; Charles R. Van Hise, *The Conservation of Natural Resources,* New York, 1913, p. 12.

[5] Slattery to Pinchot, February 28, 1921, Pinchot Papers, Box 1846. Admiration of Slattery and his work was well-nigh universal among the pro-

# 3

Inevitably there were things which divided the conservationists as a whole: disagreements over methods and over goals, sectional rivalries, disputes between Democrats and Republicans, the clashing of personalities. Also, any issue or event could impinge upon conservation with divisive results.

In general, those accepting the designation of "conservationist" were progressive, believing in the necessity of strong executive leadership and federal action. In some instances they were radicals or outright socialists. On the other hand, they sometimes emphasized as heavily as did President Taft the authority of Congress, the statutory system that must be erected, the quieting of any doubts as to constitutionality. And it was not unusual for a conservationist to consider himself a conservative—one who believed in decent and orderly processes. Representative James R. Mann of Illinois, for example, might be linked politically with "Uncle Joe" Cannon's Old Guard, but the Pinchot forces treasured him as one of their most dependable allies.[6]

There were regional variations. The southerner who favored conservation differed from the northerner or westerner. Southerners were influenced by traditions of agrarianism and anti-monopoly action as well as by the fact (unkindly noted by Pinchot) that the lands to be conserved and "saved" were mostly outside their region.

One charge was endlessly repeated against the conservationists with the effect of creating cleavages in the ranks. The Pinchot policy, it was alleged, resolved into keeping resources in cold storage, or under lock and key, or hermetically sealed. Critics implied that Pinchot and his adherents had no interest in jobs and opportunities for the people of the West; that they cared nothing for necessary development.

---

gressives and conservationists. See, for example, Wiliam Kent to Pinchot, May 18, 1922, *ibid.*, Box 457; Robert M. La Follette, quoted in Belle C. and Fola La Follette, *Robert M. La Follette*, 2 vols., New York, 1953, II, 942–943.

[6] Slattery to Pinchot, August 21, 1919, Pinchot Papers, Box 1842. For an examination of the diversity of opinion on conservation see Elmo R. Richardson, *The Politics of Conservation: Crusades and Controversies, 1897–1913*, Berkeley, Calif., 1962; also Lawrence Rakestraw, "The West, States' Rights, and Conservation: A Study of Six Public Land Conferences," *Pacific Northwest Quarterly*, XLVIII (July, 1957), 89–99.

As the *Standard Oil Bulletin* (Standard of California) saw the situation: "Unfortunately, since conservation theories have entered our politics, politicians, for want of abilities to prevent waste, deem it their duty to prevent development." The Standard Oil Company, on the other hand, had "consistently aimed at true conservation—the prevention of waste. . . ." [7]

Expressing a similar point of view, Senator Charles S. Thomas, Democrat from Colorado, was more caustic:

The average conservationist—I will not say it applies to all of them—is very much concerned about conserving other people, but when it comes to a personal application of the doctrine he is not so enthusiastic. I believe the gentleman who claims to be the great progenitor, the father of conservation is the Hon. Gifford Pinchot, at one time chief adviser to President Roosevelt, forester of the United States, and one of the founders and leaders of the late lamented Progressive Party. He it was who discovered that the way to conserve was to reserve, and that the way to develop was to keep everything petrified and stagnant. To him, so far as his actions are concerned, the American Indian . . . was the ideal conservationist. . . .[8]

From 1910 to 1912 two dramatic events had the effect of reorienting the conservation movement. First, there was the Ballinger-Pinchot controversy, in which Pinchot became a critic of the Secretary of the Interior and was fired from his job as chief United States forester. Pinchot and the progressives convinced themselves that President Taft had been a traitor to their cause; that the Secretary of the Interior, Richard A. Ballinger of Seattle, had yielded to the big interests; and that the majority report, after a congressional investigation, was a "whitewash." Democrats were delighted to echo these charges.

Whatever the exact meaning of this affair, many progressives never forgave Taft. They did not doubt that Ballinger was in league with the Guggenheims, nor forget that such a man as Edwin Denby (later Secretary of the Navy under Harding) had been among the "whitewashers" in Congress. On the other side, Taft was reported as believing that Pinchot was "a socialist and a spiritualist . . . capable of any extreme act." [9]

---

[7] "Conservation," *Standard Oil Bulletin*, III (July, 1915), 1–2.
[8] *Cong. Record*, 66 Cong., 1 Sess., pp. 4255–56, August 23, 1919. See also Representative Sylvester C. Smith of California in *ibid.*, 61 Cong., 2 Sess., pp. 5062–63, April 20, 1910; Senator Thomas J. Walsh of Montana to R. S. Hamilton, October 19, 1918, Thomas J. Walsh Papers, Library of Congress.
[9] Amos Pinchot to Gifford Pinchot, February 26, 1921, Pinchot Papers, Box

The second event was the election of 1912. As the Republicans argued and fell apart, Woodrow Wilson came to the White House. For the first time a Democratic administration had to cope with twentieth-century problems, including conservation. The relations between upper-class Republicans who had put vigor into conservation policy and the newly installed Democrats who tried to carry it forward were well-nigh predictable. Prospects of mutual satisfaction were dim.

The state of Wisconsin and its leaders played a significant role in the conservation movement and in the making of petroleum policy. Robert M. La Follette was most outstanding. In addition, there was Irvine L. Lenroot, who served first in the House and later in the Senate. Paul O. Husting, unlike the other two, was a Democrat. Elected to the Senate in 1914, he collaborated closely with Harry Slattery and Philip Wells.

La Follette and Lenroot also worked with the Pinchot group— each in his own way. The two Wisconsinites had differences, dating back to the Republican split of 1912. La Follette had sought the Republican nomination in that year, and had depended upon his old friend and fellow progressive, Lenroot, for support. But Lenroot, Pinchot, and most of the progressives went over to Theodore Roosevelt. La Follette felt that he had been betrayed, and he and the Roosevelt men were never to become fully reconciled. In Wisconsin politics, La Follette and Lenroot became bitter opponents.[10]

At the same time, however, the forces of La Follette and Pinchot could work together in a common cause. In February–March, 1919, they defeated the so-called Pittman mineral leasing bill, an anticonservationist measure which they considered obnoxious. It was La Follette who argued and filibustered successfully against the mineral leasing bill with materials supplied by the Conservation Association. And two years later (1921) it was La Follette,

---

241; Archie Butt to Clara Butt, April 12, 1910, in *Taft and Roosevelt: The Intimate Letters of Archie Butt, Military Aide,* 2 vols., Garden City, N.Y., 1930, I, 327–328.

[10] La Follette, *Robert M. La Follette,* I, 420–424; Robert S. Maxwell, *La Follette and the Rise of the Progressives in Wisconsin,* Madison, Wis., 1956, pp. 166, 192–194, and *passim.* Part of their difficulty was a conflict over foreign affairs. See "Lenroot and La Follette: A Contrast," *Outlook,* CXV (April 18, 1917), 691; Irvine L. Lenroot, "The War Loyalty of Wisconsin," *Forum,* LIX (June, 1918), 695–712.

again assisted by Slattery and Wells, who instigated the Teapot Dome investigation.

La Follette and Pinchot operated differently, though this was no discredit to either. The Wisconsinite had neither the disposition nor the opportunity for bartering favors with Wilson (after 1916), nor with Harding, Coolidge, and others of the Republican Old Guard. His forte was to attack, to filibuster, to block "giveaways," to tack on remedial amendments, to force concessions, to rally the left wing. With Pinchot it was a different story. In each Congress, in each administration, Pinchot as president of the National Conservation Association would try to place his men, would distribute his propaganda, would try to win support. Just as the special interests lobbied to influence policy, so did he. As an additional moderating influence there were without doubt Pinchot's political ambitions. He was available, for instance, for a place in Harding's Cabinet, and a conciliatory course was sometimes prudent. He would agitate from within if possible, or he would attack from without if necessary.

## 4

Woodrow Wilson's administration was a critical time for conservation policy. Essentially he inherited from Roosevelt and Taft the problem of formulating new laws so that withdrawn lands could be developed, under leases to private parties subject to federal supervision. Wilson wished to achieve a leasing system. His great difficulty came, first, from those who opposed absolutely a policy of continuing federal ownership and administration; second, from those who would not accept a system of leases unless the terms were quite liberal. Western leaders insisted that public lands of their states be opened to development.

The question of petroleum lands grew urgent. Wilson's Cabinet reflected eastern and western viewpoints and was divided; Congress was divided on somewhat the same lines. Wilson could not but give some consideration to the political aspects of this issue, to the necessity of holding together the eastern and western wings of the Democratic party. Concessions to the West might be advisable. Yet he knew too that conservation was a bipartisan policy which had gained wide acceptance and that any weakening on his part would bring criticism. The Pinchot group especially would be watching for aberrations, and they would be quick to attack.

The struggle that occurred was a many-sided one. As in preceding administrations it involved the authority of executive officers to withdraw petroleum lands and to establish naval petroleum reserves. This authority was the very basis of the new petroleum policy. It was challenged by western oil men and their lawyers and by various supporters in state or federal offices. However, after several years of doubt the United States Supreme Court in 1915 sided with the executive branch, and petroleum withdrawals were sustained.

Meanwhile three departments began to make war upon each other. The Navy and Justice Departments had been proceeding on the assumption that the land withdrawals were valid. By court action they intended to remove trespassers or probable trespassers from government land. Suits were brought claiming damages, and where necessary government receivers were envisaged. They wished also to achieve new laws fully protecting the government's interests. In these efforts, Josephus Daniels as Secretary of the Navy and Thomas W. Gregory as Attorney General received warm support from the Pinchot group and a variety of conservation leaders. Until 1919, President Wilson consistently gave his backing.

The Interior Department, however, was taking a different course. Headed by Franklin K. Lane of California, it identified itself with the western, developmental point of view. In 1915 Lane approved certain claims of the Honolulu Oil Company, inside Naval Reserve No. 2 (Buena Vista Hills, California). The Navy Department contested this decision, and with the support of the Justice Department was able to prevent the issuance of patents. Gifford Pinchot joined in the argument with a personal attack upon Secretary Lane; he also indicted Lane's chief, President Wilson. This was in 1916, during the presidential campaign.

The character of the struggle over petroleum lands had now taken shape. Progressive-conservationists in both parties were capable of working together for a bipartisan policy, but they could not forget their political affiliations, especially in election years. At the same time neither party as a political organization could withstand the relentless pressure for a liberal land policy with concessions to western interests. That pressure was to increase. Much depended upon the individuals in high office—called upon repeatedly to make decisions affecting the western lands.

## 5

The oil leasing question was an old one by 1921. In every Congress after 1909 the disposal or the administration of petroleum lands was a subject of debate. Some twenty congressional hearings were devoted to it. Senator La Follette traced his part in the affair back to 1906, when he discussed with Theodore Roosevelt a bill for the coal and oil lands. In 1921–22, therefore, when the Teapot Dome lease came under Senate investigation and ordinary citizens heard of that tract in Wyoming for the first time, many senators were well versed in the subject. Just as they debated antitrust policy with a knowledge of the origins of the Sherman Law and the Clayton Law, they debated petroleum matters with a knowledge of the background sketched in the preceding pages. The past was inseparable from the present. Political implications were keenly remembered.

In an extended debate of April 29, 1922, Senators La Follette, John B. Kendrick, George W. Norris, William E. Borah, and Henry Cabot Lodge—among others—discussed the origins of "Teapot Dome." They disagreed on many points of interpretation, but they all knew it was an old question with political overtones. George Norris expressed cogently an idea widely held. There should not be, he said, a strictly party interpretation of the oil leasing affair. The parties had been divided; the Wilson Cabinet had been divided. "I happen to know," he declared, "that there was a great contest on in that administration and that Secretary Daniels represented one side of it." The attempt at conservation of petroleum was "a policy that originated before he [Wilson] became President of the United States." Norris concluded: "To the extent that he carried it out, he is entitled to praise, if any praise is due anyone." [11]

Josephus Daniels, who could qualify as the world's outstanding expert on this subject—having been in the middle of it from 1913 to 1921—agreed essentially with Senator Norris. He refused

---

[11] *Cong. Record,* 67 Cong., 2 Sess., pp. 6097–6103, April 29, 1922.

to identify the oil scandals with the Republicans, as a party. Rather, he gave a general, fatalistic interpretation: "The trail of oil" marked the "decadence of idealism and stability in recent years" (1924); the Allies had "sailed to victory in a sea of oil," and oil had permeated the postwar world.[12]

This dispute over the leasing of public oil lands was a complex, tangled, and litigious affair. No short or facile explanation could provide much light. The beginnings went back to the Taft administration and the petroleum industry of that time, to land reformers and those who resisted reform, for whatever reason.

[12] Daniels in *Helena* (Montana) *Independent*, February 17, 1924.

# Groping for a New Oil Policy

CHAPTER II

---

*Human nature is very much the same everywhere. It is the same in my State; it is the same in Wyoming; it is the same in California. The ordinary citizen feels that anything that he can divest his Government of and give to himself with color of honor he ought to do it.*

Representative Scott Ferris (Democrat, Oklahoma), May 25, 1918

---

1

The oil policy of the United States originated as an integral part of the nineteenth-century land system. This meant "catch as catch can" exploration and discovery. But as the oil industry flourished and spread from coast to coast, the United States was sharply modifying its attitude toward public lands. Progressives and realistic thinkers were aware that some degree of government supervision had become necessary. It was apparent, too, that opportunities for the imaginative and daring prospector, or venturesome corporation, must not be eliminated. New sources of supply must be found. As oil men themselves saw the situation, in spite of some disagreement, the role of government must be kept to a minimum.

By its nature, the oil business was speculative, competitive, exploitative, and materialistic. W. L. Connelly has recalled the early days with Sinclair: "Oil was money, and the scramble for it was earnest and relentless." [1] Black Gold! Perhaps the very color, in a day of color-consciousness and romanticism, added to stories of sinister machinations by oil men and oil interests. One ob-

---

[1] W. L. Connelly, *The Oil Business as I Saw It: Half a Century with Sinclair,* Norman, Okla., 1954, p. 30.

server in the oil fields of Pennsylvania commented that the lust for wealth led to "every imaginable kind of misrepresentation and cheating." "In every transaction involving profit and loss, false-hood is expected, is looked upon as the rule, truth as the exception." A modern scholar has concluded that in the period around 1910, lawlessness was to be expected in each field, following the pattern of earlier ones; ". . . ruthless methods were common. Business ethics had not yet invaded the oil fields." [2]

Since oil was money and no man knew where it might be discovered, furtive operations were characteristic. The object was, if oil were discovered, to keep the secret and buy up adjacent tracts cheaply; or to keep one's eyes open and move into promising territory. Communications must be guarded, drillers must be sworn to secrecy, intruders must be chased away by shotgun fire if need be.

All of this was a source of concern to government officials. Information about drilling and production was hard to elicit. Meanwhile, oil men were intensely interested in discovering government secrets, the latest results of geological surveys, government intentions with respect to sale or leasing of its lands, or facts about prospective litigation. Information was precious. Spies might be anywhere. A case in point was the caution exercised by the commissioner of the General Land Office in a letter written in 1912. He told his chief, the Secretary of the Interior, about certain claimants to public oil land in Wyoming. The government was preparing a suit, and the commissioner revealed details of his strategy for the benefit of the Secretary's office. He went on to suggest, however, that these details should not be disclosed, that the information should be employed only in a general way. "When this has been done this correspondence [should] be returned direct to this office without passing through the Mails & Files Division, to be placed with the confidential records in the case in the General Land Office." [3]

Whatever was true of the oil industry, or was thought to be true, contributed to shaping the attitudes of government officials.

---

[2] Quotation in John Ise, *The United States Oil Policy*, New Haven, Conn., 1926, p. 36; Carl C. Rister, *Oil! Titan of the Southwest*, Norman, Okla., 1949, pp. 156, 186.
[3] Fred Dennett to Walter L. Fisher, August 23, 1912, Secretary's File, Department of the Interior, National Archives.

They could not but be influenced by suspicions of dishonesty and fraud where malpractices were known to be common. From independent oil men and from investigators and scholars they heard another charge: *monopoly!* The Standard Oil Company, or its so-called community of interest, was usually the butt of these attacks.

What were the facts, as best they may be ascertained, about the power of Standard Oil? At the turn of the century it was the dominating influence in the industry. Of many evidences, the best is that in its refineries were manufactured more than 75 per cent of the nation's oil products. Gradually its importance declined as petroleum fields were opened up in Texas, Kansas, Oklahoma, Louisiana, Arkansas, Wyoming, and California. Powerful new companies came into existence such as Gulf, the Texas Company, Phillips Petroleum, the Midwest Oil Company (Wyoming), Sinclair, the Southern Pacific group in California, and the organizations of E. L. Doheny. Also the Standard Oil Company was investigated, "exposed" in government reports, attacked in state and federal courts, and finally dissolved in 1911 by decision of the United States Supreme Court. Its thirty-three subsidiaries officially became independent. But according to a report of the Federal Trade Commission in 1915 citing dates, names, and figures, "a majority of the stock" of the numerous companies was still controlled by "a small group composed of the same individuals, trustees, or corporations." [4]

The Standard interests had their units and agents virtually all over the country. In a few instances a former affiliate grew so rapidly as to constitute in its own right a powerful monopoly; for example, Standard of Indiana. Considering the notoriety of Rockefeller and his Standard associates before 1911, and the continuing power of these men, it is not surprising that governmental leaders distrusted and feared them.

New companies operating independently of Standard Oil adopted the methods of that pioneer in monopolization. In particular areas, they were more powerful than Standard. Each had

---

[4] U.S. Federal Trade Commission, *Report on the Price of Gasoline in 1915,* Washington, 1917, pp. 144–146; cf. Ise, pp. 226–227, Rister, pp. 188–189; Gerald T. White, *Formative Years in the Far West: A History of Standard Oil Company of California and Predecessors Through 1919,* New York, 1962, pp. 376–385 and *passim.*

its properties and lease-holdings, its staff of lawyers, geologists, and scientists, its pipeline system, its various installations, its strategically placed friends. The pipelines were often vital. In 1914 David T. Day of the United States Geological Survey commented: "It has been a characteristic feature of the United States petroleum industry, and *not* characteristic elsewhere in the world, that no matter how remote from transportation an oil field may be located, if the field is considerable in size, it will be promptly connected with some pipeline transportation company, usually associated with the Standard Oil Company." [5] Local pipelines could, of course, be managed in a discriminatory fashion. Indeed, interstate pipelines were also used to the discouragement of independents through forcing them to sell before transporting their oil. Thus, prices could be dictated. The Interstate Commerce Commission, at least until 1914, exercised no effective control. [6]

## 2

It was the public oil lands which stirred government officials into action. Here they had a direct responsibility for conservation of resources and for honest and orderly development. Oil was being overproduced and wasted in the public land states, notably California and Wyoming. The problem became serious and urgent. So a new policy evolved, from the pressure of petroleum discoveries and from a growing realization of the tremendous importance of oil products.

How rich were the publicly owned oil lands? The recoverable oil of the United States in January, 1917, was fixed by the Geological Survey at 5,965,000,000 barrels. Of this, privately held lands were thought to contain 5,280,000,000, so that the public lands had less than one-eighth of the estimated total. [7] Yet no one knew where a gusher might be struck. These lands were precious enough, if one could get them. Moreover, according to law at least until 1909 they were open for the taking—virtually free.

---

[5] David T. Day, "Fuel Oils: Their Origin, Production and Treatment," *United States Naval Institute Proceedings*, XL (January–February, 1914), 96.

[6] John A. DeNovo, "Petroleum and the United States Navy Before World War I," *Mississippi Valley Historical Review*, XLI (March, 1955), 652–654; Day, "Fuel Oils," p. 96.

[7] George Otis Smith, memorandum for the Secretary of the Interior, June 23, 1917, Secretary's File.

Prospectors were active. Politicians, having jurisdiction at least potentially, were interested.

California after 1900 took its place as one of the exciting new petroleum states. Estimates by the Geological Survey gave California two-thirds of the oil supply in all public lands of the United States. In its private lands this single state was thought to have one-third of the national supply.[8] Small wonder that Californians were interested in oil and the government's oil policy. This state, whose population increased from 1,485,053 in 1900 to almost double that in 1914, and whose delegation in the House of Representatives jumped from eight in 1912 to eleven in 1914, was to be the center of the controversy over oil in the Wilson period.

Second in importance among the public land states was Wyoming, a promising area of feverish activity. Its production by 1917 reached almost 9,000,000 barrels—one-tenth of California's output, but an impressive showing.

The center for the petroleum offices and oil men's gatherings in the entire Rocky Mountain area was Denver, while on the West Coast, San Francisco was the focus of the oil business. A metropolis of commerce and finance, it had just risen from the earthquake of 1906. Los Angeles also grew rapidly, along with the oil business. To these cities, or to towns such as Bakersfield, California, and Casper, Wyoming, came a stream of interested people: lawyers representing the oil companies, naval officers concerned with protecting their petroleum reserves, special assistants to the Attorney General, investigators for the General Land Office.

Of basic importance in the western land situation was the mining law, or placer law, for only by its terms could patents ordinarily be obtained. This law had originally been passed for surface metals like gold, and much trouble resulted from the attempt to use it also for liquid petroleum in pools underground. Almost everyone agreed that the law was defective.

The main problem was "discovery." To be successful the prospector had to find oil in a quantity sufficient for commercial operation. Having made discovery, he could file in the Land

---

[8] *Ibid.* See also Ralph Arnold, "The California Oil Industry," *Journal of Geography,* IX (June, 1911), 270–272; Robert Glass Cleland and Osgood Hardy, *March of Industry,* San Francisco, 1929, pp. 167–193.

Office. He was then a "locator" and could proceed to patent. An individual might acquire twenty acres, or eight members of an association might share in the possession of 160 acres. It was necessary to have a total expenditure of $500 in developing any claim and to pay the government $2.50 an acre for the land. There was no limit to the number of claims that might be asserted, provided only that the requirements were met for each.[9]

Manifestly, the law contained complexities and ambiguities. It was not intended to prevent waste. It reflected a nineteenth-century faith in competition. Oil men raced each other to make discovery, whether oil was in demand or not, seeking merely to perfect their claims. An expert in the Geological Survey had this comment (1917): "Under a law which forces the operator to drill for oil lest he lose his land and to produce it lest his neighbor drain it from him, production has exceeded market demands during most of the last ten years." [10] Senator Thomas J. Walsh of Montana gave his analysis: "Oil prospecting is an altogether different affair [from gold mining]. . . . When the oil prospector strikes oil—that is, makes his discovery—he has ordinarily spent many times $500. . . . Then the ground about becomes the scene of feverish activity. . . . It is not the man who first begins, but the man who first gets oil, who takes the ground. What chance has the ordinary man in such a race with the Standard Oil?" [11]

Dissatisfaction was widespread. Scientists in government service, progressives, and conservationists began to agitate for a system of leasing. The government would retain title to its land, and could then impose conditions upon lessees. As early as 1906 Senator La Follette proposed a leasing system for coal and oil lands. By 1908 the Geological Survey and highly placed officials of the Interior Department, such as George W. Woodruff and Frank Pierce, were trying to formulate an acceptable plan. This

[9] For good descriptions see Max W. Ball, *Petroleum Withdrawals and Restorations Affecting the Public Domain,* Department of the Interior, U.S. Geological Survey, Bulletin 623, Washington, 1917, pp. 27–41; J. O. Richardson, U.S. Navy, "Naval Petroleum Reserves No. 1 and No. 2," *United States Naval Institute Proceedings,* XLII (January–February, 1916), 97–100.

[10] Ball, *Petroleum Withdrawals,* p. 20.

[11] Walsh, address before a conference of the Mining and Metallurgical Society of America, in the auditorium of the Smithsonian Institution, December 16, 1915, Senate Document 233, 64 Cong., 1 Sess., vol. 41, Washington, 1916, p. 70.

effort was to continue in the Taft and Wilson administrations.

The advocates of leasing knew whereof they spoke. Some were intelligently concerned with the most critical problems of price, supply, and conservation—only partially solved today.

Lieutenant Commander J. O. Richardson of the Bureau of Engineering, United States Navy, was such a person. He pointed out that the discovery of new oil fields meant overproduction, low prices, and the use of high-quality oil for fuel when it should not have been used for this purpose. He posed a possible solution: "If the production of oil could be so regulated that only enough oil would be produced to supply the legitimate demands for petroleum products, the price would always be so high as to prevent fuel oil from entering into competition with coal for industrial purposes in many parts of the country, yet not so high as to render it excessively expensive as a fuel for the Navy . . . and the result would be that the nation's deposits of petroleum would not be so rapidly depleted and there would always be an adequate supply of fuel for naval needs." [12]

Max W. Ball of the Geological Survey remarked that there was "no magic in leasing as such." Various fields had been developed under a leasing system, as in Oklahoma, with results as bad as those under the placer law. Unless certain fundamental principles were embodied, the new policy would fail. Most important was "adequate acreage." Without this, oil men on small plots must race for discovery, wasting oil and gas and drilling many dry holes. Philip Wells agreed. Small holdings for oil men produced a situation similar to that on the open range, where the year's crop of grass (1917) was being destroyed by fierce competition.[13] There can be little doubt that the believers in leasing, as a group, favored a departure from *laissez faire*. The most advanced among them called for an active government role, including public operation of certain fields.

One of the difficulties affecting government lands was the lack of knowledge concerning their contents. Only in 1906 did a systematic effort toward classification get under way. This lack of

[12] Richardson, "Naval Petroleum Reserves No. 1 and No. 2," p. 95.
[13] Max W. Ball, memorandum for the director of the Geological Survey on H.R. 406, March 30, 1916, Gifford Pinchot Papers, Library of Congress; Wells to Pinchot on a copy of Wells's letter to Ball, July 25, 1917, *ibid.;* Franklin K. Lane in *Annual Report of the Department of the Interior, 1915,* 2 vols., Washington, 1916, I, 16.

certainty meant that an oil man hopefully prospecting could suddenly be apprised that a homesteader had beat him to it; or he could learn that discovery of a substance like gypsum had given another prospector a prior claim.

All sorts of controversies arose. Government officials exhibited much sympathy for the oil men. In 1907, in one effort to help, certain public lands were withdrawn from agicultural entry, while oil men continued to prospect. However, the overproduction of oil soon dictated a use of the withdrawal power to ban oil men as well as others. In this way the drilling of new wells could be prevented, and conflicting claims could be kept to a minimum. Meanwhile, classification would go on and perhaps the placer law could be abandoned in favor of a leasing system.

Experts in government bureaus argued most effectively for land withdrawals. Dr. George Otis Smith, director of the Geological Survey, and his petroleum experts were most influential. An important step was taken in February, 1908, when Smith wrote to the Secretary of the Interior, emphasizing the superiority of liquid fuel for naval vessels. Most important, he recommended that all public petroleum lands in California be withdrawn from private entry: "The present rate at which the oil lands in California are being patented by private parties will make it impossible for the people of the United States to continue ownership of oil lands there more than a few months. After that, the Government will be obliged to repurchase the very oil that it has practically given away." If anything was to be done, he continued, it must be done fast, "for prospecting is now going on at an unprecedented rate throughout the West." [14]

Later in the year David T. Day and two associates in the Survey stressed the dangers of overproduction. They had become convinced that the sharply competitive drilling and overproduction could be halted only by withdrawing *all* petroleum lands from entry. This action was an immediate necessity.[15]

By September of 1909 things were approaching a climax. In a letter to Richard A. Ballinger, Smith reiterated his recommendations of the year before with respect to oil lands of California, adding a strong argument in behalf of a new law. The overproduction of oil and allied evils, he said, made necessary a new

---

[14] Quoted in Ball, *Petroleum Withdrawals,* p. 104.
[15] *Ibid.,* p. 117.

method of conservation and development. Meanwhile the Navy Department had shown its interest in a supply of fuel oil. At last the Secretary of the Interior indicated his willingness to act, and President Taft added his approval while touring in the West. An executive order of withdrawal was then issued on September 27, 1909. This order covered 3,041,000 acres of land in California and Wyoming, of which only 170,000 acres were in Wyoming. According to estimates about half of the land was in private ownership; that is, public and private lands were interspersed, or "checkerboarded," within the withdrawn areas.[16]

This withdrawal policy was adopted only after much deliberation. Obviously it was intended to be enforced. As the acting Secretary of the Interior commented: "My withdrawal prevents all forms of acquisition in future and holds the land in statu[s] quo pending legislation." [17] Through the fall of 1909 and during 1910 the government withdrew other lands in the western states. The process of classification continued, with some areas being restored to private entry upon reports that they were nonpetroleum.

## 3

The next logical step seemed to be the creation of special reserves for the Navy. To a later generation these reserves may appear to have been foolish and visionary, for we know now that there was no danger of running out of oil, as naval men feared in 1912. However, no one could be sure of this in the first decades of the century. Expert opinion supported the demand for special reserves where oil would be kept safely in the ground for the use of fighting ships.

The whole question was immensely complicated. By no means were naval officers of one mind on the subject. First, they were not

---

[16] *Ibid.,* pp. 133–135, 149; DeNovo, "Petroleum and the United States Navy Before World War I," pp. 641–645; Frank Baldwin of *The Outlook* to Richard A. Ballinger, December 2, 1909, enclosing a clipping from the *New York Sun,* Ballinger (telegram) to Baldwin, December 3, 1909, Secretary's File.

[17] Frank Pierce, quoted in Ball, *Petroleum Withdrawals,* p. 149; George Otis Smith and others, *The Classification of the Public Lands,* Department of the Interior, U.S. Geological Survey, Bulletin 537, Washington, 1913, p. 44. See "Leasing System for Mineral Lands," *Oil Age,* V (February 2, 1912), 9, for an indication of western support.

sure that oil was superior to coal as a fuel. As late as 1910, the Secretary of the Navy could say: "It is not probable that the use of oil fuel will materially increase in the future." Very soon he was to know better. There is quite a story in the series of experiments conducted with oil fuel from 1902 to about 1913. In 1902, for example, Ensign John Halligan, Jr., commanded the torpedo boat *Rodgers* as it went through various tests. A report of the Liquid Fuel Board to the chief of the Bureau of Engineering urged the continuation of such experiments. Halligan and other naval engineers did continue, and by 1913 they had won the argument for fuel oil.[18]

Second, not all officers agreed that special tracts of land should be set aside as naval petroleum reserves, yet the trend was favorable. The Geological Survey had called attention to military needs. Naval planners and experts did likewise, and the Secretary of the Navy made up his mind.

Something must be done, he wrote to the Secretary of the Interior in June, 1912. If the Navy abandoned its ships with coal bunkers in favor of oil burners with storage tanks arranged in remote places, these vessels could not be reconverted suddenly for the use of coal. A decision must be made one way or the other. The General Board of the Navy, whose advice was important on such matters, expressed its view that private sources of supply were inadequate and too costly. Special naval reserves were required: "The rise in price of oil in the bids for naval supply for the fiscal year 1913 is about 60%, and moreover the Texas Oil Company, the only one making a satisfactory bid, declines to guarantee more than 21,000,000 gallons (about 70,000 tons)." [19]

By 1912 President Taft was ready to act. Geologists in the

---

[18] George v. L. Meyer to the chairman of the Senate Committee on Naval Affairs, March 24, 1910, printed in U.S. Congress, Senate, *Reserve Oil Supply for United States Navy*, Senate Report 481, 61 Cong., 1 Sess., Washington, 1910; Report of the Liquid Fuel Board, Bureau of Steam Engineering, U.S. Navy, October 1, 1902, printed in *Annual Report of the Navy Department, 1902*, Washington, 1902, pp. 757, 769, and *passim;* E. H. Peabody, "Developments in Oil Burning," *Transactions of the Society of Naval Architects and Marine Engineers*, XX (proceedings of the twentieth annual meeting of the Society, 1912), 246–247; E. H. Peabody, "Recent Developments in Oil Fuel Burning," *International Marine Engineering*, XVIII (February, 1913), 62–63.
[19] Quoted by Richardson in "Naval Petroleum Reserves No. 1 and No. 2," pp. 106–107.

Department of Interior selected sites for the reserves in California, and the President then issued the appropriate orders. Later President Wilson in the same way established Teapot Dome in Wyoming.

From the beginning, naval petroleum reserves were a problem. The orders of withdrawal said that these tracts were to be "held for the exclusive use or benefit" of the Navy. Such use, however, was subject to "valid existing rights" of private occupants and claimants. In each reserve there were claimants; they seemed to be everywhere, in spite of the fact that government geologists had tried to select oil-bearing land on which there seemed to be a minimum of valid claims.

In other respects, the Navy's position was anomalous. The reserves had a legal status that was subject to doubt and controversy: they continued under the jurisdiction primarily of the Department of the Interior. There was also an ambiguity in the stated purpose of the reserves. According to the chief of the Bureau of Engineering, the oil "should not be drawn upon so long as it is possible to purchase oil in sufficient quantity." [20] This implied that the Navy might go into the oil business. Whether it did or not would apparently depend upon relations with the oil companies.

The petroleum withdrawals in the state of California were strung along the western side of the San Joaquin Valley. Bakersfield lay just inside the southern edge. Some thirty miles west of Bakersfield were the two naval petroleum reserves that Taft had created in 1912: Elk Hills, or Reserve No. 1, containing 37,760 acres, and Buena Vista Hills, or Reserve No. 2, to the south, containing 30,008 acres. The total area covered 106 sections of land, or a little more than a hundred square miles. On the southern edge of the reserves lay Taft, a small mining and supply center.

Petroleum withdrawals in Wyoming were scattered mostly in the central and north central areas. The great Salt Creek field and Teapot Dome were located in Natrona County, the east central part of the state.

Teapot Dome was not established until 1915. Having put the Navy on its new course with oil-burning ships, Wilson's Secretary

---

[20] *Ibid.,* pp. 105–106.

of the Navy, Josephus Daniels, sought additional oil reserves, and solicited the cooperation of the Secretary of the Interior. Teapot Dome was suggested as a possibility, even though it was not a proven oil territory. Daniels decided the Teapot would do. As he explained: ". . . the Navy Department considers it advisable to select this area rather than one where the presence of oil has been determined by actual producing wells, as in the latter case there would be adverse claims and consequent litigation, strong opposition to the creation of the Reserves, and danger of wells remaining in private ownership so as to make it possible to drain a large part of the Reserve." [21]

Teapot Dome, or Reserve No. 3, contained only 9,481 acres. Adjoining it to the north was the richly productive Salt Creek field, an area of withdrawn public lands in which many oil operators were active. Casper, Wyoming, was about thirty miles south of Teapot Dome.

## 4

The withdrawal of petroleum land precipitated a bitter contest in which the government was hard-pressed to maintain its policy. Max W. Ball observed that the withdrawals "knocked the breath, for the moment, from the California oil industry." [22] Oil men were in every stage of activity: preparing to enter public lands; in diligent prosecution of work looking to drilling and discovery; actually engaged in drilling; actually having made discovery but anxious to put down additional wells; claiming the rights to 160 acres as an "association" through the activities of "dummy locators," and claiming discovery when oil in commercial quantities had not been discovered. The possibilities for dispute and litigation were endless. Strictly speaking the government had put up "no trespassing" signs: only those who already had obtained patent without fraud or those who already had pressed to discovery were in a safe position. As to the latter,

[21] Quoted in R. G. Tracie, senior petroleum engineer, Navy Department, "History of the Naval Petroleum Reserves," unpublished manuscript, compiled in 1937, copy in Josephus Daniels Papers, Box 264, Library of Congress. See also Daniels to Attorney General Gregory, June 2, 1915, Navy Records, National Archives; "Big Merger Progresses," *National Petroleum News,* Oil Producer's Section, VII (May, 1915), 23.
[22] Ball, *Petroleum Withdrawals,* p. 21.

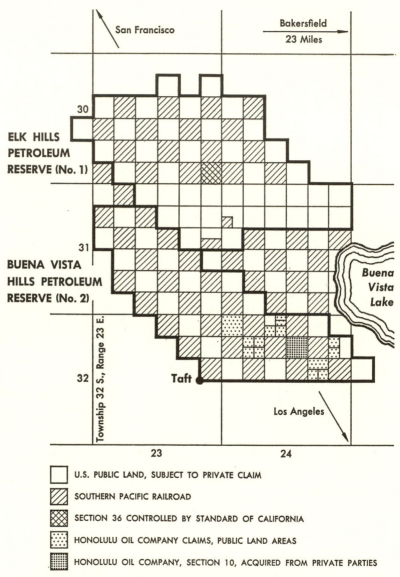

San Joaquin Valley

MAP OF CALIFORNIA NAVAL PETROLEUM RESERVES, 1916

Showing Pattern of Public Lands and Private Holdings
(Selected Disputes Only)

the total area which might be obtained was often in doubt.

Oil men quickly regained their breath. Though some obeyed the government orders, hundreds did not. The industry as a whole—many believing that the government had acted unconstitutionally—was determined to force concessions. The means to be employed were not a novelty in United States history. They would play the old frontier game, tooth and claw, if necessary. If politicians were apprised of the injustice and absurdity of the situation, they would be moved to act. If Land Office officials and others were swamped with disputes, which were costly and time-consuming, something would have to give.

In the California situation the government suffered an incubus, in the form of one huge block of private holdings. These were land grants to the Southern Pacific Railroad, patented, then later attacked on grounds of fraud. Totaling about 170,000 acres, they extended almost a hundred miles through the best petroleum lands from Coalinga in the north to the southeast below Maricopa. They ran directly through the two naval petroleum reserves, of which the railroad controlled in most quarters every odd-numbered section.

The big question was, how much drilling would the railroad do? Drilling on its sections probably would result in drainage from the adjacent even-numbered sections. These were public land sections, controlled either by the government or by claimants. However, as a naval officer commented, the railroad's theory on drilling tended to be conservative; it was practically the same as the Navy's: "They do not drill wells as long as they can buy oil at a fair price, and they do not drill wells on their own lands until some man drills on the lands adjoining. Their purpose in holding that land is to save it and reserve it so as to be able to use it when they can not buy oil at a fair price in the market. If there were nobody there except the railroads and the Government, both would be saving." [23]

Government leaders decided to take no chances. As early as 1910, the Justice Department instituted proceedings to cancel the Southern Pacific patents, but until the cases finally were decided in 1919, a great many questions remained in doubt.

[23] U.S. Congress, Senate, *Leasing of Oil Lands*, Hearings Before the Committee on Public Lands on H.R. 406, an "Act to Authorize Exploration for and Disposition of Coal, Phosphate, Oil, Gas, Potassium, or Sodium," 64 Cong., 1 Sess., Washington, 1916, p. 207.

The Southern Pacific seemingly had few friends. Oil men frequently charged that the principal beneficiary of land withdrawals would be the railroad. Its lands would be relieved from competitive drilling on the adjacent, even-numbered government sections—now withdrawn.

In hearings before the Public Lands Committee of the House, conducted in May, 1910, a number of "gentlemen from California" used this argument. One of the most influential, Thomas A. O'Donnell, displayed a map of the San Joaquin Valley, with the Southern Pacific sections marked in red. This, he said, should bring forcibly to their attention "the impossibility of conservation except for the benefit of the red sections." Others agreed. There were further quips about the government's conservation program, such as, conservation was "kind of an epidemic all through this country just now." These men did not blame the Southern Pacific particularly for its policies. All of them, said one lawyer, tried "to get the oil out of each other's land." At this there was laughter.[24]

These hearings contributed to an act for the relief of claimants, passed on June 25, 1910. The Pickett Act (named after a representative from Iowa) attempted to protect the interests of those claimants who, when lands were withdrawn, had not discovered oil, and in theory was a fair and necessary act. Under the placer law claimants had no rights; the new law provided that prospectors who had been and who continued "in diligent prosecution of work leading to discovery of oil or gas" should suffer no impairment of their rights.[25] The result was a new problem: while those who had invested thousands of dollars in legitimate operations would be protected, the door might be opened to claimants who had barely set foot upon the ground. It had been difficult enough to determine whether, in certain cases, actual *discovery* of oil had been made. Now, as an official of the Interior Department observed, every case involving the "diligence" of work "must be adjudicated upon the particular facts presented." [26]

---

[24] U.S. Congress, House, *Oil-Land Withdrawals and the Protection of Locators of Oil Lands,* Hearings Before the Committee on Public Lands on H.R. 24070, to "Authorize the President to Make Withdrawals of Public Lands," 61 Cong., 2 Sess., Washington, 1910, p. 58 and *passim.*
[25] Quoted in Tracie, "History of the Naval Petroleum Reserves."
[26] Frank Pierce to A. J. Carr, August 31, 1910, Secretary's File.

The Pickett Act also gave congressional sanction to land withdrawals by the President, which provision was of dubious value. Powerful precedents existed leading to the belief that the President already had the necessary authority. Furthermore, those who opposed the withdrawal of 1909 and attacked its validity continued to do so. Not until the Supreme Court handed down its decision in the Midwest case of 1915 was the question more or less settled. One thing is clear: the Pickett Act was only the beginning of a quest for legislative relief.

The evidence is powerful indeed that California oil men paid little attention to government withdrawals. Many were determined to exploit the rich oil fields of the San Joaquin Valley regardless of government meddling. Some "had a bear by the tail" in their struggle for these lands and simply refused to let go, while others jumped into the struggle with both feet after it had begun. The *Oil and Gas Journal* (Tulsa), describing a meeting of California oil men, seems to have sized up the situation with remarkable accuracy: "The big companies," its editors believed, "have decided to go ahead with the development and take out all the oil they can without applying for any patents, holding on to the land as long as the government refrains from hoisting them by active legal proceedings or physical force. It is believed that they are convinced that it will be possible to carry on business for years in this way, and that in the end there is no real danger of their losing out." [27]

A California newspaperman, Walter V. Woehlke, became convinced that in all the history of Western "sooners" and "boomers" and claim-jumpers there had never been anything to compare with what happened in the San Joaquin Valley, starting about 1907. These latter-day prospectors, these pioneers, drove through the sagebrush in fast runabouts. Though they carried guns, their principal weapon was the checkbook. If possible, the simplest means were used. They located corners of their claims and filled out forms describing the land. Thereafter they asserted their "rights" as against jumpers. Legally none of them had any rights until they made discovery of oil or, under the Pickett Act, until they were diligently drilling or making preparations for drilling. But if they could hold the land, or forcibly dislodge

---

[27] "Organization for Conservation," *Oil and Gas Journal*, IX (August 25, 1910), 8.

the first occupants, or produce a checkbook and buy out the prior occupants, they would have that possession which was nine points of the law.

For a time chaos reigned. So-called claims were asserted to every acre of the withdrawn lands, and in spite of a constant process of buying out "claimants" there frequently were many adverse claimants for the same land. In a battle of checkbooks, however, it was obvious who would win: a dozen or so large corporations and wealthy individuals achieved the best claims to the withdrawn land.[28]

In the Salt Creek field of central Wyoming much the same situation existed. For a generation prospectors had wandered over the area. There had been the assertion of claims and conflicting claims, sometimes in the form of location notices "stacked up five or six deep." In the main, this was without discovery of oil. Finally, a new group entered the field financed from California. William M. Fitzhugh of Berkeley, a petroleum engineer, energetically set about the job of acquiring control of the entire field. Like Balboa when he "waded into the Pacific Ocean," as one authority puts it, Fitzhugh claimed all. Significantly, he had the ability and foresight to sink a number of shallow wells. His claims and rights, acquired in 1909 or shortly thereafter, were soon passed on to the Midwest Oil Company, financed from Denver.[29]

## 5

Officials in the Taft administration were convinced that many companies and individuals were operating illegally upon withdrawn land. George Otis Smith noted that, since the withdrawals, there had been a "large number of locations" in the California and Wyoming fields. He added: "It can be stated as a general

---

[28] Walter V. Woehlke, "Petroleum and the Placer Claim," *Outlook*, XCVI (December 24, 1910), 952–954 and *passim;* Walter V. Woehlke, "Grabbing the West's Liquid Fuel," *Technical World Magazine*, XVII (June, 1912), 372–383. A mining journal observed: "So deeply has litigation entered into our mining system that a claim whose rights have never been disputed would probably be set down offhand, by a miner of the old school, as of no value." "Title to Mining Lands," *Salt Lake Mining Review*, XVI (August 15, 1914), 16–17.
[29] See especially Harold D. Roberts, *Salt Creek Wyoming: The Story of a Great Oil Field,* Denver, Colo., 1956, pp. 13–19, 37, 44–51, and *passim.*

proposition, I believe, that it is the larger companies that have disregarded the withdrawals by the Secretary, while the individual prospectors and operators have shown more respect for these orders. It is probably true that the larger interests felt better able to defend their positions by an expensive legal fight." [30] E. C. Finney, an assistant to the Secretary of the Interior, and also Secretary Ballinger himself, were convinced that a number of operators had disregarded the government's orders, and that some were calmly pumping out government oil, creating a serious situation.[31]

Thus the problems proliferated. In addition to claimants of more or less validity antedating government withdrawals there were brazen ones who came in later—perhaps five or ten years later—still asserting claims and seeking "relief."

The Taft administration, in spite of the troubles of Secretary Ballinger, exerted itself to establish a new oil policy. It was Ballinger who authorized the withdrawals of 1909. However, by the end of 1910 he was wavering. He sought the opinion of the Attorney General, George W. Wickersham, he worried over differing interpretations of the withdrawals, and he seems to have favored some adjustment of the question. Ballinger was almost a minority of one in his own department. His advisers, such as George Otis Smith and E. C. Finney, insisted that their policy was legally unassailable and must be upheld against the land-grabbers.[32]

Nevertheless, in March of 1911 an important legislative concession was made to the oil operators. This related to the many "paper claims," asserted without discovery of oil and therefore without definite legal rights. Could such claims be transferred to other parties? A decision of the Land Office in the H. H. Yard case had been against the validity of these transfers. Oil men remonstrated, and Congress passed a remedial bill. It simply provided that if a claim were legal and valid in every other respect its

---

[30] Smith to the Secretary of the Interior, December 22, 1910, Secretary's File. See also J. H. G. Wolf to Secretary Lane, March 19, 1914, Navy Records.
[31] Finney to Frank Pierce, first Assistant Secretary of the Interior, December 19, 1910, Ballinger to the Attorney General, December 24, 1910, Secretary's File.
[32] Finney to Frank Pierce, December 19, 1910, Smith to Ballinger, December 22, 1910, *ibid.* See "Government Oil Land Suits," *Oil Age,* VI (July 26, 1912), 8, and other editorials, or articles, in issues of 1912-13.

transfer previous to discovery did not make it invalid.[33] The problem of conveyances and acquired rights, perhaps involving charges of fraud, was to be a continuing one.

Secretary Ballinger's replacement, Walter L. Fisher of Chicago, brought a new firmness to his post—the "Trouble Portfolio," he called it. A vice-president of the National Conservation Association and ex-president of the Conservation League of America, he was a friend of James R. Garfield and Pinchot. His record as attorney and civic leader in Chicago had been outstanding. Almost to the last day of his administration in March, 1913, Fisher and his advisers were resisting pressures to make further concessions within the withdrawn lands. At the same time he was making recommendations for a leasing system and giving his attention to other problems in a manner seemingly moderate and fair-minded.

Ten years before Albert B. Fall leased Teapot Dome, Fisher discussed in a Cabinet meeting the problem which would provide Fall with his main excuse. This was the drainage of oil—or the alleged drainage—out of government lands into wells nearby on private lands. Was it legal or advisable, Fisher asked, to permit leases on the government tracts? By so doing, they might lessen the drainage and loss of public resources. The President, Attorney General, and Secretary of State seemed to be in favor of such leases, and this was the prevailing view. But the question was left open for further study.[34]

At the conclusion of Taft's administration, most of the administrative problems relating to petroleum had been set forth, but few had been solved. In truth the Democrats inherited a headache. The pains, however, had been incurred in a program that seemed essentially sound. There was little to do but press ahead, paying no heed to the headaches of officialdom, hoping to achieve a more rational system on the public lands.

[33] *U.S. Statutes at Large*, XXXVI, Part I (1911), 1015; Representative Denver S. Church of California in *Cong. Record*, 63 Cong., 2 Sess., p. 15295, September 17, 1914.

[34] Walter L. Fisher, "Autobiography," manuscript copy, presented by his son, Walter T. Fisher, Chicago, in possession of the author; *The Autobiography of Lincoln Steffens*, New York, 1931, pp. 422–429; Charles Hilles to Fisher, March 1, 1913, Fisher to Taft, March 1, 1913, and miscellaneous re oil lands of Wyoming 1912–13, Secretary's File; Philip Wells, chief law officer, Reclamation Service, memorandum, November 15, 1912, *ibid.*

# Return of the Democrats: The Policy Grows and Falters

**CHAPTER III**

*The entire West, and Montana in particular, is vitally concerned in seeing at the head of the Interior Department some man who comprehends the public land laws and the conditions out of which they grow, from having lived his life or at least a considerable portion of it in the region in which they are operative.*

Thomas J. Walsh to William Jennings Bryan, November 12, 1912

1

It was difficult to say in 1912 just what Woodrow Wilson's election would mean. As the campaign had proven, he was a very able man and a brilliant, inspirational speaker. His "New Freedom" provided a platform about which Democrats and reform-minded citizens might rally. Yet the new President had problems. He lacked a popular majority. He had lost key states, such as California, to Roosevelt's Progressives. Perhaps most important of all were the problems in his own party. The Democrats were a heterogeneous bunch, long out of power; to weld them together would be no easy task.

Wilson knew well that sectional attitudes could not be ignored. He was himself a native of Virginia and proud of the fact, although his career as professor, college president, and governor of New Jersey had broadened his outlook. In any case, predominant influences in the new administration seemed to be southern. Five of the ten Cabinet posts went to southerners, or to transplants from that region. Colonel House, most powerful man in Washington next to the President, was a Texan. One writer observed that the accent in the administration was unmistakably southern: "In Washington you feel it in the air, you note it in the changed and changing ways of business; you listen to evidence of it in the mellow accent with which the South makes our English a musical tongue; you hear strange names of men to whom leadership and importance are attributed, and if you ask, you almost invariably learn that they are from the South." [1]

There was a danger here. Franklin K. Lane expressed his concern that Wilson might become "surrounded by Southern reactionaries—men of his own blood and feeling, who are not of the Northern and more progressive type." [2]

Sectional, state, and local interests demanded attention. Western leaders, like Senator Walsh of Montana, were vehement on this point. Moreover, they were interested in shaping to their own ends conservation ideas spreading from the East. They could not resist the conservation movement entirely, even if they wished to do so, but they could avoid federal programs to some extent by their own state measures. They could also hope for appointment of westerners to key places and for resulting sympathetic treatment. In Congress they could powerfully influence bills for leasing of the public lands or for management of resources.

## 2

Wilson's appointments were of utmost importance. More than western leaders could suspect, the oil leasing question would hinge upon the ideas and personalities of a few leaders in the government. Two announcements went far toward relieving western anxiety. William Jennings Bryan, still national leader of the agrarians, became Secretary of State. The Nebraskan had friends without number beyond the Mississippi River and much support as well below the Mason and Dixon Line. Through him, it seemed, the West would have a powerful voice.

Franklin K. Lane of California was appointed as Secretary of the Interior—the second western man in thirty years to get that coveted spot. Westerners conducted a vigorous campaign to get

[1] Judson C. Welliver, "The Triumph of the South," *Munsey's Magazine*, XLIX (August, 1913), 740. See also A. Maurice Low, "The South in the Saddle," *Harper's Weekly*, LVII (February 8, 1913), 20.
[2] Lane to Timothy Spellacy, September 30, 1912, in *The Letters of Franklin K. Lane*, edited by Anne W. Lane and Louise H. Wall, Boston, 1922, pp. 104–105.

Lane, or someone like him, appointed, and it was by luck as much as anything else that they succeeded. President Wilson offered the job, first, to Newton D. Baker of Ohio. When he turned it down, Lane got the place on Colonel House's recommendation.[3]

"Frank" Lane was not a newcomer to Washington. Appointed to the Interstate Commerce Commission in 1905, he became chairman under Taft and was by 1913 a familiar personality in town, "an impressive rather than a dominating figure," concluded one journalist: "Solidly built, enough inclined to corpulency to suggest good fellowship, with a large, round, genial face, a high brow, and prematurely white hair, eyes that combine earnestness with humor, a habit of talking straight to you . . . a force latent behind the friendly manner." [4]

Lane had entered public life as lawyer, newspaperman, and Democratic reformer. He was associated with James D. Phelan (later senator), Gavin McNab, and others who endeavored to clean up San Francisco and rid the city and state of corrupting influences. He served as city and county attorney and in 1902 was defeated narrowly in a race for the gubernatorial chair. During a trip to Washington representing the city of San Francisco, he met President Roosevelt, and the two men got along famously. Although a Democrat, Lane was now in line for his appointment as interstate commerce commissioner.[5]

Lane's appointment to the Interior Department in 1913 was well received. Burton J. Hendrick wrote that "the whole of Washington" felt grateful to President Wilson. The Californian, he continued, was beloved of the newsboys and those who knew him well in the capital, while he was also respected by the general

---

[3] Arthur S. Link, *Wilson: The New Freedom*, Princeton, N.J., 1956, p. 18; Elmo R. Richardson, *The Politics of Conservation: Crusades and Controversies, 1897–1913*, Berkeley, Calif., 1962, pp. 145–159.

[4] "Notes from the Capital—Franklin Knight Lane," *Nation*, CII (January 20, 1916), 70. See also "Lane, the White Hope of the Wilson Cabinet," *Current Opinion*, LV (September, 1913), 164; Arthur Wallace Dunn, "An Interested Westerner," *Sunset*, XXXII (May, 1914), 1097.

[5] For sketches of Lane see Henry W. Wiens, "The Career of Franklin K. Lane in California Politics," unpublished Master's thesis, University of California, Berkeley, 1936; Burton J. Hendrick, "The American Home Secretary," *World's Work*, XXVI (August, 1913), 396–405. Wiens is suggestive as to Lane's possible weaknesses and inconsistencies in the California period.

public as a somewhat austere, "aggressive" champion of the people's interests.[6]

There were occasional hints as to the complexity of Lane's personality and the troubles that might lie in store for him. He was a hard worker and a fighter, it was said; but he was also extremely convivial. He was a progressive and a reformer believing in the extension of governmental powers; but he revealed himself as an individualist, full of admiration for the pioneer in American history, that "mystic materialist," that "patriot" of the soil. Rich people were all right, he once declared, if they earned their money.[7] He was an admirer of the government service; but he talked much of eliminating bureaucracy, cutting red tape, and introducing methods of business efficiency into government.[8] As a conservationist, Lane once made the surprising statement that this movement was primarily a matter of common sense on which men of good will sitting around a table could agree. If the Secretary believed that, he was highly unrealistic.

As Burton K. Hendrick commented, Lane's new assignment was a difficult one. The recent Ballinger troubles gave warning. One or two new mistakes in the Interior Department "might easily wreck the Wilson Administration." It was Hendrick's belief, however, that no such controversy would arise under Lane.[9]

In the course of the Wilson administration, up to 1919, two Attorneys General held office. Each was concerned with the problem of petroleum lands. If oil men were to be restrained, or expelled, by judicial proceedings, the Justice Department came into the picture. James Clark McReynolds of Tennessee was the first Democrat to serve and he held office from 1913 to August, 1914, when he was appointed to the United States Supreme Court.

---

[6] Hendrick, "The American Home Secretary," p. 396. See also James Hay, Jr., "The Fighting Commissioner," *Cosmopolitan*, L (March, 1911), 569–570.

[7] Address by Lane, "The American Pioneer," San Francisco Exposition, February 20, 1915, Gifford Pinchot Papers, Box 1856, Library of Congress; Franklin K. Lane, "Some Results of This War," *Harper's Weekly*, LX (April 3, 1915), 318; Franklin K. Lane, "Land Is Land: An Ancient Fallacy Exposed," *Independent*, LXXVIII (April 6, 1914), 18–21.

[8] Honoré Willsie, "Mr. Lane and the Public Domain," *Harper's Weekly*, LVIII (in 4 pts., August 23, 30, September 6, 13, 1913; pt. 4 subtitled "A Renaissance in Washington," September 13, 1913), 6–7; Hendrick, quoting Lane, in "The American Home Secretary," p. 402.

[9] Hendrick, quoting Lane, in *ibid.*, pp. 402–405.

McReynolds undertook a careful investigation of the situation in petroleum lands. He concluded that the government withdrawals had been "very generally disregarded" in California and Wyoming.[10] Three suits immediately were brought against important operators in California and a fourth against the Midwest Oil Company in Wyoming. The latter case was intended as a test to settle whether the government's withdrawals were or were not constitutional.

In his brief period of office McReynolds settled very little. But having become convinced of the correctness of the government's position, he acted vigorously to uphold it against illegal operations.[11]

The next head of the Justice Department was Thomas W. Gregory of Texas (1914–19), who was to be for many years in the thick of the petroleum controversy. Often remembered as "that wartime Attorney General" who treated dissenters harshly, he deserves to be remembered for other things.

Gregory established his reputation in Texas as a "trust-buster." He represented the state against the Waters-Pierce Company, a subsidiary of Standard Oil; Waters-Pierce was driven out of Texas and compelled to pay a fine of $1,623,900.[12] In 1913 Gregory came to Washington as a special assistant to the Attorney General, where he prosecuted the New York, New Haven, & Hartford Railroad under the Sherman Law. This veteran "trust-buster" was a man of quiet and self-effacing ways, but in the oil disputes he was to show firmness, even stubbornness.[13]

By birth, training, and tradition Gregory was a southerner. His father, a "Captain of Infantry in the Thirty fifth Mississippi . . . died in the Confederate Army";[14] Gregory was solicitous of his memory—also of that of the Confederacy. Nevertheless,

[10] *Annual Report of the Attorney General, 1913*, Washington, 1913, p. 40.

[11] *Annual Report of the Attorney General, 1914*, Washington, 1914, pp. 37–38; E. J. Justice, San Francisco, special assistant to the Attorney General, to the Attorney General, February 16, 1914, Ernest Knaebel, Assistant Attorney General, to Justice, February 27, 1914, Records of the Department of Justice, National Archives.

[12] Carl C. Rister, *Oil! Titan of the Southwest*, Norman, Okla., 1949, pp. 187–188; "Thomas W. Gregory," obituary in *Newsweek*, I (March 4, 1933), 19.

[13] See William G. McAdoo, *Crowded Years*, Boston, 1931, pp. 184–185.

[14] Gregory (telegram) to Governor Clifford M. Walker, Atlanta, May 5, 1925, Gregory to P. E. Crowley, president of the New York Central Railroad, July 12, 1926, Thomas W. Gregory Papers, Library of Congress.

this man was not a parochial type or a southern reactionary. A friend of Louis Brandeis, he recommended him for his place as an associate justice in 1916. He declared on the subject: ". . . I believe the appointment was the very wisest that could have been made from every standpoint. I know Brandeis as I know very few men, and my respect for him has been increasing during the last three years. He is a man who cares nothing for money, and for the last twenty years his life-work has been standing for personal liberty as against property rights. He is a radical, but one radical in nine is not a bad thing on the Supreme Bench. . . . His rejection [in the Senate] would fortify many men in the mistaken belief that no one but reactionaries and persons attached to large interests can go on the Federal bench. . . ." [15]

The only Cabinet officer directly concerned with public oil lands, and who remained at his post throughout the Wilson years, was Josephus Daniels. Partly for this reason he has been better known than Gregory or Lane. He also is remembered as an ambassador to Mexico under Franklin D. Roosevelt and as an "editor in politics" from Raleigh, North Carolina. For thirty-five years after entering Wilson's Cabinet this slightly rotund, smiling newspaperman was a familiar sight in Washington, D.C., and in political gatherings.

On many subjects, including the public oil lands, Daniels and Gregory could agree. In the racial disturbances of the 1890's, Daniels' *News and Observer* fought the fight for white supremacy, although after that time his ideas on racial questions became increasingly moderate. Daniels was an antimonopolist. He was intensely loyal to the Democratic party. He was a good friend and conspicuous admirer of Bryan.[16]

The "good Josephus," kindly, humorous, sentimental—and apparently easygoing—soon became a mark for blue bloods in politics. Even young Franklin D. Roosevelt, Daniels' Assistant Secretary, sometimes subjected his chief to ridicule. Daniels' efforts at democratic reform in the Navy also aroused opposition. Yet he proceeded to confound his critics, proving once again the

[15] Gregory to R. L. Batts, March 1, 1916, *ibid.* See also Gregory to Judge George W. Anderson, October 23, 1930, *ibid.*
[16] Jonathan Daniels, *The End of Innocence,* Philadelphia, 1954, pp. 31–40; E. David Cronon, "Josephus Daniels as a Reluctant Candidate," *North Carolina Historical Review,* XXXIII (October, 1956), 457, 464–465.

virtues of an unpretentious, honest man, determined to succeed and devoted to the public service.[17]

The oil question affords an excellent illustration of the crucial role often played by subordinates. Three such officials in the Wilson administration were Clay Tallman, commissioner of the General Land Office, and two lawyers in the Department of Justice: Ernest Knaebel, Assistant Attorney General in charge of the Public Lands Division, and E. J. Justice, special assistant to the Attorney General.

Tallman, who held his office throughout the Wilson administration, was a believer in lenient terms for the development of resources. A lawyer and former state senator from Nevada, he was a personal and political friend of the powerful Senator Key Pittman. In his post Tallman had responsibility for the many district land offices, and was charged with the difficult task of adjudicating in the Interior Department various claims to the public lands. His influence on Secretary Lane may be surmised, and to some extent defined.

Ernest Knaebel was a Republican carry-over from the Taft administration. An eastern man and a graduate of Yale, he had been practicing law in Denver when called to Washington and placed in charge of the Public Land Division of the Justice Department (1909). In the first years of the Wilson administration, his legal talents were to count for much.

E. J. Justice, from Greensboro, North Carolina, had the very important assignment of handling oil cases in California, including those against the Southern Pacific Railroad. He had served in his state house of representatives and in the state senate, and his fight in North Carolina for antitrust legislation and other reforms led Josephus Daniels to refer to him as "a progressive of progressives." [18]

Another group of subordinates had a continuous influence upon oil policy. They were naval officers in the Bureau of Engineering, assigned to duty in connection with the oil reserves. Admiral Robert S. Griffin, who served as chief of the Bureau

---

[17] Daniels, *End of Innocence*, p. 32 and *passim;* Cronon, "Josephus Daniels as a Reluctant Candidate," pp. 464–468, 471, 478; *Roosevelt and Daniels,* edited by Carroll Kilpatrick, Chapel Hill, N.C., 1952, especially editor's Introduction.

[18] Josephus Daniels, *Editor in Politics*, Chapel Hill, N.C., 1941, pp. 618–619 and *passim.*

from May, 1913, through the entire Wilson period, put much
effort into trying to establish and maintain fuel reserves. Griffin
apparently combined a practical knowledge of public affairs with
a sense of humor. One young officer was assigned to the oil reserve question for a very special reason: his father, who was
known to be unfriendly toward federal land policy, was none
other than the Democratic senator, John F. Shafroth of Colorado.[19]

A number of officers received assignments to the "oil desk"
in the Bureau of Engineering. Periodically they might go away
on other duty, and return. Among the more important were J. O.
Richardson, H. A. Stuart, and Nathaniel H. Wright.

In July, 1915, Lieutenant Commander Irvin F. Landis received
his assignment to San Francisco as the officer in charge of the
reserves both in California and Wyoming, and he remained until
1922. Landis devoted his time almost entirely to California, es-
tablishing an office in the post office building in San Francisco.
A careful, conscientious officer, he undertook field investigations
and specialized studies of the reserves, reporting frequently to
Washington in long, detailed letters.

As specialists in these petroleum matters, Landis and other
officers were highly influential. Try as they might, they could not
be wholly formal and official in their correspondence. They provided a running commentary on the battle over petroleum lands,
as well as insights into their own changing "battle strategy." [20]

## 3

Immediately upon assuming office, Secretary Daniels wanted
something done about oil lands, and jogged the Justice and Interior Departments into action. Purposes of the naval petroleum
reserves in California must be fulfilled. The Navy should be
given control over these reserves. Claimants should, in some
way, be removed. Moreover, in view of the fact that oil prices
paid by the Navy had doubled from 1911 to 1913 it "should become a producer and refiner of oil for its own use." This would

---

[19] Author's interview with Admiral J. O. Richardson (ret.), March 27, 1961.
Griffin was promoted from captain to rear admiral in 1916.
[20] See especially the correspondence of Irvin F. Landis, Navy Records, National Archives; also Daniels to E. J. Justice, July 28, 1915, *ibid.*

be nothing revolutionary. The Navy already produced some of its own ships and maintained industrial navy yards, a gun factory, and a clothing factory, "all of which," Daniels said, were "indispensable to the supply of superior articles for the Navy and for the control of prices from commercial concerns furnishing similar articles." [21]

With his ideas quickly crystallizing, Daniels sought the advice and cooperation of the Interior Department and informed the Attorney General that he was anxious to have legal proceedings instituted as soon as possible to protect the naval petroleum reserves against drainage. As to conservation policy in general, Daniels stated his position rather clearly in a speech at Denver (August, 1913). Administrators of the public domain must steer a difficult course. They were compelled on the one hand to guard against private monopoly of resources and on the other against a form of federal tyranny which would hamper local development in the West.[22]

Attorney General McReynolds meanwhile was trying to find out what this complicated oil question was all about. Ernest Knaebel sent him in June, 1913, a long memorandum explaining that there were three classes of cases affecting the oil lands. The first two involved the Southern Pacific Railroad and its extensive patented holdings in the San Joaquin Valley of California, where the railroad was charged with fraud. In two distinct cases there, the government was moving to set aside Southern Pacific patents. Then there was a third category of cases arising under the presidential withdrawals, where no patents were involved. The question was, what were the rights of various claimants to the withdrawn land?

Knaebel went on to describe to his chief the perplexing situation involving oil claimants. During a recent trip to Denver Knaebel had talked over these matters with A. I. McCormick, the United States attorney for Los Angeles. A "very large area" of

---

[21] *Annual Report of the Navy Department, 1913,* Washington, 1913, pp. 14–16. See also Daniels to Representative Lemuel P. Padgett, January 15, 1914, Navy Records.

[22] Daniels to James Clark McReynolds, June 12, 1913, Ernest Knaebel, memorandum, December 8, 1913, Records of the Department of Justice; Daniels to William C. Redfield, February 2, 1924, Josephus Daniels Papers, Box 578, Library of Congress; Daniels' speeches, August, 1913, *ibid.*

the land that had been withdrawn in California was occupied by claimants; "many wells" had been completed, and others were being sunk; "vast quantities" of oil had been removed. Knaebel gave further illustrations of the complexity of the situation. In one government suit against the Consolidated Midway Oil Company, involving less than 640 acres, there were thirteen corporations and seventeen individuals as defendants. Government bills revealed "not only a complex of contracts, conveyances, leases, assignments, and mortgages and other liens, but also in some instances, distinct and apparently conflicting claims to the same parcels of land." Possibly as many as fifty or a hundred suits might be necessary to halt the drilling and extraction of oil on withdrawn lands in California.

Like his chief, Knaebel lacked an intimate personal knowledge of conditions in California. Possibly for this reason, he showed a tendency to be lenient. In certain instances, he wrote, the claimants might have moral equities, even though they did not come within the protecting phrases of the Pickett Act. In justice to these individuals and for the welfare of their states, it might be advisable occasionally to relax the withdrawal orders.[23]

The Attorney General needed further information, and thought of sending a special investigator to the California fields. At this point, Josephus Daniels suggested E. J. Justice, whom he praised highly and referred to as one of his "closest friends." [24] This suggestion was welcomed. McReynolds sent Justice to California, and soon relied heavily upon his advice.

Justice's first assignment was to visit the California fields and reconnoiter. On returning to Washington early in 1914, he was urged to take charge of the government's cases in the West. Justice complied. Making his headquarters in the post office building in San Francisco, he threw himself into his work and mastered almost every detail of the labyrinthine cases.

---

[23] Knaebel to McReynolds, June 13, 1913, Records of the Department of Justice. See also testimony of E. J. Justice in U.S. Congress, Senate, *Oil-Land Leasing Bill*, Hearings Before the Committee on Naval Affairs on "So-called Relief Provisions of the Leasing Bill Relative to the California Naval Petroleum Reserve," 64 Cong., 2 Sess., Washington, 1917, p. 6; and for frequent comment on developments of the early Wilson period see *The Oil Age* (Los Angeles), and *Standard Oil Bulletin* (San Francisco), *passim.*
[24] Daniels to Admiral Charles F. Pond, July 28, 1914, Navy Records. See also Daniels to William C. Redfield, February 2, 1924, Daniels Papers, Box 578; E. J. Justice in U.S. Congress, Senate, *Oil-Land Leasing Bill*, p. 54.

His first suggestions will illustrate why he became a valued assistant. Justice proposed that McReynolds confer with two lawyers from California representing two distinct types of oil interests in their state. They were Oscar Sutro, an attorney for Standard Oil of California, "one of the four pipe line companies," and A. E. Bolton of San Francisco. The latter represented a class of producers who were dependent on Standard and the other pipeline companies to purchase their oil, some of which came from public lands. Justice explained further: "Both Sutro and Bolton will want to say things to you that they do not want the other to hear. . . . Sutro and his clients are more interested in knowing what the Government wishes than in having the terms made easy. On the other hand, Bolton and his clients and others who are interested only as producers and sellers of oil are interested in getting a policy adopted by the Government which will be most favorable to them."

These two men and others they might bring along would supply much information. Otherwise the Justice Department might have to obtain it through agents of the Land Office. Justice continued that, while the Californians would want many things which the Attorney General could not approve, there might be a degree of compliance which would save time and expense.[25]

With this capacity for analysis and his other abilities, Justice was given almost complete control over the millions of dollars worth of litigation in California. Justice's impression was that he had a "wide discretion," and need not obtain authority from Washington "except in extraordinary cases." Knaebel confirmed this. However, the Department did desire to be kept completely informed of developments.

On this basis Justice proceeded. The suits against the Southern Pacific Railroad were continued. He instituted new suits against certain violators of the presidential withdrawals, until by 1916 there was a total of thirty cases, twenty-seven of which were in California. Various cases were settled against the trespassers, with the court directing that the amount of damages due the government be determined by a master. In many instances a settlement

---

[25] Justice, Greensboro, N.C., to McReynolds, January 27, 1914, Records of the Department of Justice. See also Justice, San Francisco, to McReynolds, February 16, 1914, *ibid.*

was delayed, and the receipts from the sale of oil or the oil itself
were placed in the hands of a receiver.[26]

## 4

In 1913–14, everything considered, the conservationist point of
view seemed to predominate. Even the Department of Interior,
sometimes disparaged as a "sluice gate" of corruption, had been
reformed; or so it seemed. Secretary Lane was an honest, well-
intentioned administrator. In his annual reports of 1913 and
1914 the Secretary summed up a point of view which, in spite of
a few ambiguities, was that of an idealist and a reformer.

The report of 1913 gave greatest prominence to "the fuller and
freer use" of the national resources. As was well known, a feeling
existed in the West that its needs and its problems merited more
consideration in Washington than they had received. The explanation of western discontent was simple, said Secretary Lane.
This country had embarked upon a new policy toward its public
lands, and rightly so, but without developing "adequate machinery." It had "closed opportunities to the monopolist" without providing adequate opportunities to the "developer."

With reference to petroleum, Lane cited the inadequacies of
the placer law, the frauds and subterfuges encouraged by it, and
the necessity for a better system. It would be wise to stimulate the
discovery of oil in some manner. He suggested giving patents
to an explorer for a portion of his discovery; the greater portion
could then be developed through leasing.

He showed his awareness of the Navy's fuel oil problem. His
belief was that the government should retain a "sufficient" amount
of proven oil lands to make its ships "independent of the world
and as fully competent as their rivals." Lane also wrote to the
Secretary of the Navy giving unequivocal support to the idea of
naval reserves. Only through the development of its own reserves,
he suggested, could the Navy gain "relief" from high commercial
prices on oil. He concluded: "It is believed that the Department
of the Navy may rely upon the reserves already existing [in
California] for a supply of fuel oil for a period greater than the
life of any battleship to be constructed within the next decade." [27]

---

[26] Knaebel to Justice, February 27, 1914, *ibid.; Annual Report of the Attorney
General, 1916*, Washington, 1916, pp. 45–46.
[27] *Annual Report of the Department of the Interior, 1913*, 2 vols., Washington,
1913, I, 3–5, 15–18; Lane to Daniels, March 31, 1913 (copy), Navy Records.

In his private correspondence of 1913, Lane acted tougher toward claimants and trespassers than did officials of the Justice
Department. Writing to Knaebel in July, Lane enclosed a letter
from an independent oil man in California. He commented that
this letter would give Knaebel "an idea of the situation in the
California oil fields. . . ." The enclosure was an indictment of
"the octopus [Southern Pacific] and its allies, namely the Kern
Trading & Oil Company, the Associated Oil Company, and other
large producers who are holding and producing oil from thousands of acres of land which legitimately belongs to the United
States government." At the same time there was surplus production in the state, with the resultant low prices. Why could not
the government stop this illicit production on its own lands
and thus eliminate the surplus? This point of view was one which
Lane shared. He proposed to the Justice Department that they
make application "for out and out preliminary injunctions" in
each case of what was thought to be illegal operations.[28]

## 5

Just as the administration aimed at protection of oil lands, so
claimants waged a determined opposition. Increasingly they
asked, or demanded, more of the government. Oil men came to
Washington, it sometimes seemed, in droves. In a typical reference one representative noted that "25 or 30 oil men" had recently appeared before the Committee on Public Lands.[29]

What the oil men wanted was largely Congress's to give. Congress was the focus of the controversy—in meetings of the Committees on Public Lands and Naval Affairs, in special committee
hearings, on the floor of both houses. Every shade of opinion
was heard, representing oil companies and claimants, the Na-

---

[28] Lane to Knaebel, July 3, 1913, enclosing a letter from M. V. McQuigg of
Los Angeles to Lane, May 27, 1913, Knaebel, quoting Lane, to A. I. McCormick, June 18, 1913, William Denman to McReynolds, February 14, 1914,
Records of the Department of Justice. See also Lane, quoted in "Marketers
May Refuse Oil from Government Land," *Oil Age*, VII (April 25, 1913), 1–2.
[29] Scott Ferris in *Cong. Record*, 63 Cong., 2 Sess., p. 15430, September 19, 1914.
The government's policy for withdrawn lands antagonized those who purchased controverted oil, as well as those who produced it. Thus, for example,
the Standard Oil Company was made a codefendant with certain oil producers. Shortly thereafter, announcing it could not continue such purchases,
it castigated the government's procedure; and it continued to do so. See
"Standard Oil Company's Position as Result of Oil Land Litigation," *Standard Oil Bulletin*, I (October, 1913), 1–2, and *passim* in issues of 1913–14.

tional Conservation Association and other reform groups, the Department of Interior, the Navy Department, and so on. Initially discussions were fairly amicable. Oil interests had been temporarily appeased by the government's early concessions and its willingness to grant them a hearing. Nevertheless, the main points remained at issue.

The Pickett Act of June 25, 1910, continued to be the point of departure. Were claimants fairly protected by its phrase that there should be no impairment of the rights of those "in diligent prosecution of work leading to discovery of oil or gas"? Certain terms needed to be defined. What, for instance, was the interpretation of diligence? Should this question and others be determined solely in the Land Office and in the courts? Or by new legislation? As it developed, the Land Office was busy, the courts were busy, and new legislation also was necessary.

A special kind of temporary relief was given in August, 1914, to certain parties already producing oil whose rights were as yet undetermined. There were those who by contract, lease, or transfer had obtained locations originally fraudulent. Had they obtained these locations in good faith? Might they be allowed temporarily to produce oil under agreements with the Secretary of the Interior? There was also the question of companies which bought this "tainted" oil. Standard of California, an important purchaser, would, along with other companies, be aided by government leniency.

Oscar Sutro of California Standard visited Washington in February, 1914. He impressed upon the Attorney General, Secretary Lane, and others that relief was needed. While the Justice Department might act through the courts, regulating the production of oil in certain disputed cases and impounding the proceeds, this was not enough. The situation would continue "chaotic." The Secretary of the Interior should be empowered to make special operating agreements, and action by the Justice Department and courts and by the Department of Interior should continue simultaneously.

Sutro offered a proposal for a bill containing the basic ideas and a few of the expressions which became law on August 25, 1914. The Secretary of the Interior was given wide discretion to "enter into agreements" providing for the disposition of oil, gas, and the proceeds of sales in these disputed cases. The bill was

passed with almost no opposition in Congress, although the
Navy and Justice Departments raised objections.[30] Later, Secretary Lane's administration of the law aroused a great deal of
criticism.

## 6

The larger question continually before Congress was new laws
for the development of withdrawn land. Bills were of two types,
so far as petroleum was concerned. First, relief bills. Claimants
might be awarded preferential leases, and even patents on the
basis of their claims. Second, there were bills for general development in areas not under claim. Prospecting in such areas
might be allowed by government permit.

Relief bills were highly controversial, while bills for general
development were not. It was obviously desirable to consider the
two separately. However, relief bills inevitably got tacked onto
general bills, in 1914 and thereafter.

The initiative for leasing bills came from Secretary Lane and
his congressional allies. Like Woodrow Wilson, Lane asserted his
executive leadership. On occasion members of Congress protested
against being told "20 or 30 times" or "a hundred times" in a
single debate that the Secretary or his department thought thus
and so. After all, protested Mann of Illinois, the "bright minds"
of Congress were supposed to come together and produce the
laws, under certain advantages not enjoyed by the Secretary of
the Interior.[31]

Such criticisms helped to reveal Lane's power and influence
in 1913–15. For the most part members of Congress, as well as
others, were full of admiration for the dynamic Secretary. His

---

[30] Oscar Sutro to Attorney General McReynolds, February 18, 1914, with
enclosure, Records of the Department of Justice; Secretary Lane to Scott
Ferris, April 10, 1914, quoted in U.S. Congress, House, *Locators of Oil and Gas
on the Public Domain*, House Report 519, 63 Cong., 2 Sess., vol. 2, Washington, 1914; Lane to Ferris, April 17, 1914, quoted in U.S. Congress, House,
*Oil or Gas Lands*, House Report 695, 63 Cong., 2 Sess., vol. 2, Washington,
1914; *Cong. Record*, 63 Cong., 2 Sess., pp. 8769–70, May 18, 1914; Gerald T.
White, *Formative Years in the Far West: A History of Standard Oil Company
of California and Predecessors Through 1919*, New York, 1962, pp. 442–444.
[31] Mann and Frank Mondell in *Cong. Record*, 63 Cong., 2 Sess., p. 15556,
September 22, 1914.

recommendations carried weight. Bills leaving wide discretion to the Secretary received a more favorable hearing because Lane was the Secretary.

In the House of Representatives, Scott Ferris of Oklahoma, only thirty-six years old but chairman of the Committee on Public Lands, tended strongly to follow Lane's lead. In the Senate, Walsh of Montana and others worked closely with the administration, conferring with Lane and his subordinates, with members of the House, and with other interested persons. They aimed toward a leasing system.[32]

In April, 1914, Ferris introduced a general development bill. This won the approval of Pinchot and many conservationists, but not all. Its passage would have made possible the exploration and development of coal, phosphate, oil, gas, potassium, and sodium lands. The discoverer of oil, for example, would have been permitted to receive patent to one-fourth of the land included within his prospecting territory, while the government might grant leases on the remaining three-fourths.

At the same time a relief bill was separately introduced by Representative Denver S. Church, a Democrat from Fresno, California, in the heart of the oil country. Church felt so poignantly about the rights of oil men, and injustices suffered by them out on the California desert, that he turned in one speech to poetry. Government men and land agents, he implied, were preying upon helpless pioneers.

> Never stoops the soaring vulture
> On his quarry in the desert,
> On the sick or wounded bison,
> But another vulture, watching

[32] See, for example, Ferris in *ibid.*, p. 15283, September 17, 1914; *Christian Science Monitor*, May 6, 1914, in *ibid.*, pp. 13249–51, August 4, 1914; Walsh of Montana in U.S. Congress, Senate, *Leasing of Oil Lands*, Hearings Before the Committee on Public Lands on H.R. 406, an "Act to Authorize Exploration for and Disposition of Coal, Phosphate, Oil, Gas, Potassium, or Sodium," 64 Cong., 1 Sess., Washington, 1916, pp. 12–13; McGregor (A. J. McKelway), "Unlocking the Far West," *Harper's Weekly*, LVIII (April 4, 1914), 15; James Middleton, "A New West: The Attempts to Open Up the Natural Treasures of the Western States—Utilization and Conservation vs. Monopolistic Greed—the Department of the Interior," *World's Work*, XXXI (April, 1916), 669–680. Gifford Pinchot had opposed the appointment of Scott Ferris as chairman of the House Public Lands Committee. Pinchot to William Jennings Bryan, December 31, 1912 (copy), Harry A. Slattery Papers, Duke University Library, Durham, N.C.

From his high aerial lookout,
Sees the downward plunge, and follows;
And a third pursues the second,
Coming from the invisible ether.
First a speck, and then a vulture,
Till the air is dark with pinions.
　So disasters come not singly;
But as if they watched and waited,
Scanning one another's motions,
When the first descends, the others
Follow, follow, gathering flockwise
Round their victim, sick and wounded
First a shadow, then a sorrow,
Till the air is dark with anguish.[33]

As Secretary Lane explained the Church bill, which he favored, it was the natural culmination of a need for relief. The law of 1911 had guaranteed that transfer of oil land previous to actual discovery would not invalidate the transfer. Operating agreements, negotiated under the plan of 1914, would give temporary relief to many oil producers whose rights were in doubt. But some permanent plan for relief was necessary.

The Secretary explained relief provisions of the Church bill. They would authorize "locators or their successors in interest in cases where oil or gas has been discovered, was being produced, or upon which drilling operations were in actual progress January 1, 1914, upon lands the claims to which was [sic] initiated prior to July 3, 1910," to receive leases in lieu of patents upon their surrender of patent rights in the "defective location." Claimants could lease in no case more than 2,560 acres. They would pay a royalty "not exceeding one-eighth" of the production of oil and gas.

He frankly stated that people with defective locations would be eligible. But he said that granting leases in this fashion would "afford relief to operators who . . . have in good faith made large expenditures in the development of oil or gas from such lands." Moreover, the Land Office would be relieved of a great deal of work and expense in examining and adjudicating these cases.[34]

---

[33] *Cong. Record,* 63 Cong., 2 Sess., p. 13200, August 3, 1914.
[34] U.S. Congress, House Reports 519, 668, and 695, 63 Cong., 2 Sess., vol. 2; Lane to Scott Ferris, April 17, 1914, quoted in House Report 695; Gifford Pinchot, "Open Letter to the Honorable Franklin K. Lane, Secretary of the Interior, Concerning the Navy's Oil Lands," August 12, 1916, Pinchot Papers.

Here was the most wide-open proposal ever made formally and seriously by the Interior Department for oil men's relief. Various leaders, particularly from eastern states, could not accept such a bill. The "claims"—any and all claims apparently—if initiated previous to July 3, 1910, would be recognized by granting leases on remarkably lenient terms. The *maximum* royalty of one-eighth was generous. Naval petroleum reserves, like other lands, could be leased.

Walter V. Woelke, editor of *Sunset* magazine in San Francisco, gave his appraisal of this bill. It would legalize "land burglary"; it would play into the hands of those who had acquired shadowy claims to withdrawn petroleum lands:

> In its practical working-out the Church Bill, if passed will enable the man who has no legal right whatever to the land he claims, to retain seven-eighths of the oil which does not belong to him. This class of claimants will be the only ones to make use of the leasing privilege. Those who had a real right to the land before the second withdrawal order [July 2, 1910] will fight the efforts to oust them and will obtain patent to their holdings in the courts. The bill puts a premium on evasion of the public-land laws. Instead of providing relief for those entitled to it, the bill confirms speculators without the shadow of a right in the possession of the loot, asking them only to return not more than one-eighth of that which is not theirs.[35]

The Church bill failed in the House, in spite of Lane's endorsement. It then showed up naturally as a relief amendment to the general bill, which was concurrently receiving favorable consideration in the House.

The debate on this bill, with relief amendments, reached its climax in the House in mid-September, 1914. It revealed the attitudes of conservationists, as compared with those of oil claimants and their friends, six years before this issue was settled by the Congress. The striking fact was that conservationists wanted a leasing bill. Their mood was generous: they did not oppose development of resources, as so often charged.

Ferris of Oklahoma, Mann of Illinois, and Lenroot of Wisconsin represented a conservationist view. In seeking relief, Church of California was joined by his colleague John E. Raker of Susanville, California (a Democrat), and by Frank Mondell of Wyoming. Mondell, a Republican of the Old Guard variety,

---

[35] Walter V. Woelke, "Legalizing Land Burglary," *Sunset*, XXXIII (July, 1914), 159–160; Pinchot, "Open Letter to the Honorable Franklin K. Lane."

was strongly pro-western and states' rights in philosophy. He had been Ferris' predecessor as chairman of the Public Lands Committee, and the two men understandably were keen rivals. According to Gifford Pinchot, Mondell was "pure poison" to the conservation movement.

In the debate of September 17, Mondell gave an illustration of why he might be called "poison." During debate on the general bill, he offered an amendment which would give oil men a maximum of relief. Representative Church was off the floor at the moment, but Mondell's amendment and his were almost identical. Ferris and the eastern Democrats, as well as conservationist Republicans, were surprisingly acquiescent. They wanted a few changes, in line with ideas of the Pinchot group, but clearly they did not try to block this legislation.

Having done his bit for the oil men, assuming the bill should pass, Mondell got up to denounce it as a whole:

I want to call attention to the fact that, so far as this bill affects oil, it is not a leasing bill to any extent. (Applause.) It is, in some respects, the most wide-open bill for absolute fee-simple ownership that ever was considered on the floor of this House. (Applause.) If I had brought this bill before the House, I would have expected my motives to be impugned. I am not impugning anyone's motives; but, knowing what I know about public lands, I believe I would have been subject to the charge that I was attempting to give an opportunity to loot the public domain if I had brought in legislation of this kind.[36]

Mondell's comments were among the many evidences that the bill was too liberal toward oil men and that the combination of leasing and patent in fee was undesirable.

Nevertheless, the conservationists sought only a few changes. Ferris succeeded in getting several amendments on September 19, one of which was regarded by Pinchot as having especial significance. Where it had been stated that the Secretary of the Interior "shall" grant leases to claimants, the wording was changed to "the Secretary of the Interior may, within his discretion, lease on such reasonable terms and conditions as he may prescribe. . . ." Pinchot believed in giving an executive such as the Secretary of the Interior ample power and responsibility—and he intended to hold him responsible. This change was quite a safeguard, he thought, partly because at this time apparently he

[36] *Cong. Record,* 63 Cong., 2 Sess., p. 15541, September 22, 1914; *ibid.,* pp. 15293–94, September 17, 1914, and *passim.*

trusted Secretary Lane. Ferris also succeeded in reducing the maximum area which could be leased by any single person, corporation, or association from 2,560 acres to 640 acres.[37] The wisdom of such a reduction was questionable.

James R. Mann objected to the royalty provisions. The Mondell-Church amendment had set the royalty at a figure not "exceeding" one-eighth of production, and Mann argued that nobody could tell what that meant, whether one-twentieth of production or what. He proposed to amend the amendment so as to provide for royalties of "not less than one eighth." Without opposition, his amendment was accepted.

The naval reserves were not protected in this bill, which permitted the leasing of land to claimants on the California naval reserves under the same conditions as elsewhere. Considering the furor later to arise over the leasing of naval reserves, this is surprising. There was little opposition, even from Mann and Lenroot.

The explanation seems to lie partly in the fact that the Secretary of the Interior would have discretionary power to lease or not to lease. Secretary Lane had expressed his concern for a fuel supply for the Navy and, in general, had won the confidence of the conservationists. They were willing to trust him.

But the naval reserves at this time had little importance, in the eyes of Representative Mann and many others. Lenroot did reveal an awareness that the reserves were slightly distinctive. He proposed that receipts from royalties in the reserves should go into a special naval petroleum fund in the Treasury, for the needs of the Navy. He got almost nowhere. Mann, among others, could see no sense in such a provision. If the Navy needed money, the Congress would appropriate it. Why have a special fund? If the Navy needed oil, the government would see that it got that too. Lenroot was successful only to the dubious extent of getting an amendment that "any moneys which may accrue to the United States under the provisions of this act from lands within the naval petroleum reserve, shall be deposited in the Treasury as miscellaneous receipts"; that is, rather than going into the Reclamation Fund with the other royalties.[38]

---

[37] *Ibid.*, pp. 15413–15, September 19, 1914; Pinchot, "Open Letter to the Honorable Franklin K. Lane."

[38] *Cong. Record*, 63 Cong., 2 Sess., p. 15296, September 17, 1914; *ibid.*, p.

One can imagine Church and Raker of California and certain oil men fairly gleeful at the liberality with which they were treated. They had gotten practically everything they demanded. But they had not yet won the fight.

The Ferris bill, having passed the House, went to the Senate, where it was amended. Finally in the closing moments of the Sixty-third Congress (March, 1915) the House and Senate could not agree, and the bill failed.[39] A substitute bill offered by Senator Clarence D. Clark of Wyoming also failed. All the arguments now had to be repeated in the new Congress.

# 7

By the spring of 1915 the controversy over petroleum lands was somewhat clarified. A Democratic administration had not been able to achieve agreement. In the Cabinet, Secretary Lane of California was moving toward an open break with Secretary Daniels of North Carolina and Attorney General Gregory of Texas. In Congress Senator Pittman, Representative Church, and others for oil men's relief were residents of public land states. Conservation leaders in Congress, or moderates on the question, came from farther east.

As if to complete the picture of a sectional division, the Supreme Court handed down its decision on February 23, 1915, in the case of *United States* v. *Midwest Oil Company*. By a five to three decision the eastern justices held that the petroleum withdrawal of 1909 had been constitutional. Powerful support was thus added to the new public land policy which had originated in the executive branch of the government. Oil men and various western politicians expressed their indignation. The struggle would now reach a new intensity.

---

15555, September 22, 1914, and *passim*. J. O. Richardson, as a young naval officer, found much indifference on the subject of fuel for the Navy. Author's interview with Admiral Richardson, March 27, 1961.
[39] *Cong. Record,* 63 Cong., 3 Sess., p. 5155, March 2, 1915; *ibid.,* p. 5440, March 3, 1915.

# The Division in Wilson's Cabinet, 1915–20

CHAPTER IV

*Attorney General Gregory has the suits, Secretary Daniels has the Naval Reserves, and Secretary Lane has the administration of the lands.*

Representative Scott Ferris, May 25, 1918

1

As Arthur S. Link has commented, by 1916 one of the "bitterest controversies" of the Wilson administration had arisen over the petroleum lands question,[1] in the center of which was Franklin K. Lane. This controversy continued and intensified until Lane's position became almost untenable: that of a loyal westerner and Californian in an administration whose point of view was eastern conservationist. Lane's policies were surveyed by his western friends, as well as by critics in or out of the government, and he was almost compelled to take a stand on issues and details about which there was violent disagreement. Sometimes he agreed with the advanced conservation group. Sometimes he let subordinates take the responsibility for a bill or a proposal unacceptable to the conservationists. He was a hard man to pin down,[2] and he failed to satisfy either the oil men or their opponents.

---

[1] Arthur S. Link, *Wilson: The New Freedom*, Princeton, N.J., 1956, p. 132.
[2] Lane, "Memorandum for the Press," July 3, 1916, Lane to Senator Charles S. Thomas, January 10, 1917, remarks by Thomas, Senator Reed Smoot, and Senator John D. Works in *Cong. Record*, 64 Cong., 2 Sess., pp. 1249–50, January 12, 1917; Gifford Pinchot, "Open Letter to the Honorable Franklin K. Lane, Secretary of the Interior, Concerning the Navy's Oil Lands," August 12, 1916, Gifford Pinchot Papers, Library of Congress.

Lane's failings were partly personal. He wanted too much to be a success. He exulted in his high office and his high acquaintances. He liked too much to talk about them and wished too deeply to keep them. In 1917 he indulged in a little self-revelation: "The world is all people to me. I lean upon them. They induce thought and fancy. Thrown on myself I am a stranded bark." Loving people and parties, extremely ambitious, unable to retire "into the garden" for strength and solace, Lane was distressed when disagreements occurred and when some of his friends grew visibly cool and distrustful.[3] In the midst of what appeared to be a successful career, an able, gregarious, hard-hitting administrator was headed for bitter disappointments.

The petroleum fight continued on several fronts at once, in the courts, in the Congress, and in the departments. Generally speaking, the period 1915–16 was discouraging for oil claimants and their friends. The Supreme Court decision in the Midwest case was a shock. Then came the case of the Honolulu Consolidated Oil Company and its claims to public lands within Naval Reserve No. 2.

Secretary Daniels commented that the Honolulu case was the origin of the dispute between himself and Lane which continued until Lane left the Cabinet in 1920. Senator Charles S. Thomas of Colorado pointed to another aspect of the Honolulu affair: President Wilson and Attorney General Gregory took sides with the Navy Department. The "humiliating" result, said the senator, was the "fact that the Secretary of the Interior, so far as we can judge from this condition, does not control the department over which he has been appointed to preside."[4]

Western senators like Thomas were bitter over this state of affairs. Lane was unhappy. The chances for agreement on a leasing bill were diminished. And yet it is possible that this situation might never have developed, for Attorney General Gregory came within a whisper of acquiescing in Lane's view; had he done so the Honolulu people would have received patents from

---

[3] *The Letters of Franklin K. Lane,* edited by Anne W. Lane and Louise H. Wall, Boston, 1922, pp. 8, 46, 75, 88, 102–103, 202, and *passim.* See also Jonathan Daniels, *The End of Innocence,* Philadelphia, 1954, p. 168 and *passim.*
[4] Daniels to William C. Redfield, February 2, 1924, Josephus Daniels Papers, Box 578, Library of Congress; *Cong. Record,* 65 Cong., 2 Sess., p. 10493, September 19, 1918.

Lane rather than the leases they got from Secretary Fall in 1921.

## 2

Another matter antedated the Honolulu case and contributed to the atmosphere in which it exploded. This was the decision of the Supreme Court in the case of the Midwest Oil Company (February 23, 1915). Conservation leaders saw the decision as a landmark; or as Gregory described it later (1929), it "certainly [was] one of the greatest victories won by the Department of Justice in the last 20 years." [5] It was, indeed, a landmark: the power of executive withdrawals at last was firmly endorsed by the high court. Advocates of leasing legislation were stimulated to continue their efforts, while diehards believing in sale of federal land were correspondingly discouraged. As Senator Walsh of Montana saw the new situation, private acquisition of withdrawn lands had become well-nigh impossible. There would be no "lifting of the ban." [6]

The government's victory in the Midwest case was due to Assistant Attorney General Ernest Knaebel more than to anyone else. However, Solicitor General John W. Davis gave assistance. Davis was to have a notable career as ambassador to the Court of St. James, Democratic presidential nominee in 1924, and leader at the bar. For Knaebel, the Midwest decision was a high point. He once remarked of his great victory: "I was the attending physician at the birth of the midwest case. Not only then, but even at its conception."

This statement occurred during a hearing before the Senate Committee on Public Lands. Hard-eyed western senators were not impressed. Thomas of Colorado and the two Californians, John D. Works (progressive Republican) and James D. Phelan (Democrat), gave Knaebel rough treatment as he continued his

---

[5] Gregory to Attorney General William D. Mitchell, August 31, 1929, Thomas W. Gregory Papers, Library of Congress; E. A. Sherman, "The Supreme Court of the United States and Conservation Policies," *Journal of Forestry,* XIX (December, 1921), 928–930; William E. Colby, "The New Public Land Policy with Special Reference to Oil Lands," *California Law Review,* III (May, 1915), 269–291.

[6] Walsh to Senator Charles S. Henderson, September 2, 1919, Thomas J. Walsh Papers, Library of Congress; J. Leonard Bates, "The Midwest Decision, 1915: A Landmark in Conservation History," *Pacific Northwest Quarterly,* LI (January, 1960), 26–34.

testimony. Their attitude was evidence of the impact, legal and emotional, of the Midwest decision.[7]

The Justice Department had selected this case for its simplicity as to the facts involved. It seemed a clear-cut test of whether President Taft's withdrawals were or were not constitutional.

Six months after Taft's petroleum withdrawal of September 27, 1909, the Fitzhugh-Henshaw group from California had entered upon a certain quarter-section of the Salt Creek field in Wyoming. They explored, discovered oil, and assigned their interest to the Midwest group. However, their entry and discovery admittedly occurred some six months after the presidential proclamation. What were their rights? Legally, the government maintained, they had none.

A bill of equity was filed against the Midwest Company, seeking to regain the land and to require an accounting for some 50,000 barrels of oil extracted. On motion of the defendants, however, Judge John A. Riner, federal district judge for Wyoming, dismissed the bill, ruling that an order of the President could not invalidate normal location of land under the mining law.

So the government first met defeat. Knaebel commented that he had expected it. In his brief he had done the best he could in a "short time, under much pressure, and without any great preliminary preparation for the task." In the meantime Judge Maurice T. Dooling, a federal district judge in California, had decided in a parallel case that the presidential order was unlawful. But the Justice Department had proceeded to appeal to the Circuit Court of the Eighth Circuit, which in turn rendered no decision but certified the questions to the Supreme Court.[8]

---

[7] U.S. Congress, Senate, *Leasing of Oil Lands*, Hearings Before the Committee on Public Lands on H.R. 406, an "Act to Authorize Exploration for and Disposition of Coal, Phosphate, Oil, Gas, Potassium, or Sodium," 64 Cong., 1 Sess., Washington, 1916, pp. 360–366. Senator Walsh had declared in 1914: "Out in the western part of the country we have suffered most grievously by the abuse of the power of the executive officers of the government to withdraw lands from entry, and many of us have got into such a frame of mind that the least suggestion about empowering the officers of the government to withdraw even a little bit of a tract of 20 acres of ground for the most necessary public purpose throws us into a state of panic." *Cong. Record*, 63 Cong., 2 Sess., pp. 3323–24, February 11, 1914.

[8] Except where otherwise noted, this account is based upon the decision

Before the Supreme Court in 1914 the questions were fully and elaborately argued. "Friends of the court," from California, were included in the defense. Lawyers for the defense argued, as the lower courts had decided, that the President had no power to change or suspend the operation of a federal law, namely, the mining law. The United States government was one of limited and delegated authority. The President's powers were specified by the Constitution. Withdrawal of land was not included, and insofar as he had any power in this sphere, it depended upon congressional acts or sanction. But the defense even argued that the Pickett Act of June 25, 1910, "did not validate, or authorize the validation of, any previous withdrawals." Thus the Fitzhugh-Henshaw group and the Midwest Company had acquired rights previous to June 25, 1910, which "could not be affected even by act of Congress, much less by an executive order."

The vote as announced on February 23, 1915, was five to three, with McReynolds abstaining. Joseph R. Lamar of Georgia wrote the majority opinion, concurred in by Chief Justice Edward D. White of Louisiana and Justices Mahlon Pitney of New Jersey, Charles Evans Hughes of New York, and Oliver Wendell Holmes, Jr., of Massachusetts. William R. Day of Ohio wrote the dissenting opinion with Willis Van Devanter of Wyoming and Joseph McKenna of California concurring.

The majority took a position squarely behind the withdrawal of 1909. Scores and even hundreds of such actions had occurred, they decided, without either general or specific authority from the Congress. But Congress had acquiesced; implicitly it had approved. While it was true that the Constitution did not expressly permit executive withdrawals, "government," they declared, "is a practical affair intended for practical men." Indeed, "when it appeared that the public interest would be served by withdrawing or reserving parts of the public domain, nothing was more natural than to retain what the government already owned." The Executive acted as an "agent" for the protection and management of the public domain; and Congress had "uni-

(59 Law. Ed., 236 U.S. 673, 1915). See also Knaebel to A. I. McCormick, June 18, 1913, Records of the Department of Justice, National Archives; Colby, "The New Public Land Policy," pp. 276–285; Harold D. Roberts, *Salt Creek Wyoming: The Story of a Great Oil Field*, Denver, Colo., 1956, pp. 47–61, 98–101, and *passim*.

formly and repeatedly acquiesced" in these withdrawals of land.

The crucial date, therefore, was that of the presidential order, rather than of later legislation. The act of June 25, 1910, neither abridged nor enlarged the claims previously existing; it "left the rights of parties . . . to be determined by the state of the law when the [executive] proclamation was issued." What this meant then was that the Midwest Company and its assignor, having entered the lands in question after withdrawal, had no legal rights. Similar claimants were in the same anomalous position —unless they could find relief in the Congress.

In this decision the eastern point of view prevailed. As a California lawyer remarked, the majority of justices (eastern men) had been "influenced" by the "modern conservation policy." In strikingly vivid language they had endorsed the Rooseveltian doctrines of executive leadership and federal supervision of the public domain. Western lawyers, on the other hand, believed almost unanimously that the withdrawals had been illegal.[9] They were correct in saying that the decision was a strained one, based upon implied powers and the theory that "government is a practical affair intended for practical men."

## 3

Feelings ran high over the Midwest case, and the reactions to it were significant. The Justice Department prior to the decision had been severely hampered in its efforts to defend the withdrawn lands. Thus E. J. Justice had complained early in 1915: "There is very little I can do until the Supreme Court has decided the Midwest case." When that decision came, there was a great deal the government could do. As the commissioner of the Land Office said, the "general situation" had been "greatly clarified." A policy which had been encouraged and furthered by both the major parties since 1909 had faltered, bordering on collapse. Now the Supreme Court threw its great prestige behind that policy.

On all fronts United States officials—but especially those in the Navy and Justice Departments—pursued their objectives

---

[9] Colby, "The New Public Land Policy," pp. 277–281. See also Roberts, *Salt Creek,* pp. 54–55, 101, and *passim;* "The President and the Public Lands," *Outlook,* CIX (March 24, 1915), 657.

with new vigor and determination. Almost immediately the Navy Department asked for and got the establishment of a new petroleum reserve, Teapot Dome in Wyoming. Also Commander Irvin F. Landis at this time received his orders to "take charge" of the reserves with headquarters in San Francisco. Attorney General Gregory now obtained a special appropriation of more than $100,000 to enable him "to represent and protect the interests of the United States" in petroleum land disputes. As Gregory described the situation, the pathway had been opened. His department proceeded "earnestly and systematically," ascertaining the merits of various claims.[10]

Oil men, lawyers, and politicians in the West responded with the greatest indignation at their treatment. Senator Clarence D. Clark of Wyoming asserted on March 2, 1915, that the recent Supreme Court decision had put "a stop to the largest and greatest industry" of his state. He proposed immediate congressional action to relieve the situation. The *Standard Oil Bulletin* protested against this recent decision by a divided court, which had left the "unfortunate producer of oil from public land" without the patents which he deserved.[11]

One of the biggest lobbying operations in the history of the United States now developed. The Oil Industry Association of California claimed to represent 90 per cent of all petroleum producers in the state and was the center of this agitation. By the fall of 1915 its leaders were sponsoring meetings in San Francisco, Bakersfield, Taft, and many other sites through the oil fields. "No effort" was being spared, said Commander Landis. Not only oil operators and corporations were expected to join, but also the employees. "All employees," he said, were urged and "in fact compelled" to join. The initiation fee was $1.00. If they refused, they were blacklisted.[12]

---

[10] Justice to Secretary Daniels, January 5, 1915, Navy Records, National Archives; Department of the Interior, *Report of the Commissioner of the General Land Office*, Washington, 1915, p. 9; Department of Justice, Attorney General, *Withdrawn Oil Lands of the United States*, Supplement to the Annual Report for the Fiscal Year 1915 Embodying a Report upon the Litigation, Document 593, 64 Cong., 1 Sess., Washington, 1916.

[11] *Cong. Record*, 63 Cong., 3 Sess., p. 5154, March 2, 1915; "A Plea for Peace," *Standard Oil Bulletin*, II (April, 1915), 1–2.

[12] Irvin F. Landis to the Secretary of the Navy, December 24, 1915, Landis to J. O. Richardson, November 29, 1915, Navy Records. See also "The Oil Industry Association," *Standard Oil Bulletin*, III (November, 1915), 1–2; Gerald

The Association appealed to Governor Hiram Johnson of California. It had the satisfaction of winning his friend, the progressive Lieutenant Governor John M. Eshleman, to their side as a Washington lobbyist. James N. Gillett, ex-governor of California, and Francis B. Loomis, formerly an Assistant Secretary of State of the United States (more lately of Standard of California), were numbered among their lobbyists.

With headquarters in the Palace Hotel, San Francisco, and the Westory Building, Washington, D.C., this was a formidable group of people. They fought, in effect, to defeat the Supreme Court decision in the Midwest case. Congress, if not the Supreme Court, would recognize their claims. Senator Walsh of Montana referred to these oil interests, caught by the Supreme Court decision, "piteously pleading" now for the right to lease the properties they had occupied.[13]

Influenced to some extent by the agitation in California, Secretary Lane expressed sympathy for the oil claimants. In his annual report of 1915 he pointed out that "many of the most competent members of the bar" had believed the Taft withdrawals to be void. He emphasized the hardships faced by those who had violated the withdrawal order. His practical solution of the problem of legislative relief was to draw the line at the second executive withdrawal of July 2, 1910, subsequent to the Pickett Act.[14]

In the lower courts meanwhile claimants were finding little cause for comfort. One admitted in a Senate hearing that they

T. White, *Formative Years in the Far West: A History of Standard Oil Company of California and Predecessors Through 1919*, New York, 1962, pp. 444–445 and *passim*.

[13] Senator Walsh, address before a conference of the Mining and Metallurgical Society of America, in the auditorium of the Smithsonian Institution, December 16, 1915, Senate Document 233, 64 Cong., 1 Sess., vol. 41, Washington, 1916, p. 79. See also Hiram Johnson to W. F. Chandler, Fresno, November 23, 1915, and identical letters to others familiar with the California oil industry, Eshleman to Johnson, November 15, December 7, 1915, Oil Industry Association of California, "The Unhappy Condition of the Oil Industry of California, November, 1915," and various other materials, Hiram Johnson Papers, Bancroft Library, University of California, Berkeley; Francis B. Loomis Folder in the Chester Rowell Papers, Bancroft Library; Timothy Spellacy to Secretary Lane, November 27, 1915 (copy), Woodrow Wilson Papers, File VI, Box 505, Library of Congress.

[14] *Annual Report of the Department of the Interior, 1915*, 2 vols., Washington, 1916, I, 17–18.

had their stomachs "full of litigation" and did not "want any more of it." They hoped for aid from Congress. Looking around the committee room this oil man was encouraged by all the "Kentucky blood" present—Senator Smoot, who had many friends in Kentucky, Senator Marcus A. Smith of Arizona, born in Kentucky, and Senator Fall of New Mexico, also born in Kentucky. "When I saw Senator Fall, I began to feel that I was at home." [15]

Decisions both in the state courts and lower federal courts upheld the authority of the federal government, the necessity for diligent prosecution of "actual work" toward discovery of oil for legitimate location of a claim, and the need finally for discovery of oil. In the California case *Borgwardt* v. *McKittrick Oil Company* (February, 1913) the justices of the California Supreme Court affirmed that "until the inchoate location is perfected by discovery, the locator has no vested right Congress is obliged to recognize." But if the location were in good faith, and if work continued toward discovery, there was a right of possession as against other parties which was transferable.

Attorney General Gregory believed that claimants were in a predicament. His special report of 1916 summed up the situation. Those who had entered withdrawn lands in defiance of the orders of withdrawal would "doubtless be given little or no help by the courts without some additional legislation in their favor by Congress." He quoted from a recent opinion delivered by United States District Judge Bledsoe (California):

. . . all of these defendants went upon these lands at a time when they knew that they had been withdrawn from entry and settlement by order of the President of the United States. . . . The Government of the United States did nothing to lead them to believe that the withdrawal order was invalid, and to hold that a party may deliberately refuse to recognize a valid Executive order and thereby and because of such refusal profit himself is to put at once a premium upon disregard of law and constituted authority; to make it the rightful privilege of everyone to misconceive and disregard the law, if in so doing he will thereby advantage himself. . . .[16]

In the Sixty-fourth Congress there were renewed efforts to reconcile differences between oil men and conservationists, and to pass a leasing bill. The most important of several bills under

---

[15] U.S. Congress, Senate, *Leasing of Oil Lands,* pp. 129–132.
[16] Department of Justice, Attorney General, *Withdrawn Oil Lands,* p. 13.

consideration was H.R. 406, introduced by Scott Ferris in the House in December, 1915. Fairly moderate men like Ferris pressed hard for a compromise. Oil men, however, were demanding more than they ever had at a time when conservationists in and out of the government increasingly were convinced that they had yielded too much in the past.

Mann of Illinois had this to say, objecting to further relief: "I want to say to the gentleman in charge of the bill [Ferris] that I think we have gone quite the full length in favor of these people, who have no legal rights, or if they have legal rights are unwilling to stand upon them—that we have gone quite as far as we ought to go, indeed a little further than we ought to go, in this provision in the bill. (Applause.)" [17]

When the bill passed the House, Senator Phelan and others in the upper house made further attempts to liberalize it. The Interior Department favored relief. The Navy and Justice Departments increasingly fought it. Through 1916 these departmental differences over legislative relief were intermixed with the bitterness resulting from the Honolulu case.

## 4

When the Honolulu case first came to public view, it was a source of hope to oil claimants. Soon, instead, it symbolized for them the unfairness of distant officials and of conservation zealots. For charges were made that some, if not all, of the Honolulu Company's claims were fraudulent and could not be allowed. To do so might set a dangerous precedent. Further, the naval petroleum reserves might be destroyed.

The Honolulu claims would never have assumed such importance except that they lay inside Buena Vista Hills, or Naval Reserve No. 2, the only reserve proven to be rich in oil. One section (a square mile) in the middle of the reserve, privately controlled by Standard Oil, was known to have produced 12,-000,000 barrels of oil in two years. Still only partially developed, its gushers were among the most famous in the country.[18] Very high indeed were the stakes in public land sections nearby.

---

[17] *Cong. Record*, 64 Cong., 1 Sess., p. 1092, January 14, 1916.
[18] J. O. Richardson, U.S. Navy, "Naval Petroleum Reserves No. 1 and No. 2," *United States Naval Institute Proceedings*, XLII (January–February, 1916), 122.

Buena Vista Hills was not a large area, but politically and strategically it had large implications. Senator Charles S. Thomas of Colorado put the matter this way: the petroleum land withdrawals of 1909 were a "sort of declaration of war"; the naval reserves became the "war zone." [19] In the Wilson years nearly all the fighting actually occurred over Buena Vista Hills.

The reserve was covered by claims except where the land already had been patented. Large companies, generally speaking, were in the dominant position, including the Southern Pacific Railroad or its affiliated companies, Standard of California, and the Honolulu Company. According to them, Buena Vista Hills had been rendered untenable as an oil reserve. According to the Navy, if illegal and fraudulent claimants got out, No. 2 would be a wonderful reserve. Each side was adamant, and in 1915–17 the entire dispute over oil lands hinged upon Naval Reserve No. 2.

The Honolulu claims were vigorously asserted. They were based upon alleged occupancy of certain locations previous to the presidential withdrawals of 1909 and upon fulfillment of other requirements: diligent work toward discovery of oil, actual discovery, and expenditures comparable to $500 for each separate location, all intended to earn patents on the land in question. In 1915 the Honolulu Company presented its case for seventeen claims to the commissioner of the Land Office (Clay Tallman). Before the year's end he gave his decision. He "clearlisted" for patent thirteen of these claims, which covered twelve and a half quarter-sections in the heart of Reserve No. 2. In arriving at his decision Tallman concurred almost entirely with the sworn statements and affidavits of William Matson, former sea captain and now president of the Honolulu Company.

Captain Matson was best known as president and founder of the Matson Navigation Company, with its home office in San Francisco. Born in Sweden in 1849, Matson had gone to sea at an early age. By the 1880's he was identified with the shipping industry in San Francisco, and in the twentieth century he became the outstanding shipowner in the port.

Matson's interest in oil lands developed naturally from a de-

---

[19] U.S. Congress, Senate, *Leasing of Oil Lands*, p. 288. See also memorandum, probably from Geological Survey, June 21, 1917, Interior Department Records, National Archives.

sire to control his own supply of fuel oil, which he required for his ships, for his sugar plantations in the Hawaiian Islands, and for other businesses. Matson was attracted to the Buena Vista Hills area near Taft, and entered into certain arrangements: first, with the private owners of one section, and second, with locators on a number of public land tracts. All of this, Matson asserted later, was legally done in 1908–09, long before the executive withdrawals.[20]

In 1910 Captain Matson gave some idea of his views on conservation when he testified, along with many oil men, in hearings on the Pickett bill. Why should the government keep its lands withdrawn and keep people "all the time waiting for fuel"? he asked. What could the government do with these lands anyhow? Frank Mondell, who was in the chair, said—very likely with a grimace—perhaps "the next generation" would get this oil. Matson replied: "Well, they say it is a good thing to look out for those who come along next, but I believe in looking out a little for yourself first." There was "laughter."[21] Matson had a reputation for being a rough and ready type.

Matson's claims were supported by Congressman Julius Kahn of San Francisco and others. According to Kahn, Captain Matson's word was "looked upon as good as his bond with any business man in San Francisco."[22]

James D. Phelan, one of the most honored citizens of San Francisco, used his powerful position as a Democratic senator in Washington to further the Honolulu Company's interests. Phelan was a rich man of culture and humanitarian impulses. He had been the reform mayor of his city from 1897 to 1902 and con-

---

[20] Matson affidavit, quoted in Tallman to Lane, December 15, 1915, in U.S. Congress, Senate, *Oil-Land Leasing Bill*, Hearings Before the Committee on Naval Affairs on "So-called Relief Provisions of the Leasing Bill Relative to the California Naval Petroleum Reserve," 64 Cong., 2 Sess., Washington, 1917, p. 127. Documents relative to the Honolulu case run from pages 123 to 167 of this hearing. See sketches of Matson in William Martin Camp, *San Francisco: Port of Gold*, Garden City, N.Y., 1947, pp. 225, 405, and *passim*; also "Successful Oil Burning Steamer Test," *Army and Navy Journal*, XXXIX (May 31, 1902), 983.

[21] U.S. Congress, House, *Oil-Land Withdrawals and the Protection of Locators of Oil Lands*, Hearings Before the Committee on Public Lands on H.R. 24070, to "Authorize the President to Make Withdrawals of Public Lands," 61 Cong., 2 Sess., Washington, 1910, p. 63.

[22] Julius Kahn to Attorney General Gregory, April 15, 1916, Records of the Department of Justice.

tinued as civic leader in many good causes. When elected, however, to the Senate in 1914 he was not bashful in pursuing the patronage. He spoke proudly if not arrogantly as a native Californian, representing his great state in Washington. Phelan was noted also for his lovely country estate Villa Montalvo, south of San Francisco, and his parties were given in the grand manner both in California and Washington.

Oil claimants had few more loyal spokesmen than Senator Phelan. For example, in a rather amusing exchange during Senate hearings on the leasing bill (February, 1916), Phelan and two other Democratic senators indicated their opinion of E. J. Justice (at this time Justice was strongly opposing the Honolulu claims):

Phelan: I do not wish to be disrespectful about this gentleman in California, but he was sent from the South into the West, just as in other years men were sent from the North into the South.
Clark [Wyoming]: He is not a native son?
Phelan: He is not a native son.
Smith [Marcus A. Smith, Arizona]: They tell us that some wise men came out of the East.
Phelan: But they carried presents.[23]

Captain Matson had to present an argument to Tallman in the Land Office, seeking his patents. It was of dubious validity, consisting of an array of facts designed to show that the Honolulu Company had pursued a "unit" plan of operations since 1908. That is to say, Matson did not assert that on every tract claimed there had been diligent work toward discovery of oil, as ordinarily required by law. But he did assert that operating from Section 10, which the company acquired from private parties, they had legitimately extended their operations into other quarter-sections nearby on the public lands. This he said they had done as quickly

---

[23] U.S. Congress, Senate, *Leasing of Oil Lands,* p. 338. See also *ibid.,* pp. 365–366; Phelan to Woodrow Wilson, May 8, 1913, Phelan to Joseph Tumulty, June –, 1913, and *passim,* Wilson Papers, File VI, Box 321; George E. Mowry, *The California Progressives,* Berkeley, Calif., 1951, p. 130 and *passim;* Gertrude Atherton, *California: An Intimate History,* New York, 1927, Dedication and pp. 309–314; Gertrude Atherton, *My San Francisco: A Wayward Biography,* New York, 1946, pp. 29, 73, 100–105, and *passim.* A recent scholar considers Phelan clearly a conservative and a "thorough believer in exploitation"—who had as one of his major concerns the welfare of California oil men. Robert Edward Hennings, "James D. Phelan and the Wilson Progressives of California," unpublished Ph.D. dissertation, University of California, Berkeley, 1961, pp. ii, 239–242, 367, 421.

as roads could be constructed, water could be hauled into the desert, and other equipment and supplies made available.

All was part of a unit plan. They were operating in territory remote from supplies and where oil as yet had not been discovered. In June, 1909, their first well, drilled on their Section 10, "blew out with dry natural gas, producing an estimated quantity of 8,000,000 cubic feet per day" and "blowing wild" for several months before being brought under control. On February 1, 1910, after further drilling, they reached the oil formations and production ran at about 100 barrels daily.

This was in 1910 on their privately owned land. There was no claim that oil had been actually discovered or even drilled for on public land in their possession previous to the executive withdrawals. Everything depended, therefore, on the case which could be made for diligent work and heavy expenditure of money aiming at discovery, according to the unit theory. Matson declared that up to December, 1913, his company had spent over $3,000,000 in developing the located lands.

Commissioner Tallman did not base his decision solely on Matson's testimony. He cited evidence from reports of agents in the Land Office tending to corroborate Matson's statements. He debated the merits of Matson's theory of "unit development." Furthermore, on some of the claims, "periods of several months elapsed with no work leading to the discovery of oil" and with no improvements. The subject of "diligence" had to be carefully considered. Finally the commissioner accepted Matson's contentions that preliminary work, such as road building, could be regarded as applicable to many claims and that, given the difficulties of operation in remote desert country, actual continuous work was not required.[24]

On four claims Tallman denied patent, pending a further investigation by the local land office. The charge had been made that the original locators were dummies. Four years later he concluded that the charge had been correct, and patent was denied.[25]

Far more important was Tallman's approval of thirteen Hono-

[24] Tallman to Lane, December 15, 1915, quoted in U.S. Congress, Senate, *Oil-Land Leasing Bill*, pp. 127–140; Gregory, memorandum for President Wilson, February 27, 1919, Records of the Department of Justice.
[25] *Ibid.*; Irvin F. Landis to J. O. Richardson, Bureau of Engineering, Washington, December 31, 1915, Navy Records.

lulu claims. The commissioner hardly came to this decision with an open mind. He was extremely friendly and lenient toward oil claimants, and perfectly willing to give rights to those who entered government lands after withdrawals. He once proposed making February 23, 1915 (the date of the Midwest decision), the effective date rather than September 27, 1909. According to this proposal those who entered government lands as late as 1915, and who violated the executive orders and the Pickett Act, would be given preferential rights for leasing. Tallman, moreover, was not willing to differentiate between those acting in good faith and those perpetrating a fraud. To do so, he said, was too difficult and expensive.

Tallman apparently had no interest in the integrity of the naval petroleum reserves. Claimants there should be given the same consideration as anywhere else. He refused to admit that the Navy had gained significant rights in these so-called reserves. They had been created merely by executive order; their status was uncertain. He also believed that an "operating reserve" would be better than trying to keep the oil in the ground. Tallman's position resembled that of the western politicians and oil men.[26]

## 5

To many, Tallman's decision on the Honolulu claims was a surprise and a shock. Officials of the Justice and Navy Departments had presented written arguments against these claims and had hoped for the best. They were convinced of weaknesses in the opposing contentions, and they knew that in California the field agents for the Land Office itself were disinclined to accept at face value Captain Matson's affidavits and arguments.

The next question was, would Secretary Lane uphold the decision of his subordinate? Quickly they learned that, so far as the Department of the Interior was concerned, this case was disposed of. Secretary Daniels recorded that one day before a Cabi-

---

[26] U.S. Congress, *General Leasing Bill,* Proceedings of the Special Joint Conference of the Committees on Public Lands and Representatives of the Departments of Justice, Navy, and Interior on H.R. 406, 64 Cong., 2 Sess., Washington, 1917, pp. 118–120. See "No Naval Reserve Lands," *Oil Age,* VI (November 22, 1912), 8–9; "A Plea for Peace," *Standard Oil Bulletin,* II (April, 1915), 2, 16.

net meeting Lane remarked, "Oh, by the way, Josephus, I've been going carefully over the Honolulu Oil case and I'm afraid you're going to lose." [27] There was nothing to do, Lane felt, but support the commissioner's decision. Ordinarily in such a case the company would have received its patents quickly.

At this point, however, a protest movement began. E. J. Justice, who was busy trying railroad cases in California, took time to wire his objections in detail, attacking the idea of unit development. How could anyone know, he asked, whether work in one location actually was related to a distant claim? The purpose of such work was "locked in [the] breast" of the Honolulu officers and "the difficulty of meeting such proof" was obvious. He warned that if the Honolulu Company won on a basis such as this other companies having claims in Buena Vista Hills would hasten to establish that they also had unit plans of operation: "As Standard Oil Co. is always building pipe lines and roads and is claiming much unpatented land it would be hard for government to meet claim now or hereafter made that company was doing such work with view of acquiring lands it now wants."

Others, including subordinates in the Interior Department, expressed their disagreement with Commissioner Tallman. In Washington Knaebel declared that he could not accept the unit theory, the idea that many claims could be acquired by general work involved in what was said to be an over-all plan. Out in San Francisco, Commander Landis noted that local agents of the Land Office had recommended proceedings adverse to the Honolulu Company. One of these agents, C. D. Hamel, did express views considerably different from Tallman's, in spite of the fact that the commissioner's decision had been based partly upon Hamel's reports. Hamel concluded that the Honolulu people had made a good many "misleading statements" as to the facts. At most, they deserved only six of the locations they claimed.[28]

---

[27] Cf. Josephus Daniels, *The Wilson Era: Years of Peace, 1910–1917*, Chapel Hill, N.C., 1944, pp. 373–374; Daniels, *End of Innocence*, p. 184. See also Landis to Richardson, December 31, 1915, Navy Records; Lane to Gregory, December 24, 1915, Knaebel to Daniels, December 27, 1915, Knaebel to Justice, December 28, 1915, Records of the Department of Justice.

[28] Justice (telegram) to Gregory, December 20, 1915, Knaebel to Gregory, December 23, 1915, *ibid.;* Landis to the Bureau of Engineering, December 21, 1915, Landis to Richardson, December 31, 1915, Navy Records; Hamel to Justice, February 14, 1916, quoted in U.S. Congress, Senate, *Oil-Land Leasing Bill*, pp. 150–166.

Secretary Daniels made up his mind to resist the Interior Department, and sought Gregory's cooperation. The result was a series of letters and conferences between officials of the two departments, aimed at stopping the Honolulu Company—at least temporarily. Daniels and Justice had strong views, while Gregory seems to have approached the issue with considerable objectivity.

But on January 29, 1916, Gregory wrote to Secretary Lane asking delay in the issuance of patents. The "whole situation," he said, was unusual. "Grave differences" of opinion existed, and he believed that a final verdict should wait if possible for judicial opinion in parallel cases then pending. If, however, so much delay were out of the question he would like the opportunity personally to examine the case and try to form an "independent" and, he should hope, "impartial" opinion. If patents should be issued, he pointed out, "the step would be practically irrevocable, both as an elimination of these immensely valuable lands from the naval reserve and as a precedent to be cited and followed in all similar cases." [29]

Lane acceded to the request. Soon Gregory brought another man into the case, who he assumed would be absolutely impartial—Solicitor General John W. Davis. Formerly a congressman, Davis was well known and highly regarded for his legal abilities, judgment, and character.

## 6

Now came a counterreaction from men of the West. Just at this time the Senate Committee on Public Lands was holding a hearing. The main subject of consideration was the leasing bill, which had recently passed the House, but much of the testimony and discussion related to the Honolulu case. Some oil men were optimistic, because of Tallman's "large view" in the matter.[30] The prevailing mood, however, was one of bitterness and frustration.

Officials of the Justice and Navy Departments were subjected

---

[29] Gregory to Lane, January 29, 1916, Records of the Department of Justice. See also Daniels to Gregory, December 22, 1915, Gregory to Knaebel, December 25, 1915, Knaebel, memorandum for Gregory, December 28, 1915, *ibid.*
[30] U.S. Congress, Senate, *Leasing of Oil Lands*, p. 72 (February 2, 1916); C. H. Gilman, "Important Decision," *Oil and Gas Journal*, XIV (January 13, 1916), 60.

to harsh criticism. This understandably did not add to their love of oil men and "oil senators," when they knew that the law and the courts were on their side. For doing their duty, it seemed, they were being persecuted. Knaebel was scorched for frank but accurate statements he made about the Midwest case. He might desire to change his "language" when he looked over his remarks, said Senator Works.[31]

Daniels and Justice were referred to several times as "carpetbaggers"—quite a word to apply to hard-working North Carolinians of the Reconstruction generation. Hardly a kind word was said for leaders in the government, except for Secretary Lane, who was often lauded, and for Tallman. References to "heroic," long-suffering oil men were numerous.[32]

James N. Gillett, ex-governor of California, and Lieutenant Governor John M. Eshleman of California were among those who attacked the Justice Department. Eshleman declared: "The Attorney General says . . . that a man who had not made a discovery—a discovery, if you please—at the time of the withdrawals has no rights whatsoever." He cited the Attorney General's supplemental report of 1916 as evidence for his charge. As a matter of fact, Gregory had said something quite different. He stated explicitly that there were three classes of claimants: first, those who had valid locations based on discovery; second, "those who were and continued in diligent prosecution of discovery work"; and, finally, "those . . . who had neither made discovery or location nor were diligently working when the order took effect, or who, if working at that time, saw fit to cease their diligence, but who afterwards, in the face of the withdrawal resumed work and appropriated the oil." [33]

Gregory also testified before the committee. With reference to diligence, he said that he did not interpret the Pickett Act to mean that a man had to work daily and never leave his tract. Diligence had "to be construed reasonably." He commented on the Honolulu case. The Solicitor General was threshing out that question at the moment, he said, and he had not made up his own mind about it even though the Secretary of the Navy had. On

---

[31] U.S. Congress, Senate, *Leasing of Oil Lands*, pp. 360–361.

[32] *Ibid.*, pp. 151, 335–338, 379, and *passim*.

[33] *Ibid.*, p. 114; Department of Justice, Attorney General, *Withdrawn Oil Lands*, p. 12.

the "unit theory" he added: "Personally I have never held that the work counted by the Pickett Act is necessarily confined to work done within the boundaries of the tract claimed." [34]

Gregory gave every indication of trying to be fair. There seems to have been no legitimate basis for the extreme attacks made on him and his subordinates.

Josephus Daniels and his naval reserves were subjected to quite a barrage. Ex-Governor Gillett attempted to prove that Buena Vista Hills was so cut up by private claims that the Navy should abandon it. The Navy had no right to the land in the first place, he declared, unless it could be claimed that "under international law the Navy has the right to take a prize if it can get it." Why pick on California anyway? There were other lands that might be held in reserve. But conditions being what they were, claims inside the reserves were "just as sacred" as those outside the reserves. Gillett had a solution: those whose claims antedated the withdrawal should get a patent; those whose claims occurred later should obtain a preferential lease.[35]

Daniels came in person to reply. He denied that Buena Vista Hills was cut up and ruined as a reserve. If the government won the Honolulu case and the Southern Pacific cases they would have a most valuable property. Implicit in his discussion was the right of the Navy to this land. Private claimants who had a genuine equity could protect themselves, he said, under existing law, through judicial procedure.

Turning to the current leasing bill, Daniels expressed his concern. The naval reserves must be excepted from it in every way, shape, and form. "I insist that it is wrong practice to require the leasing of lands to all these people without judicial investigation." [36] He believed that people operating illegally on the reserves had taken enough oil already to more than compensate themselves for money invested. This could be judicially determined. If the leasing bill before the committee were passed, however, it would reward many claimants who had "no legal or equitable rights," and much of the reserve would be lost. Worst of all, if relief amendments proposed by Senator Phelan were

---

[34] U.S. Congress, Senate, *Leasing of Oil Lands*, pp. 347–351.
[35] *Ibid.*, pp. 137–146; see also pp. 288, 335, and *passim*.
[36] *Ibid.*, p. 208 and *passim*.

added to the bill they would take away "not only the cream but the milk." [37]

Daniels knew that if the Honolulu Company, for example, failed to obtain patents it would then seek leases under this new legislation. He was convinced that it did not deserve either leases or patents. Up to a point Commissioner Tallman agreed. The Honolulu Company would seek leases. Furthermore, he declared, they would be entitled to them.[38]

## 7

All efforts at this time toward compromise on a leasing bill were failures. The fate of the Honolulu claims now hinged upon individuals in the executive departments, and upon one individual especially—E. J. Justice.

During the Senate hearings just described, in February of 1916, a friend of the oil men spoke more wisely perhaps than he knew. Their most determined and resourceful opponent in the government, he said, was Assistant Attorney General Justice in California. This man was fighting them; it had been his protest against Tallman's decision which "resulted in it being held up." [39] In the months to come, Justice quite possibly played the deciding role in blocking patents for the Honolulu Company.

That company came very close to having its way. In February–March, 1916, John W. Davis was investigating this whole case in accordance with Gregory's decision to "let an entirely new man take up the problem with a perfectly open mind on the subject." On March 3 Davis put his recommendations into a memorandum for the Attorney General. Assuming, he said, that Commissioner Tallman had correctly stated the facts in his decision, he believed that the case had been "properly resolved" in favor of the Honolulu Company. He did, however, recommend that Tallman review the evidence as stated by Hamel and Justice.[40]

Gregory was on the verge of giving in. He wrote to Lane and

---

[37] *Ibid.*, p. 213.
[38] U.S. Congress, *General Leasing Bill*, pp. 103–114 (December, 1916).
[39] Lieutenant Governor Eshleman of California in U.S. Congress, Senate, *Leasing of Oil Lands*, p. 375.
[40] Gregory to Daniels, February 16, 1916, Davis, memorandum for the Attorney General, March 3, 1916, Records of the Department of Justice.

said that he would be "quite content" to abide by Lane's decision, after such re-examination of the case as Lane might wish to make. However, this letter was not sent. And Davis' original recommendations were never disclosed, although rumors circulated that he had favored Honolulu.[41]

About this time Justice arrived in Washington from California and conferred with Davis. After one conference he wrote a long-hand letter to Davis, saying that he was hesitant about offering "so many and material suggestions" and stressing that he was offering *"respectfully"* his views. "As I said yesterday I may not be able to free myself from the atmosphere of the situation which has grown out of my being an attorney and the partisanship of the position—." There were other conferences between policy-makers in the Justice Department, but it seems safe to conclude that Justice was the deciding influence in preventing a surrender to Lane and Tallman.[42]

As a good many attested, Justice was a forceful personality, an idealist, earnestly concerned about conservation matters and the preservation of democratic opportunities. But as Senator La Follette observed him, he was also "a man of calm, well-poised judgment." La Follette continued: "I never saw a man, upon such limited acquaintance, in the results of whose deliberate and ample investigation of any matter I would have more confidence."

From 1914 to 1917 Justice was attaining a mastery of the facts in the oil cases, which could not but impress the less informed.[43] Justice believed—although certain information he hesitated to put into print—that fraud and monopoly were the rule in the San Joaquin Valley. Large companies dominated Buena Vista Hills; the smallest was a million-dollar corporation. The time for "small operators" had passed long before, he said. Large companies in California were "associated together in fixing prices for the consumer and producer. . . . That is the prices rise and fall

---

[41] Gregory to Lane, March 6, 1916 (not signed and marked "not sent"), *ibid.;* Senator Thomas in *Cong. Record*, 65 Cong., 2 Sess., p. 10487, September 19, 1918.

[42] Justice to Davis, March 9, 1916, Gregory to Lane, April 12, 1916, Records of the Department of Justice.

[43] Senator Swanson in U.S. Congress, Senate, *Oil-Land Leasing Bill*, pp. 56–57, 79 (January 17, 1917); Justice in *ibid.*, pp. 6–10 and *passim;* Senator La Follette in *Cong. Record*, 66 Cong., 1 Sess., p. 4752, August 28, 1919.

throughout the state simultaneously." [44] Outright fraud was common, and he could talk at length about clear-cut examples. In many instances these large outfits had shamefully conducted their operations, trying to get at the oil, and had let water into the oil sands, destroying the public resources.

In Reserve No. 2 at the time of Taft's withdrawal only two wells had been drilled into the oil sands, both of which went to patent. Since that withdrawal big operators had sunk 215 wells, many without lawful authority. And now on the basis of these alleged rights, they were trying to destroy the naval reserve.

Justice said of the Honolulu Company that they had spent no money which he considered legitimate for holding their claims to public land. They had spent money on Section 10, which they owned and on which they drilled their first well. [45] Probably in 1915–16 Justice suspected more than he knew about Section 10 and the part it played in the Honolulu claims.

Justice's arguments, and perhaps those of Daniels, were sufficient to convince John W. Davis. Gregory's doubts were also resolved. On April 12 Gregory wrote Lane a new letter eight pages long, arguing powerfully against giving patents to the Honolulu Company. He could not accept the idea, after "painstaking investigation," that a claimant could scatter his diligence; could "make one unit of reasonable diligence . . . suffice to hold an indefinite number of claims by unifying them in his plan of operations." He went on: "The beginning of work upon a single road might thus become the means of acquiring what would amount to an option upon an entire oil field."

What Gregory sought was a further delay in granting patents, pending decisions of the courts in similar cases. In asking such a delay, he said, he had in mind the fact that no hearing had ever been had in this case and that there were certain matters "susceptible of proof" that had been mentioned by the special agent (Hamel) but not by Commissioner Tallman. [46]

Finally, President Wilson had to intervene. At his request, early in 1917, Lane set aside the commissioner's decision, and

---

[44] Testimony in U.S. Congress, Senate, *Oil-Land Leasing Bill*, pp. 12–14.
[45] *Ibid.*, pp. 8, 10, 28–29, 42–47, 78, and *passim;* testimony of Howard M. Payne of San Francisco, receiver in California oil cases, in U.S. Congress, Senate, *Leasing of Oil Lands*, pp. 153, 174–179 (February 8, 1916).
[46] Gregory to Lane, April 12, 1916, Records of the Department of Justice.

the Honolulu case was reopened for consideration of the facts and the law.[47]

Nevertheless, by 1916 Lane and Tallman had taken a position from which they would never retreat. Lane declared that as to the "controlling facts" in the case there was "little, if any, dispute." Arrayed against him were Gregory and his subordinates, Daniels and his subordinates, conservationists in both parties, the special agents Hamel and George Hayworth in Tallman's own Land Office, and finally Woodrow Wilson. From 1916 to 1920 the President refused to abide by Lane's judgment in the case, and grew increasingly wary of Lane's advice. Lane himself complained that the President did not trust him.[48]

For the first time, in this Honolulu fight, many observers came to have doubts about Lane. The Pinchot group openly attacked him. Perhaps most humiliating of all, this squabble within the administration was public knowledge. Lane stood revealed before his own friends as a Secretary of the Interior frustrated by his colleagues and overruled by his chief.[49] Why he did not resign in these circumstances is a real question.

Developments in the Honolulu case from 1916 to 1920 tended further to show that Lane had been mistaken, that Matson and the Honolulu interests had misrepresented their "diligence" and their rights. In the summer of 1917 Assistant Attorney General Francis J. Kearful went to California and discovered new evidence, which was to count heavily thereafter with most officials informed on the subject. As Gregory put it, this new "unquestioned documentary evidence" showed clearly that the so-called diligent work performed by the Honolulu people "was merely a cheap pretense and intended for the purpose of excluding bona fide prospectors until the completion of a well on adjoining land in private ownership [Section 10] might demonstrate the oil-bearing character of the claims in question."

---

[47] Gregory, memorandum for President Wilson, February 27, 1919, *ibid.*

[48] *Ibid.;* Daniels, *End of Innocence,* p. 290 and *passim.* See also Lane to Wilson, February 9, 1920, Wilson to Lane, February 11, 1920, Wilson Papers, File II, Box 167; "Memorandum of an Interview with Mrs. Woodrow Wilson—January 4, 1926," "Interview with William B. Wilson, Former Secretary of Labor, January 12, and 13, 1928," Ray Stannard Baker Papers, Series I, Box 58, Library of Congress.

[49] Senator Thomas in *Cong. Record,* 65 Cong., 2 Sess., p. 10493, September 19, 1918; Francis J. Kearful to President Wilson, June 28, 1920, Records of the Department of Justice.

Matson, it developed, had been concentrating his efforts on this Section 10. While he had kept up an appearance of work on public land sections, he had avoided expenditures there. At the same time he was determined to keep rivals off, employing a patrol with orders to shoot if necessary. Matson's letters and his contracts with earlier locators revealed these activities. He was under no obligation to develop these claims, according to his contracts, unless Section 10 proved productive. His so-called "unit" development work was therefore fraudulent.[50]

A series of new officials in both political parties were convinced of the fraudulent intent of the Honolulu Company. They included Assistant Attorneys General Leslie C. Garnett and Henry F. May; Secretary of the Interior John Barton Payne, who succeeded Lane in 1920; and Harlan Stone and Owen Roberts of the Coolidge administration.

Not among this number were Harry Daugherty and Albert B. Fall of the Harding administration. They succeeded in 1921 in giving the Honolulu Company leases to all seventeen quarter-sections of land for which it had failed to receive patents. Three years later (1924) an Assistant Attorney General under Harlan Stone summed up the disillusioning conclusion of this case: "Thus did the Honolulu Company, by its 'good faith' and 'diligence' in holding possession (as against other explorers) by cabins, lumber for derricks, armed men, etc., while experimenting on other and patented lands, secure a lease at minimum rates, for the full development of 17 quarter-sections of government oil lands in Naval Reserve No. 2. And this was made possible by retroactive legislation, modifying the law to the company advantage, and by the sympathetic attitude of the Interior Department under Secretary Lane and the profound sense of *justice* which moved Secretary Fall." [51]

---

[50] Gregory, memorandum for President Wilson, February 27, 1919, *ibid.* See also Gregory to the commissioner of the Land Office, October 19, 1917, enclosing an eleven-page brief prepared for the Attorney General by Francis J. Kearful, and memorandum by Henry F. May, Assistant Attorney General, March 4, 1920, *ibid.;* Nathaniel H. Wright to Irvin F. Landis, November 21, 1917, Navy Records. The Honolulu Company also acquired a reputation of being the most stubborn and recalcitrant of the oil companies, so far as cooperation with officials of the Navy or Justice Department was concerned. See Landis to J. O. Richardson, August 16, 1916, *ibid.* Timothy Spellacy referred to the Honolulu Company as holding land with Winchester rifles. Spellacy to Secretary Lane, November 27, 1915 (copy), Wilson Papers, File VI, Box 505.
[51] W. W. Dyar, memorandum, May 7, 1924, Records of the Department of

8

In the short span of one year, from February, 1915, to early 1916, the issues in the petroleum dispute had crystallized. The Supreme Court, by upholding the executive withdrawals of 1909, did much to establish future lines of argument. Oil men fought back, creating the Oil Industry Association of California. Secretary Lane and Commissioner Tallman of the Land Office increasingly threw their weight on the side of western claimants. Economic sectionalism, it would seem, underlay these disputes over the public lands.

The petroleum question by 1916 had become a personal matter for many people. The outstanding fact was that Secretary of the Interior Lane stood repudiated by his own administration in the Honolulu case. About the same time he was falling into disfavor in Wilson circles because of personal characteristics and weaknesses, including a tendency to spill Cabinet secrets to his friends in California. The Pinchot group meanwhile was losing confidence in him. Secretary Lane had become, in his own right, an issue of importance in this long-lived controversy.

---

Justice. See also Leslie C. Garnett and Henry F. May, petition for rehearing in Honolulu case, undated but 1920, James E. Crawford to Kearful, June 5, 1919, Owen Roberts to C. Bascom Slemp (Coolidge's secretary), May 3, 1924, Coolidge to Attorney General Stone, May 6, 1924, Stone to Curtis D. Wilbur, January 24, 1925, and *passim, ibid.*

# Pinchot, Lane, and the West in 1916

**CHAPTER V**

*The trouble with Mr. Pinchot is that every man who disagrees with him concerning the disposition of our natural resources is either himself a thief or the defender of and an apologist for thieves. Congress, under the leadership of Mr. Wilson, has been doing things, and solving problems, the Republicans found themselves unable to cope with.*

Senator Thomas J. Walsh to C. S. Jackson
of the *Oregon Journal*, September 6, 1916

1

Gifford Pinchot and his group followed closely almost everything connected with conservation. They made a practice, for example, of collecting Secretary Lane's speeches and memoranda issued from the Interior Department. They came to believe that Lane used too many "words, words, words" which failed to square with the facts. In their eyes he was too much a spokesman of the West. He was untrustworthy. One can imagine Pinchot and his friends talking among themselves about the following speech, which Lane delivered at the Panama-Pacific Exposition, in San Francisco, on February 20, 1915.

Lane's subject was "The American Pioneer." The pioneer, he said, was for him "the one hero of this day":

Without him we would not be here. Without him banners would not fly, nor bands play. . . . Here he stands at last beside this western sea, the incarnate soul of his insatiable race—the American pioneer. Pity? He scorns it. Glory? He does not ask it. . . . In his long wandering he has had time to think. He has talked with the stars, and they have taught him not to ask why. . . . Perhaps strained nerves may some-

times think the gesture of the pioneer to be abrupt, and his voice we
know has been hardened by the winter winds. But his neighbors will
soon come to know that he has no hatred in his heart, for he is without
fear; that he is without envy, for none can add to his wealth. . . .

And his last lines extolled the American pioneer as that "mystic
materialist." [1]

Lane wrote dozens of speeches and articles, or permitted them
to be written about himself, in a similar turgid style, waxing
most eloquent about the glories of the great West. He was also
capable of rising to philosophic heights and of winning the praise
of such a man as Justice Oliver Wendell Holmes, Jr.[2]

Attitudes toward Lane were important in 1916. If there were
many who reacted negatively, there were also many who respected him. To westerners he often seemed the epitome of justice
and moderation in the federal government. Undoubtedly his
being in the Cabinet was politically helpful to the President.
This was the year in which President Wilson was re-elected over
Charles Evans Hughes, by a margin of a few thousand votes. It
would be possible to say—though difficult to prove—that conservation issues associated with Lane were a deciding factor in the
election. It is even conceivable that western petroleum interests
made the difference, that they could have swung the election
against Wilson had they thought his administration hostile or
had they believed the Republicans more friendly. But they did
not. Westerners often thought in terms of a simple choice: it
was Wilson and Lane, or Hughes and Pinchot.

In some respects, the happenings of this year bore directly
upon petroleum disputes. No less important were the implications and long-range effects.

---

[1] Address by Lane, February 20, 1915, Gifford Pinchot Papers, Box 1856, Library of Congress. See also Slattery to Pinchot, January 16, 1917, enclosing
"Memorandum for the Press" from the Department of the Interior, *ibid.*,
Box 1838; *The Letters of Franklin K. Lane*, edited by Anne W. Lane and
Louise H. Wall, Boston, 1922, pp. 165–168. Lane's literary style, even in his
official reports, drew widespread comment. An amusing indication of this
is "In the Driftway," *Nation*, CVII (December 14, 1918), 730.

[2] See *Letters of Franklin K. Lane*, pp. 91–94 and *passim;* Honoré Willsie, "Mr.
Lane and the Public Domain," *Harper's Weekly*, LVIII (in 4 pts., August 23,
30, September 6, 13, 1913); Will Erwin, "Franklin K. Lane, the Story of a
Presidential Impossibility," *Collier's*, LVI (February 26, 1916), 12–13, 30, 32–33,
36.

## 2

The key to Franklin Lane's policies, and to some of his difficulties, was a conception of progress roughly similar to Herbert Hoover's. Enterprising men, he believed, would create ever-continuing opportunities in the industrial age. He once said, referring especially to Indian policy, "the Indian is no more entitled to idle land than a white man." [3] In the case of petroleum he never believed, as experts often asserted, that the supply would last only a generation. Encouraged by the government, oil men would make new discoveries in the field and so would chemists in the laboratories. America would go pushing ahead to ever distant frontiers. Lane belonged to the New Era school of optimists and materialists and had their virtues as well as their weaknesses. In the final analysis, although he wished to be fair to all, he was pro-business.

Lane and Attorney General Gregory afford an interesting contrast, so far as attitudes toward business and wealth are concerned. Lane believed that "the law must not be severe or lenient with any man simply because he is rich nor because he is poor." In practice he favored relaxing the law so as to benefit powerful oil interests in the name of progress. Gregory evinced a deep distrust of money men and money power and a sympathy for the underdog. He was suspicious of anyone having a tendency "to snuggle up to any convenient millionaire." [4] And he once declared of an opposite tendency, "I have always thought that sympathy for the weak and the oppressed was the finest characteristic a public man could have; the powerful need [no] sympathy even if they are entitled to it."

Lane, an admirer of the rich and the successful, aspired in his youth for a palace on Nob Hill and in his maturity for a home like Monticello, or perhaps like that of his friend Senator Phelan at Villa Montalvo in California. He would work for develop-

---

[3] *Annual Report of the Department of the Interior, 1914*, 2 vols., Washington, 1914, I, 12; *Letters of Franklin K. Lane*, pp. 208–209.

[4] Lane to Orva G. Williams, April 7, 1904, *ibid.*, p. 46; Gregory to George W. Anderson, June 4, 1924, Thomas W. Gregory Papers, Library of Congress. See also Ralph H. Gabriel, *The Course of American Democratic Thought*, 2nd ed., New York, 1956, pp. 163, 168, and *passim* for a brief analysis of the "Gospel of Wealth." Strong overtones of such ideas and of an old-fashioned faith in business leadership are to be found in Lane's thinking.

ment of the West without worrying particularly where the profits went. Gregory and others had a different conception of progress.[5]

President Wilson, Gregory, Daniels, La Follette, and the Pinchot group were more suspicious than Lane was of progress and enlightenment through the leadership of businessmen. Progressives all, they differed among themselves, and significantly with Lane on matters of detail which led to broad policy.

The dominant theme in Secretary Lane's annual reports was development of the West, which was to be achieved primarily through the new leasing program for water power sites and nonmetallic mineral lands. Lane sponsored various bills, but they were soon stalled. The Secretary then strove for reorganization of the Department, for elimination of red tape, and for developmental measures of more or less importance.

In 1914 Lane reported that three unusual things had occurred in the preceding year: ". . . the passing of the Cherokee Nation, the opening of Alaska, and the advancement of a series of measures aimed to promote the further development of the West." It was characteristic of Lane that he showed a real grasp of Indian traditions and of the difficulty of assimilating these people "into a harsh competitive world of business" while he also approved of allotting their lands (thus placing them in that competitive world). And notwithstanding his intelligence and sympathy, he waxed eloquent about the great progress being made. This was in a transitional period when an orgy of exploitation was occurring in Oklahoma. Said Lane: "The word of the white man has been made good. These native and aspiring people have been lifted as American citizens into full fellowship with their civilized conquerors. . . . Surely there is something fine in this slight bit of history. . . ." [6]

Of Lane's Alaskan policy, the leading scholar, Ernest Gruening, has declared that Lane understood better than did Pinchot the

[5] Gregory to Daniels, February 19, 1924, Gregory Papers; Secretary Lane, speech before a conference of the Mining and Metallurgical Society of America, in the auditorium of the Smithsonian Institution, December 16, 1915, Senate Document 233, 64 Cong., 1 Sess., vol. 41, Washington, 1916, pp. 12–14; *Letters of Franklin K. Lane*, pp. 89–90; Jonathan Daniels, *The End of Innocence*, Philadelphia, 1954, pp. 167–169.

[6] *Annual Report of the Department of the Interior, 1914*, I, 3, 8, and *passim*; *Letters of Franklin K. Lane*, pp. 208–210; Angie Debo, *And Still the Waters Run*, Princeton, N.J., 1940, pp. 213 ff., 230 ff., 281, and *passim*.

needs of that backward area. Pinchot, he holds, was unrealistic in his fears of exploitation of Alaska. The result was that he delayed necessary development. Lane, on the other hand, argued that "the Territory of Alaska is being held prisoner in fetters of red tape, which will have to be struck off before the vast wealth of this portion of the United States can be realized." Lane called for a development board of presidential appointees confirmed by the Senate who would take over many of the functions then scattered among the Forest Service, the Road Commission, the Bureau of Mines, the Bureau of Education, and the office of the Secretary of the Interior. Nonsensical red tape would thus be eliminated.

This plan, however, did not go into effect, and Gruening comments apropos Lane's part in the failure: "Secretary Lane had a number of agencies operating in Alaska in his own Interior Department—more, actually, than any other cabinet officer. He required no legislation or the approval of any other cabinet officer or of anyone else to deal with them. . . . Yet nothing was done about it in the seven years of Secretary Lane's stewardship of the Interior Department." [7]

Perhaps Lane's greatest failing was quite simply that he talked too much. In the case of Alaska, he did inaugurate a coal leasing system and the Alaskan railroad project. He strongly supported the national parks, and the National Park Service was established under him. In other respects there were also concrete achievements. But his effervescent language, his promises beyond his capacity to deliver, his effusions about a new day in Washington, made him vulnerable to attack by the well-informed. Also—as it turned out—luck was against him.

## 3

In the summer of 1916 Pinchot publicly assailed Secretary Lane as an anticonservationist, in spite of the "widespread impression" which had been created that he was "the champion" of conservation. In the form of an open letter (published as a pamphlet), Pinchot spared few details, devoting fourteen of

---

[7] Franklin K. Lane, "Red Tape in Alaska," *Outlook*, CIX (January 20, 1915), 136–138; Ernest Gruening, *The State of Alaska*, New York, 1954, pp. 130 ff., 229; *Annual Report of the Department of the Interior, 1914*, I, 13–15.

seventeen pages to a point-by-point analysis of the oil land question. He tried to prove that Lane had actively supported oil trespassers and that at the moment he favored the Phelan oil bill, which would give these claimants what they wanted.[8]

Pinchot and his associates had the virtue of consistency. Long before Lane came to the Interior Department as Secretary they had decided upon important criteria for the administration of this office, whether the Secretary was Garfield, Ballinger, Fisher, Lane, John Barton Payne, or Fall. They watched each to see how he measured up. In 1909 during the Ballinger-Pinchot dispute Pinchot wrote to Taft: "The Secretary of the Interior has larger responsibilities than any other Cabinet officer in the conservation of natural resources. . . . [His attitude] necessarily gives direction to a multitude of decisions, few of which may involve by themselves serious injury to the Conservation movement, but which taken together may promote or retard it in a most vital way." And Pinchot continued, with words no less applicable to his later differences with Lane: "Unless he is vigorously friendly to the conservation policies and prompt to defend our natural resources against the unending aggression of private interests, the public interest must suffer. If he does not defend it in certain matters, no one else can. In these matters, indifference differs little from hostility in its final results. . . ."[9]

Most crucial, therefore, was the executive officer. First of all, did he believe in conservation? Second and little less important, was he a believer in executive responsibility and stewardship of natural resources? Pinchot had strong ideas on this subject, based upon his own experience in the government. All practical discretion should be left in the hands of administrative officers, he said. Take away the power to do bad, and you also take away the power of effective and constructive action. Specifically, in the leasing bills, he proposed to leave much discretion in Lane's hands; for Lane had seemed to epitomize the man of action, the powerful and vigilant administrator. It came as something of

---

[8] Gifford Pinchot, "Open Letter to the Honorable Franklin K. Lane, Secretary of the Interior, Concerning the Navy's Oil Lands," August 12, 1916, Pinchot Papers. Also see Lane, "Memorandum for the Press," July 3, 1916, Pinchot to Lane, July 15, 1916, *ibid.*, Box 1859.

[9] Pinchot to Taft, November 4, 1909 (copy), Harry A. Slattery Papers, Duke University Library, Durham, N.C.

a shock, therefore, when Lane opposed the attempt to give him or his department much power or discretion in the handling of leases. It seemed out of character for him to avoid responsibility.

This conflict over administrative theory lay behind the Pinchot-Lane feuding. The conservationists believed also that Lane had been weaned away from them, that he had gone over to the other side even though he refused to admit it.[10]

It can be argued that compromise with oil men and other interest groups was inevitable, that Lane—more than Pinchot—was following a logical and constructive course. Yet Pinchot's criticisms were solidly based on facts. His open letter of August, 1916, is an impressive document.

Pinchot could not prove that Lane supported the Phelan bill as such. What he did show convincingly was the long involved story of leasing measures, in which Lane had acquiesced to virtually everything the Phelan bill contained, except under different names. He pointed out, too, that Lane had spoken for relief in such terms that many anticonservationists assumed he was on their side, although Lane denied that he was. Lieutenant Governor Eshleman of California had once brought to him a proposal such as the Phelan bill, he said, and he told him he "would not stand for it." Lane also denied the existence of any disagreement with Daniels and Gregory except over the merits of a legal decision (in the Honolulu case).[11]

Pinchot's indictment was a powerful one. Lane, he maintained, had been trying since 1914 to give preferential treatment to claimants in the naval reserves, and this was the heart of Senator Phelan's current bill. He cited Lane's support of the Church bill in 1914, of the Ferris bill including an alleged "joker" in 1916,

---

[10] Pinchot testimony in U.S. Congress, Senate, *Water-Power Bill*, Hearings Before the Committee on Public Lands on H.R. 16673, an "Act for the Development of Water Power," 63 Cong., 3 Sess., Washington, 1914, p. 235; Lane testimony in U.S. Congress, House, *Water-Power Bill*, Hearings Before the Committee on Public Lands on H.R. 14893, for "Development of Water Power," 63 Cong., 2 Sess., Washington, 1914, p. 293; Pinchot, "Open Letter to the Honorable Franklin K. Lane"; Jerome G. Kerwin, *Federal Water Power Legislation*, New York, 1926, pp. 190 ff.

[11] Pinchot, "Open Letter to the Honorable Franklin K. Lane"; Lane, "Memorandum for the Press," July 3, 1916, quoted in *Cong. Record*, 64 Cong., 2 Sess., p. 1249, January 12, 1917. For an exaggerated attack on the Phelan bill see George Creel, "The Oil Story," *Pearson's Magazine*, XXXVI (September, 1916), 197–202.

and his unwillingness to accept a discretionary power to lease which might have enabled him to save the reserves. He noted Lane's developing coolness toward the idea of naval reserves. Lane "would not assume" to say what the policy ought to be, although at the same time he and his subordinates gave aid and comfort to those trying to appropriate the reserves. He quoted Eshleman of California: "The Department of the Interior, in whose jurisdiction these things properly belong, has said officially, and takes the position, that whatever the relief may be, we ought to have it." [12]

In the face of such charges and insinuations, Lane's position was weakened by his California connections and his apparent political and social ambitions. For example, in the midst of his controversy with Pinchot he pondered whether to run for the United States Senate from California, supported financially by Senator Phelan and his friends.[13] The evidence also indicated that in spirit at least he favored Phelan and the oil interests and perhaps the Phelan bill, without endorsing it publicly.

The Phelan bill was extremely generous to oil men; it is not difficult to see why conservationists denounced it. The *Oil and Gas Journal* commented that it was designed "to meet the wishes of California oil men who are located on public lands." [14] Naval reserves were specifically *included*. Undoubtedly an important part of the bill provided for preferential leasing on Reserve No. 2 to such parties as the Honolulu Company. In trying to determine the worthy claimants, new loose and ambiguous language was

---

[12] Pinchot, "Open Letter to the Honorable Franklin K. Lane." See also statements of Senators Thomas of Colorado, Smoot of Utah, and Works of California in *Cong. Record*, 64 Cong., 2 Sess., pp. 1249–50, January 12, 1917; *Annual Report of the Department of the Interior, 1913*, 2 vols., Washington, 1913, I, 17; *Annual Report of the Department of the Interior, 1915*, 2 vols., Washington, 1916, I, 17–18; "Lane Says Relief Is Due California Operator," *National Petroleum News*, VII (December, 1915), 93; James H. Teller, associate justice of the state of Colorado, to Lane, November 30, 1915, Lane to Teller, December 11, 1915, Secretary's File, Department of the Interior, National Archives; Senator Paul O. Husting's Minority Report on S. 2812, unpublished, 1917, copy in Slattery Papers.
[13] *Letters of Franklin K. Lane*, pp. 216–217.
[14] "Senator Phelan's Amendment," *Oil and Gas Journal*, XIV (February 10, 1916), 26; U.S. Congress, Senate, *Leasing of Oil Lands*, Hearings Before the Committee on Public Lands on H.R. 406, an "Act to Authorize Exploration for and Disposition of Coal, Phosphate, Oil, Gas, Potassium, or Sodium," 64 Cong., 1 Sess., Washington, 1916, p. 148 and *passim*.

employed. A "substantial" amount of work was necessary previous to the first withdrawal. Pains were taken to provide that those who had acquired claims from others, even though these claims were fraudulent, would not be affected adversely unless they had knowledge of the fraud. To prove such knowledge would be virtually impossible. Claimants could first seek patents. If they failed, they still could seek leases. The royalty was only one-eighth of production.

Senators Paul O. Husting of Wisconsin and William H. Thompson of Kansas (Democrats) denounced the provisions as "farcical if they were not so serious in their results." They continued: "The fraudulent paper claim antedating discovery which, under the mining law, was absolutely void, and represented no property interest and however often assigned could confer none, is here made the means, when coupled with work done in conscious violation of the withdrawal orders, of depriving the United States of oil deposits representing an enormous sum of money and of ruining the naval reserve in California." [15]

Beside the oil question there were other grievances among the conservationists against Lane. In the spring of 1916 a fight over the leasing of water power sites was nearing its climax in the Congress. Lane's position again was ambiguous and again at odds with his previously enunciated proposals for protection of the public interest. Earlier Lane had advanced general principles for water power development, emphasizing federal regulation and suggesting such plans as flexible fees to be charged developers in accordance with their ability to deliver horsepower cheaply to the consumer. Combination and monopoly would be absolutely prohibited. Embodying many of Lane's ideas, the Ferris bill was introduced in the House and passed. The Pinchot group approved. But in 1915–16 the Senate took under consideration and passed the Shields bill, quite a different measure. Government regulation would be weak, no fee would be charged the developer, and the vagueness of the "recapture" provision made it likely that "leases" would be similar to perpetual grants. At this time

---

[15]U.S. Congress, Senate, *Exploration for and Disposition of Coal, Phosphate, Oil, Gas, etc.*, Senate Report 319, pt. 2, 64 Cong., 1 Sess., Washington, 1916. See also Husting's Minority Report on S. 2812; Woodrow Wilson to Attorney General Gregory, August 2, 1916, Wilson to Norman Hapgood, August 2, 1916, Woodrow Wilson Papers, File VI, Box 505, Library of Congress.

the water power lobby was no less active in Washington than the oil lobby.[16]

If Secretary Lane disapproved of the Shields bill, he kept the fact hidden in his breast. It was not surprising that Pinchot denounced Lane for his "silent submission" to the Shields bill, "in direct opposition to conservation principles you once approved," nor that Pinchot generously supplied his newspaper friends with ammunition to be used against the Secretary.[17]

Water power ranked with oil as the most important of conservation issues in 1916, with a history of bitter controversy. Pinchot, Wells, Slattery, and some of their friends in Congress felt passionately on this subject of power development. Seeing conservation as of a piece, they added water power disappointments to oil in their dossier of particulars on Secretary Lane.

## 4

In the course of the political campaign Pinchot broadened his attack. He followed his criticisms of Lane with an indictment of the Wilson administration. This was sent out in the form of an open letter to 5,000 editors. The campaign of 1916 is notable for the way in which Republicans and Democrats alike had to appeal to divergent groups who were mutually antagonistic. Each party had its progressives and standpatters on domestic issues, as well as its pacifists and interventionists who disagreed about the war in Europe. The question of conservation cut through political lines in a manner that almost defied interpretation.

Pinchot made his appeal primarily to progressives. President Wilson, he said, was completely untrustworthy, both in domestic and foreign affairs. In the beginning Wilson had impressed him favorably, but gradually he had come to see that no man in public life had a greater capacity than the President "to say one thing but do another, and get away with it." And he went on: "We had all heard him declare for the Conservation of our natural resources; and have seen him neglect that policy, and refuse his help to defeat the Shields waterpower bill, the most dangerous

---

[16] Kerwin, *Federal Water Power Legislation*, pp. 182–183, 195, 198–216.
[17] Pinchot, "Open Letter to the Honorable Franklin K. Lane." See also National Conservation Association releases of January 12, 1915, March 9, 1916, and *passim*, Slattery Memoranda File, 1914–16, Slattery Papers.

attack on Conservation since Ballinger's effort to turn Alaska over to the Guggenheims." Moreover, after flouting the progressives, Wilson now came to an election year and endeavored to appease and conciliate them, using "molasses to catch flies." In contrast there was Charles Evans Hughes, a man of his word.[18]

The replies were often interesting. Many, such as Harold L. Ickes, congratulated Pinchot on his statement. But Charles K. McClatchy of the *Sacramento Bee* pointed out that Charles Evans Hughes did not say anything. He proposed to campaign on his personality, which was not much of a basis for a campaign. The editor of *Better Farming*, Frederick L. Chapman, replied that if for no other reason he would support Wilson because he had appointed Franklin K. Lane as his Secretary of the Interior. Touched on his sorest spot, Pinchot fired back a copy of his pamphlet attacking Lane's policies and his advocacy of relief for oil exploiters. This, he said, would give Lane's "exact measure." [19]

Pinchot was fighting a losing battle at this time. He had to admit, in reply to one of his correspondents, that much progressive legislation had passed under the Democrats. Many progressive Republicans, including Pinchot's brother Amos, were won over to Wilson's side. They were most inclined to support him if they approved of his "pacifistic" policy of staying out of the European war. Gifford Pinchot, however, had the eastern Republican internationalist point of view, which added to the vehemence of his assaults on Wilson.[20]

As Pinchot and other Republicans appealed for the vote, Democrats did likewise. Furthermore, Democrats held the trump cards. Most of all, they had the presidency. Circumstances also seemed to favor them. For example, to the degree that Lane lost popularity in the East, he probably regained it in the West. His sins in the eyes of Pinchot were virtues in the eyes of most west-

[18] See, for example, Pinchot to M. F. Conley of the *Big Sandy News*, Louisa, Ky., September 7, 1916, Pinchot Papers, Box 1943. See also Pinchot to Lawrence F. Abbott of *The Outlook*, September 12, 1916, *ibid.;* Martin L. Fausold, "Gifford Pinchot and the Decline of Pennsylvania Progressivism," *Pennsylvania History,* XXV (January, 1958), 25–38.

[19] Ickes to Pinchot, September 15, 1916, McClatchy to Pinchot, September 11, 1916, Chapman to Pinchot, September 29, 1916, Pinchot to Chapman with enclosure, October 4, 1916, Pinchot Papers, Box 1943.

[20] Pinchot to Clarence Poe, September 16, 1916, *ibid.,* Box 1943; Senator Walsh to Amos Pinchot, October 16, 1916, Thomas J. Walsh Papers, Library of Congress.

erners. Lane was in demand as a speaker—and was clearly a political asset to the Democratic party.

The Wilson administration at this time played a skillful political game. While appealing to progressives of both parties, it had not shut the door on conservatives and special interests. And the President himself, though he had broadened his reform outlook, was still difficult to classify. One could not be sure how far he might go (or permit his followers to go) in placating local politicians, the petroleum interests, or others. A number of concessions might flow from the iron realities of politics.

## 5

Western Democrats rallied to the support of the Wilson administration. Understandably, they were loyal to, and hoped for the best from, their own administration. By communicating with the President and exerting whatever influence they could before the election, they might win support for their precious leasing bills. If that strategy failed, they had another. They would simply win the election. Then surely they could obtain backing for the bills that they needed.

In June, 1916, Senator Walsh pointed out the political advantages of passing the oil leasing bill. Writing to the President, he summed up his thinking on the subject:

You will recall that when a number of Senators called on you some three or four weeks ago to confer with you about the so-called [oil] leasing bill, we all urged upon you, and you recognized, the wisdom of getting Secretary Lane and Secretary Daniels together at once that one department should not be at war with another concerning any feature of the bill. Since that time the differences have, unfortunately, become so acute as not only to threaten the measure, whose passage would be an additional achievement for the administration, but have stimulated efforts to discredit the Interior Department and its eminently successful head before the country.

He referred to a series of articles appearing in certain papers, intended to prove that Secretary Lane's administration was "no improvement upon the method and spirit which prevailed under Ballinger." This he regarded as "singularly unfortunate" at such a "critical juncture"—just preceding the Democratic convention. It was also unfair to Secretary Lane, who had "so richly earned the confidence of the country."

Walsh hoped that the President, amid all his cares, could find time to adjust these differences within his Cabinet. If the leasing bill could be passed with a clear understanding that the Cabinet and the administration were united behind it, then criticism would be silenced and the "troublesome issue avoided."

The President gave some encouragement. He agreed that Lane had been unjustly criticized and said that he and Lane had frankly discussed the situation. Reassuring news had also come from the Navy Department. He believed that they would be able to accommodate their differences.[21] However, the oil leasing bill did not pass, and western Democrats entered the campaign with their wishes unfulfilled.

Senator Walsh went ahead to become manager of the Democratic campaign in the West, with headquarters in Chicago, and handled this job with great energy and skill. A review of his activities, and of incoming and outgoing mail, tends to show the importance of "western" issues. Democratic workers and informants believed generally that certain speakers would be highly effective beyond the Mississippi River, while others should stay away. Bryan, Lane, and Clay Tallman received a high rating. Too, a growing number of westerners believed that their section had not been treated very well and that southerners had too much influence in the Wilson administration.[22]

On the whole, Democrats were fairly well united, reserving their sharpest words for Republicans such as Gifford Pinchot. After Pinchot's attack on Lane and the administration, Senator Walsh considered a countermove. Suggestions came from Clay Tallman in the Land Office. A circular ought to be put out, the commissioner said, and the oil question ought to be discussed in such a way as to show that Lane was trying to settle things fairly.

[21] Walsh to Wilson, June 20, 1916, Wilson to Walsh, June 26, 1916, Wilson Papers, File VI, Box 505. See also Senator Phelan to Wilson, May 25, 1916, Josephus Daniels to Wilson, June 7, 1916, Wilson to Gregory, August 2, 1916, Wilson to Norman Hapgood, August 2, 1916, *ibid.;* Senator Charles S. Thomas to Joseph Tumulty, April 21, 1915, *ibid.,* Box 267; "Oil Leasing Bill Will Not Be Vetoed," *Oil and Gas Journal,* XIV (June 1, 1916), 28. Walsh meanwhile demonstrated in the Senate a remarkable grasp of the oil question in its technical aspects. He seems to have recognized as well the Navy's rights in the matter. *Cong. Record,* 64 Cong., 1 Sess., pp. 10936–38, July 13, 1916.
[22] See, for example, Walsh to Governor John B. Kendrick, Cheyenne, Wyo., September 16, 1916, Kendrick to Walsh, September 27, 1916, Walsh Papers; Fred Dubois to Walsh, October 1, 1916, *ibid.*

Further, he recommended a special appeal to oil operators. The title of a circular might be: "WHAT THE OIL OPERATORS WILL GET IF THEY GET HUGHES." Such a document, "properly handled," ought to be "tremendously effective." [23]

Walsh believed in somewhat the same approach, but he did not accept the idea of an appeal to oil men as a group. Rather, he sent a letter to every Democratic newspaper in the western states, suggesting that Democratic papers should give the "widest publicity" to current rumors and beliefs that, if Hughes were elected, his Secretary of the Interior would be Pinchot. Walsh concluded: "Ask your readers how they would enjoy having Pinchot [as] Secretary of the Interior." [24]

Late in the campaign Walsh did appeal to one oil man for financial aid. This was Verner Z. Reed of the Midwest Oil Company, to whom Walsh and Vance McCormick, the national chairman, sent this wire: "In desperate need of funds to keep up swelling Wilson tide. Will you not come to our rescue?" Reed had previously volunteered his assistance, and perhaps he supplied the funds requested.[25]

Among the Democratic leaders were several directly implicated later in the Teapot Dome scandal. E. L. Doheny of the Pan-American Petroleum Company was chosen as a Democratic elector in California. Already in the Wilson years the Pinchot group was suspicious of Doheny and his activities, although to the public at large his reputation was good.[26]

In Colorado the owners of the *Denver Post* gave their support to Wilson. Frederick G. Bonfils and Harry E. Tammen, the sort to expect quick returns on an investment, complained that their paper had not been receiving friendly treatment from the Denver post office; whereupon Secretary of the Treasury William G. McAdoo and Postmaster General Burleson almost fell over

[23] Tallman to Walsh, September 26, 1916, *ibid.*

[24] Walsh to ———, undated but about October 1, 1916, *ibid.* See also Walsh's opinion of Pinchot, expressed in a letter to C. S. Jackson of the *Oregon Journal*, September 6, 1916. Walsh said in part: "The trouble with Mr. Pinchot is that every man who disagrees with him concerning the disposition of our natural resources is either himself a thief or the defender of and an apologist for thieves." *Ibid.*

[25] Walsh and McCormick to Reed, October 30, 1916, *ibid.*

[26] Secretary of State, California, *Statement of Vote,* November 7, 1916, Sacramento, 1916, p. 2; Philip Wells to Pinchot, December 6, 1919, Pinchot Papers, Box 1700.

each other in their anxiety to smooth out any difficulties. Running a notoriously sensational and irresponsible newspaper, Bonfils and Tammen had been accused in 1914 of exacting a bribe from the Rock Island Railroad. Later in the Teapot Dome inquiry they were shown to have blackmailed Harry F. Sinclair to the amount of almost a quarter of a million dollars on the threat of exposing his secret lease of Teapot Dome.[27]

Wilsonian Democrats in 1916 felt compelled to work for the support of men such as these, as well as the progressive and more respectable factions in the West. Not long after the election had ended victoriously, Bonfils came to Washington, hailed as the dominant owner of the principal organ in Colorado which had supported Wilson, a good friend of McAdoo, and "a strong admirer and supporter of Secretary Lane." [28]

For Franklin Lane, 1916 was an eventful year. In January he was hopeful of being appointed to the United States Supreme Court to succeed Joseph R. Lamar, who had just died; but instead the place went to Louis Brandeis. Alluding to this and other matters, Lane referred to himself as "disconsolate." [29]

In July he thought seriously of running for the United States Senate from California. Senator Phelan urged that he do so and promised to "see that all the necessary money was raised." Seeking advice from his wife, Lane provided one of the best of evidences that he was quite unhappy at this time and would have been delighted to leave the Interior Department if he could go in a dignified way. "I really feel very much tempted to do it at times [to run for the Senate] because things have been made so uncomfortable by some of my fool colleagues [Gregory and Daniels] who have butted in on my affairs."

[27] McAdoo to Burleson, August 14, September 9, 1916, Albert S. Burleson Papers, vols. 17–18, Library of Congress; Burleson to McAdoo, October 14, 1916, Burleson to Tammen, October 14, 1916, Bonfils to Burleson, October 19, 1916, Ruskin McArdle (Burleson's secretary) to Burleson, October 24, 1916, McArdle to Bonfils, October 25, 1916, McArdle to B. F. Stapleton (Denver postmaster), October 25, 1916, *ibid.;* Kenneth Stewart and John Tebbel, *Makers of Modern Journalism,* New York, 1952, pp. 185–190.
[28] M. D. McEniry of the General Land Office, Denver, to Joseph J. Cotter, Department of the Interior, Washington, November 6, 1917, Secretary's File.
[29] *Letters of Franklin K. Lane,* pp. 199–202. See also memorandum of a letter from Senator Phelan to Woodrow Wilson, January 10, 1916, and Wilson's letter in reply, January 11, 1916, Wilson Papers, File VI, Box 321; *New York Times,* January 7, 1916.

Next, the attacks by Pinchot added to Lane's discomfort. He would not even reply to Pinchot, declaring: He "wrote me thirty pages to prove that I was a liar, and rather than read that again I will admit the fact." [30]

In the campaign, Lane was loyal to his President and his party, yet an occasional statement reveals what a gulf lay between this Californian and the traditional dedicated Democrat. In a letter to the President of June 8, he offered advice on the platform, which he thought should be "one long joyful shout of exalta-tion" over the achievements of Wilson's administration. But Lane went on to make the assertion that previous to Wilson the Re-publicans had been the only forward-looking party: "The Re-publican party was for half a century a constructive party, and the Democratic party was the party of negation and complaint." Such a view would never have been expressed by a Gregory, a Daniels, or a Cordell Hull, and the President himself had once proclaimed that as a southerner and a historian there was noth-ing in the history of the South of which he was ashamed.[31] Such attitudes should have been known to Lane. For an ambitious man, he was sadly lacking in discretion and reserve.

Nevertheless, in 1916 Lane proved his ability once again and his usefulness to the President. He served on the Joint High Commission which was trying to solve differences between the United States and Mexico. Amid these labors on the East Coast he watched the course of the campaign. Finally, as the Democrats dramatically seized the victory, he joined in the chorus of thanks-giving and praise.

According to Lane, the "real progressivism" of the West de-cided the election. Western men, in contrast with those in the East, could not be delivered. "The West," he said, *"thinks for itself."* California was the decisive state. Not until November 10 were the results definite. A majority of 15,000 in San Francisco contributed importantly to Wilson's statewide total, leaving him with a bare margin of 3,000 votes. This was enough to assure his victory. In the oil regions, Kern County gave Wilson a solid

---

[30] *Letters of Franklin K. Lane,* pp. 216–217, 222.
[31] *Ibid.,* pp. 211–212; quotations from Wilson in Arthur S. Link, "The Wilson Movement in North Carolina," *North Carolina Historical Review,* XXIII (October, 1946), 484, n. 7.

majority. The Democratic representative, Denver S. Church, was easily re-elected, running ahead of the President.[32]

Curiously, Thomas W. Gregory took almost as much pride in the western vote as did Lane. As a Texan, Gregory claimed the prerogative of being both western and southern. It was a great time for the Democrats, or as one of Gregory's friends proclaimed, "the greatest political event" of their lives.[33]

The election was often interpreted as a defeat for Gifford Pinchot. Thus Senator Thomas of Colorado said on the floor of the Senate that sentiment in his region was "stronger than partisanship"; they did not want any repressive federalizing policies for the resources of the West. He believed that Hughes, by accepting the support of Pinchot, had lost thousands of votes in the public land states.

Secretary Lane, having won this round with Pinchot, was feeling good. His department, he admitted, was rather "stuck up" over the results of the election. To Frank Cobb of the *New York World* he wrote in a half-jocular vein that the "states which the Interior Department deals with are the states which elected Mr. Wilson." And to another he expressed the belief: "All of us will be taken a bit more seriously now, I guess."[34]

For the western Democratic politician this election had a significance that is difficult to exaggerate. After all, the South always voted Democratic; that was to be expected. But the West had done the job this time. Only two states north of the Ohio River and east of the Mississippi (Ohio and New Hampshire) had contributed to Wilson's success. It was truly a sectional victory. Lane quoted a telegram from Bryan: "Shake. Many thanks. It was great. The West, a stone which the builders rejected, has

[32] *Letters of Franklin K. Lane,* pp. 227–228; Secretary of State, California, *Statement of Vote; New York Times,* November 10, 1916; George E. Mowry, "1916 and the Lost Election," in *The California Progressives,* Berkeley, Calif., 1951, pp. 247–277.

[33] George W. Anderson to Gregory, November 11, 1916, Gregory to Anderson, November 13, 1916, Gregory Papers. See also Paul O. Husting to Gregory, November 29, 1916, *ibid.;* Senator Walsh, Chicago, to Senator Key Pittman, Reno, Nev., November 9, 1916, Walsh Papers; Walsh quoted in *San Francisco Chronicle,* November 10, 1916; Senator Phelan to Joseph Tumulty, December 30, 1916, Wilson Papers, File VI, Box 321.

[34] Lane to Cobb, November 11, 1916, Lane to James K. Moffitt, November 12, 1916, in *Letters of Franklin K. Lane,* pp. 227–229; *Cong. Record,* 64 Cong., 2 Sess., p. 1049, January 9, 1917.

become the head of the corner." [35] But had it? Would people of the West receive benefits commensurate with their hopes and labors of 1916? They would not, and the result was to be a considerable disillusionment.

---

[35] *Letters of Franklin K. Lane,* p. 229.

# New Horizons for Petroleum

 **CHAPTER VI**

*I want to say that all patriots are not in office; some of them are oil men, and they are perfectly willing to give up what they have to the Government.*

E. L. Doheny, June, 1917

1

"The new age is primarily the oil age," declared Sheldon Clark of the Sinclair Refining Company in 1918; and he continued, speaking to a jobbers' convention: "The present war has opened up a vista which shows petroleum as the master of human destiny. . . . With the growth of the oil industry we are becoming the king breakers, for without it the war against autocracy could not be carried to a successful conclusion." He complimented his fellow oil men on their patriotic contributions to victory and expressed the hope that they would continue on their present "unselfish course." [1]

Three years later Senator William E. Borah lamented that oil men had become "kingmakers" as well as "breakers": "To promote their vast designs," he declared, "these oil magnates are capable of starting revolutions in Mexico, instigating civil wars in Asia, of setting fire to Europe and the world to crush a competitor." [2]

It may be doubted whether oil men were as ruthless as Borah

[1] Address of March 29, 1918, "Coming Age To Be One of Petroleum, Says Clark," *National Petroleum News*, X (April 3, 1918), 16.
[2] Borah to John E. Semmes, April 23, 1921, quoting a French newspaper, William E. Borah Papers, Box 202, Library of Congress.

charged. On the other hand, it would be unrealistic to think that any economic group, or industry, sacrificed itself in the patriotic surge of 1917–18. The oil industry certainly did not. Chances that oil men, in the war years, might be governed by prewar prejudices and ambitions were greater than in some other lines of enterprise. In new oil fields, or in the matter of claims, they had "a bear by the tail." The struggle for "relief" bills never ceased, while proposals of price-fixing and government operation were bitterly resisted.

The oil man's duty, as he saw it, was to find oil and produce it with a minimum of government restraint. Temporarily, some regulations must be expected, but he and his fellows would work for self-regulation of the industry. Possibly they could do more than that. As oil executives moved into key positions in the wartime agencies, they sought a fundamental change in policy: the government should rid itself of the old suspicions and punitive tactics. It should *assist* oil men in domestic and foreign expansion.

## 2

One who viewed optimistically the contribution of businessmen was Secretary of the Interior Franklin K. Lane. The war period was tremendously exciting for Lane. In 1916–17 he was among the chauvinists of the Cabinet, accepting *in toto* the stories of German atrocities, urging an all-out effort to stop the Hun. As one of the six Cabinet members in the Council of National Defense, he saw the necessity for an unprecedented mobilization of men and resources. The strength of America in this crisis, he believed, could be found in the "adventuresome spirit and the exploiting energies" of men who had pushed into frontier country and taken up government lands. Yet this was not enough. The making of modern war demanded the utmost of the chemist, the geologist, the topographer, the utmost from the brains and civilization of America. Out of such an effort America should emerge "as the center of the world's thought" and of its morality.[3]

Capable of seeing the darker side of war, Lane gave it but little thought, and was contemptuous of those who hesitated.

---

[3] *Annual Report of the Department of the Interior, 1917*, 2 vols., Washington, 1918, I, 3–13. See also *The Letters of Franklin K. Lane*, edited by Anne W. Lane and Louise H. Wall, Boston, 1922, pp. 233–241 and *passim*.

He was uninhibited by fears of what the war might bring, exhilarated by his meetings with Balfour, Joffre, railroad presidents, industrial magnates, and an endless stream of people. These were "great days," he wrote, in one of his many animated descriptions of the Washington scene.[4]

A number of new government officials were drawn to Washington by the Council of National Defense, established in August, 1916. This body included Secretary Lane and the Secretaries of War, Navy, Agriculture, Commerce, and Labor. Most of the work, however, was accomplished by an advisory commission headed by Walter S. Gifford of the American Telephone and Telegraph Company. Bernard Baruch was one of its members. He was later to head the all-powerful, coordinating War Industries Board. Early in 1917 various committees were established, one for each industry, to give assistance to the Council of National Defense. These advisers were the famous dollar-a-year men, drawn primarily from the ranks of large corporations.

Dollar-a-year men, who were numbered in the hundreds, were subjected to considerable criticism. According to Amos Pinchot, they sat in the morning as "foremost patriots," directing mobilization, while in the afternoon they conducted their own business with newly acquired inside information and often with government contracts. Harry Slattery had similar criticisms. In his office building, he said, he had been "surrounded" by "this National Council of Defense outfit," and from the first he had had his "strong suspicions about the whole bunch."[5] Such suspicions and prejudices had some basis, so far as the petroleum industry was concerned.

The Petroleum Service Committee, as it was called, was headed by Alfred C. Bedford, president of the Standard Oil Company

---

[4] Lane to George W. Lane, May 3, 1917, *ibid.*, p. 250 and *passim*.

[5] Amos Pinchot, "War Profits and Patriotism" (letter to the conference committee of the Senate and House of Representatives), New York, September 18, 1917, Gifford Pinchot Papers, Box 1859, Library of Congress; Slattery to Amos Pinchot, September 22, 1917, *ibid.*, Box 1838. See also Slattery to Amos Pinchot, October 10, 1917, Slattery to Gifford Pinchot, February 28, 1918, *ibid.*; Josephus Daniels to Franklin D. Roosevelt, February 17, 1944, Josephus Daniels Papers, Box 17, Library of Congress; Thomas W. Gregory to Woodrow Wilson, March 28, 1918, Woodrow Wilson Papers, File VI, Box 505, Library of Congress; Gregory to George W. Anderson, January 17, 1925, Gregory to W. S. Farish of the Humble Oil Company, February 20, 1929, Thomas W. Gregory Papers, Library of Congress.

(New Jersey). Among the other eight members in July of 1917 were the following: E. C. Lufkin, president of the Texas Company, John W. Van Dyke, president of the Atlantic Refining Company, George S. Davidson, president of the Gulf Refining Company, E. L. Doheny of the Mexican Petroleum Company, and Harry F. Sinclair of the Sinclair Oil & Refining Company.[6]

Independents and the industry at large gave their backing to the Petroleum Committee. The *National Petroleum News* commented: "Every man in the oil industry must absolutely give his entire confidence to this Oil Committee. . . . If necessary, we should put our entire businesses into the hands of this Committee, and it would be far better for the oil industry to do so than to put the oil industry directly into the hands of the government." [7]

At this time E. L. Doheny moved into Washington. This man enjoyed an enviable reputation among all but the eternally vigilant or jaundiced. He typified the millionaire possessed of intelligence, good humor, and charm, who seemed to care nothing for money as such and who acquired many influential friends during the war years. Doheny had struggled to success against obstacles that were truly formidable. Born in Fond du Lac, Wisconsin, of an Irish father (1856), he went to Oklahoma as a youth and continued into the far West, prospecting for gold. A studious person, he learned metallurgy and geology, and, while convalescing from a fall down a mine shaft in which he broke both legs, studied law and was later admitted to practice. A hardy outdoorsman as well, he once found it necessary to fight off a mountain lion with a hunting knife.

At the age of thirty-five, after hair-raising adventures and financial ups and downs, Doheny seemed a failure. He then went from triumph to triumph as a petroleum pioneer and public figure in California and Mexico. He explored and opened the Los Angeles district and other fabulously wealthy fields in California. Most of all, he was known for opening the Tampico dis-

---

[6] See "Mr. A. C. Bedford on Thrift and Investing," *World's Work*, XXXVI (June, 1918), 133. See also Edward Hungerford, "A. C. Bedford," *System*, XXXII (July, 1917), 48–49; "Oil Committee Deserves Trade's Solid Backing," *National Petroleum News*, IX (July, 1917), 9.

[7] *Ibid.* See also "Wilson Holds Fate of Oil Trade," *ibid.*, X (May 8, 1918), 5; speech by Alfred C. Bedford, quoted in "Bedford on War Organization of the Petroleum Industry," *Oil Age*, XIV (April, 1918), 14.

trict in Mexico with its spectacular gushers. A legend developed about Doheny: as soon as any venture became a business, simply paying well, he looked for new frontiers to conquer. "Conquest, not money, was his dominating aim," concluded one observer.[8] Nevertheless, by 1918 Doheny was among the richest men on the West Coast and liked to travel sumptuously in his private railroad car. His companies produced more oil than any single Standard company. He also attained stature in Washington as an enlightened employer of labor and a high-minded expert on petroleum matters. Doheny had arrived—an almost irresistible product of the success tradition, tempered in currents of twentieth-century reform.

Secretary Lane had a predilection for men of Doheny's type. The Secretary's attitude was ingratiating. His recommendations on specific policies, while plausibly required to win the war, were frequently pro-business.

In this respect Lane contrasted sharply with Josephus Daniels, who stubbornly resisted the blandishments of businessmen. Daniels was determined that this war should not afford bomb-proof shelters in Washington for the scions of the rich and wellborn. Nor should it bring exorbitant profits. He insisted on buying steel, petroleum, and other supplies for the Navy cheaply regardless of criticism. When assailed by the Navy League, the steel companies, the petroleum interests, the blue bloods, he yielded not one inch.[9] His natural stubbornness seems, if anything, to have been fortified by the many attacks.

On June 26, 1917, Lane, Daniels, and other officials delivered addresses before the coal operators of America, some 400 of them, gathered in the Department of the Interior. A crisis in coal production existed. The government threatened to take over output unless the operators themselves could establish a fair price and effectively regulate the industry. Daniels spoke briefly.

[8] Bertie C. Forbes, "Edward L. Doheny," in *Men Who Are Making the West*, New York, 1923, pp. 100–101 and *passim*. See also "C. A. Canfield Dead," *Oil Age*, VIII (August 22, 1913), 1; Wilbur Hall, "How Doheny Did It," *Sunset*, XIL (July, 1918), 21–23; Clarence W. Barron, "Doheny—Lord of Oil" and *passim*, in *The Mexican Problem*, Boston, 1917.
[9] Jonathan Daniels, *The End of Innocence*, Philadelphia, 1954, pp. 92, 112, 113–115, 157–158, 186–187, 227; Arthur S. Link, *Wilson: The New Freedom*, Princeton, N.J., 1956, pp. 122–125; William Kent to Ray Stannard Baker, June 24, 1925, Baker to Kent, June 30, 1925, Ray Stannard Baker Papers, Series IB, Box 41, Library of Congress.

A draft of military manpower, he said, had been imperative; and a draft of other kinds of power was no less imperative. "No man owns an oil well or a coal mine except a[s] trustee. And if this war goes on long no man can say that he owns a gallon of oil or a ton of coal."

Lane opened his oration by commenting that he had just arrived from a meeting of the Central Committee of the Red Cross and was happy to be able to report that the $100,000,000 line was about to be crossed. "These are days of big things. These are days when big things are being done in a big country by big men. . . . Are you small or are you big?"

Ordinarily, he said, he wanted to see "profits large," because he believed in "forwarding men according to their imagination and their capacity and their daring when they are doing a service." He expressed sympathy over the recent financial difficulties of the coal operators. He knew the "greatness of the American business man," his foresightedness and his services to the nation: "We who are in public office in this country have had comparatively little to do with the growth of this country." Now these were extraordinary times in which he was sure businessmen would recognize "there are things greater than making money." And although he was "not a demagogue," he had faith that the workers in the mines were no less patriotic than other Americans. He appealed to the memory of Washington and Lincoln, to the sacrifices of the soldier dead of other wars, and to every sensibility and heartstring of the magnates present.[10]

This coal crisis illustrated once again the divisions within the Wilson administration. Coal operators could not but agree to fixing the price of their product. The question remained as to where to fix it. In the immediate background was a surge of bituminous prices to record levels—in many instances 200 per cent spot rises or even as much as 300 per cent from prewar

[10] See release from the Committee on Public Information, June 26, 1917, Interior Department Records, National Archives. See also Lane's address before the Coal Production Committee of the Council of National Defense, quoted in *Manufacturer's Record*, May 24, 1917, *ibid.*; Lane's address of September 18, 1917, before the War Convention of American Business, conducted by the National Chamber of Commerce, quoted in part in "Business and the War," *Army and Navy Journal*, LV (September 29, 1917), 155; Franklin K. Lane, *The American Spirit: Addresses in Wartime*, New York, 1918.

levels. The average price in June, 1917, was about $5.00 a ton at the mine. Consumer discontent was rising. The Justice Department had registered warnings of an investigation. It was in these circumstances that a Committee on Coal Production of the Council of National Defense was organized, with Francis S. Peabody of Illinois as chairman. Shortly thereafter the meeting of coal operators was held, as already described.

Lane and Peabody took the lead in bringing about a reduction of prices, by voluntary action of the operators, to approximately $3.50 a ton. A solution seemed to have been found, and doubtless Lane had done his best. Immediately, however, Secretary of War Newton D. Baker, Josephus Daniels, and others insisted that the prices were still far too high. The final decision depended upon President Wilson, with his powers under the new Lever Act. As usual, he sided with Daniels; the price was reduced to an average of $2.35.

Lane almost resigned. Writing to Robert Lansing in 1921, when Lansing was having his own troubles with Wilson, Lane said: "I came to the brink when the President blew up my coal agreement to save three or four hundred million dollars for the people. But I was stopped by the thought, 'Give no comfort to Berlin.' " [11]

## 3

In August of 1917 the Fuel Administration assumed direct responsibility for coal and oil. It undertook the job which previously had been handled by officials such as Secretary Lane, in conjunction with committees of the Council of National Defense. In the top position of fuel administrator was Harry A. Garfield of Williams College, with Mark L. Requa of California as general director of the Oil Division.

Garfield described vividly the excitement of those days. His agency "grew with great rapidity and spread throughout the States, its force within the capital adding seriously to the teeming,

---

[11] *Letters of Franklin K. Lane*, p. 463. See also C. E. Lesher, *Prices of Coal and Coke*, Washington, 1919, pp. 22–27; "What Is a Fair Price for Coal," *Survey*, XXXVII (December 2, 1916), 247–249; editorials in *Independent*, XIC (July 7, 1917), 13–14, (August 25, 1917), 274, (September 1, 1917), 312, (September 8, 1917), 384; "The Baker-Lane Controversy," *Outlook*, CXVI (July 11, 1917), 385; Sydney A. Hale, "The Coal Problem of Today," *World's Work*, XXXVI (July, 1918), 318–328.

striving, energized, overcrowded population of the city. . . . A kind of madness seized the populace. . . . Nice discriminations were lost in the fever of production. Somehow to increase the output and to send it forward seemed to express patriotic effort." The fixing of coal prices, he later concluded, was one of the significant achievements of 1917–18.[12]

As director of the Oil Division, Requa had much influence. He was an oil man and consultant, known for his strong views on petroleum supply, and was an advocate of quick development. Writing to Secretary Lane, just preceding the outbreak of war, he volunteered his services. He also volunteered his advice. If war came, he declared, it would be vitally necessary to seize the Mexican oil fields: "From my knowledge of the situation, from a commercial and strategic standpoint, prompt seizure of these oil fields is most important." A few months earlier Requa had appeared as a witness for the Southern Pacific Railroad in the government's oil cases in California. Commander Landis, the officer in charge of the naval reserves, commented: "The impression he made as a witness would seem to justify the belief that he is very friendly to interests that are not in accord with the Navy Department's policy regarding the Naval Petroleum Reserves." Commander Wright, at the "oil desk" in Washington, replied that they had made the same estimate.

Requa urged that drilling be commenced immediately on the withdrawn lands in the West. In June of 1917 he appeared before the Senate Committee on Public Lands to express his view that some solution to the leasing stalemate must be found. Otherwise, he warned, in concert with Senator Phelan, business and commerce on the West Coast would be paralyzed by diminishing supplies of fuel.[13]

---

[12] U.S. Fuel Administration, *Final Report of the Administrator, 1917–1919*, by Harry A. Garfield, *Report of the Oil Division, 1917–1919*, by Mark L. Requa, Washington, 1921, pp. 7–8 and *passim*.

[13] Requa to Lane, March 10, 1917, Secretary's File, Department of the Interior, National Archives; Landis to the Secretary of the Navy, November 30, 1916, Wright to Landis, December 11, 1916, Navy Records, National Archives; U.S. Congress, Senate, *Leasing of Oil Lands*, Hearings Before the Committee on Public Lands on S. 45, a "Bill to Encourage and Promote the Mining of Coal, Phosphate, Oil, Gas, Potassium, and Sodium on the Public Domain," 65 Cong., 1 Sess., Washington, 1917, pp. 71–82. One of the naval officers at the "oil desk" in Washington (probably Wright) gave his estimate of Requa as the newly appointed oil administrator: Requa was, of course, "well tied up

Requa had come to the front in California as a leader of the Independent Oil Producers Agency. In its inception this was designed to protect the smaller companies from the aggressions of Southern Pacific and Standard Oil. Franklin K. Lane and his brother George were prominent members in the early 1900's, and when Franklin went to Washington, his brother continued in his capacity with the Agency. By 1913 this organization contained 175 members and produced 22 per cent of the state's oil. In alliance with the Union Oil Company it formed the Producers Transportation Company and built a pipeline to the coast. Along with Standard Oil, the Southern Pacific interests, and the General Petroleum Company, the Producers Agency monopolized the pipelines from the San Joaquin Valley.

The Producers Agency thus had joined the "system." An official report of the California Bureau of Mines concluded that the original hope of independents had not been realized through the Producers Transportation Company: "If an independent producer desires to transport his oil over the line of the Producers Transportation Company he must fulfill several requirements. He must sign a ten year contract to turn over to the Independent Oil Producers Agency all the oil produced by him upon certain defined lands. . . . He must agree that during the term of this contract the Producers Transportation Company shall be the exclusive carrier of his oil. . . ."

After describing the other pipeline companies, the report continued: "Under these circumstances it would naturally be expected that the oil pipe line companies could dictate the prices at which the independent producer should sell his oil to them.

"The record shows the companies are doing this very thing. There is a remarkable uniformity in the price offered by all of these companies for the oil of the independent producers . . . no company has ever underbid a price named by the Associated Oil Company [Southern Pacific]. . . ." [14]

with the California oil men" but, nevertheless, made a favorable impression so far as ability and "honesty of purpose" were concerned. Unsigned letter to Commander Landis, January 11, 1918, Navy Records.

[14] R. P. McLaughlin and C. A. Waring, *Petroleum Industry of California*, California State Mining Bureau, Bulletin 69, Sacramento, 1914, pp. 475, 491–494, and *passim*; "Introducing New U.S. Oil Controller," *National Petroleum News*, X (January 16, 1918), 11, and *passim* in issues of 1918. An editor of the *California Oil World* insisted that the Independent Oil Producers Agency

Representing the Producers Agency, Requa went to New York in 1915, trying, as the *Petroleum News* described it, to effect a "big merger." This involved Union Oil, General Petroleum, California Petroleum, and some other companies. He did not succeed. It is apparent, nevertheless, that the Producers Agency had become a powerful new force, opposed by many separate independents. Requa personally exemplified the big business point of view, although he prided himself on having been politically "pretty much all over the shop within the lines of the Republican party —Mugwump, Progressive, Bull Mooser." [15]

Requa's staff in the Oil Division was heavily loaded with Californians. Thomas A. O'Donnell of Los Angeles, placed in charge of production, was an oil lobbyist in the fight over leasing. In 1910 he had come to Washington with a large delegation, seeking passage of what became the Pickett Act. He was termed the "most practical oil man present." Later, deeply dissatisfied with that act, he had returned to urge the passage of further relief legislation. He had been among those who castigated Secretary Daniels for his lack of understanding and his "carpetbag" policies respecting the West. In 1917 he was an associate of Doheny's —a director of Pan-American Petroleum. Doubtless for these reasons O'Donnell "severed all active business connections" while he remained with the Oil Division. Requa made a point of this in his final report.

Frank J. Silsbee, also of Los Angeles, had been chief statistician with the Independent Oil Producers Agency. The Bureau of Domestic Consumption was placed under C. G. Sheffield of the Union Oil Company of California. S. A. Guiberson, Jr., of Los Angeles and the Associated Pipe Line Company (Southern Pacific) headed the Bureau of Pipe Lines. D. M. Folsom of the Bureau of Mines of Stanford University was Requa's representative and director for the West Coast. Thomas Cox of Oakland was a mining engineer also brought into the Oil Division.

When H. H. Welsh of Fresno joined Requa's staff as a personal assistant, the *National Petroleum News* commented: "Like nearly

---

was the "most conspicuous example of applied progressivism . . . to be found anywhere." Charles P. Fox to Chester Rowell, September 16, 1913, Chester Rowell Papers, Bancroft Library, University of California, Berkeley.
[15] Requa to William Allen White, April 19, 1924, William Allen White Papers, Box 75, Library of Congress; "Big Merger Progresses," *National Petroleum News*, Oil Producer's Section, VII (May, 1915), 23.

every other man from the California fields who has come here
to help in the Oil division he has been prominently identified
with the Independent Oil Producers Agency." [16]

## 4

From these western officials and the Oil Division came continuous
pressure for production. Warnings of diminishing stocks and of
the perilous national situation filled the air. Requa and his staff,
Secretary Lane and most of his subordinates, Senator Phelan
and other senators from the West, and diverse interests in California contributed to the agitation. Walter S. Gifford of the
Council of National Defense added his influence. Even the
skeptics were periodically alarmed.

Was there or was there not a petroleum shortage? If the answer
is affirmative, Lane and his group doubtless were justified in their
alarmist tactics, for the national security counted above all else
in the uncertain days of 1917–19.

Rather consistently there was informed opposition to this
pressure. The Navy Department, Justice Department, Federal
Trade Commission, the Pinchot group, antimonopolists in California and Wyoming, and many progressives refused to believe
that precipitate action was demanded. Production was adequate,
they believed. At crucial moments they won the support of
Bernard Baruch and the President. If action was held to be
mandatory, they offered alternative schemes of commandeering
and government operation in certain areas. Where private
claimants were permitted to continue production, in disputed
cases, they believed in a less generous policy than did Secretary
Lane.

Immediately upon the declaration of war in April of 1917, the

---

[16] "Requa Adds Another Californian to Staff," *ibid.*, X (April 17, 1918), 12.
See also U.S. Fuel Administration, *Final Report of the Administrator, Report of the Oil Division*, pp. 261–264 and *passim;* Barron, *The Mexican
Problem*, p. 125; U.S. Congress, House, *Oil-Land Withdrawals and the Pro-
tection of Locators of Oil Lands*, Hearings Before the Committee on Public
Lands on H.R. 24070, to "Authorize the President to Make Withdrawals of
Public Lands," 61 Cong., 2 Sess., Washington, 1910, pp. 5 ff., 73. Important
independent producers in California challenged Requa's impartiality and
his fitness as oil administrator. See Alfred L. Black, Los Angeles attorney, to
Josephus Daniels, May 20, 1918, Navy Records; "Fights Requa on Pipe Line
Ruling," *National Petroleum News*, X (April 10, 1918), 38; "Makes New
Appeal on Pipe Line Order," *ibid.*, X (May 29, 1918), 7.

demand for more production was inaugurated in California. The San Francisco Chamber of Commerce sent a telegram to Newton D. Baker, portraying a desperate situation. It was not only petroleum that was needed. Other minerals such as potash, "fundamental in the manufacture of explosives," were held to be withdrawn and locked up by the government's policy. The shortage of fuel oil already was beginning to threaten the efficiency of railroads, business, and industry in the West. The Southern Pacific Railroad was practically without fuel oil. Copper mines in Arizona might be forced to shut down.

They also mentioned a point which at all times was to cast doubts upon the validity of their arguments. California had millions of barrels of oil in storage. As stated in the telegram: "California is today producing about 265,000 barrels of crude oil per day with a normal consumption of about 300,000 barrels daily. On January 1, 1916, there were in storage in California 57,000,-000 barrels of crude oil. On April 1, 1917, this storage had been reduced to 41,000,000 barrels, at a daily loss of substantially 35,000 barrels. At this rate of decline *three years* would completely wipe out the present crude storage." The reason for keeping oil in storage, an independent operator in California pointed out, was to use it. This was just the time to do so.[17]

Cries of alarm continued. The Pacific Mail Steamship Company viewed "with much apprehension the rapidly depleting oil reserve threatening exhaustion of stock"; and they appealed to Secretary Lane: "Please help us." Julius Kahn, a representative from San Francisco, forwarded to Secretary Lane an appeal from the Oceanic Steamship Company of San Francisco. Ray Lyman Wilbur, president of Stanford University, wrote to Secretary Lane, enclosing communications from Governor William D. Stephens of California. The governor sent a wire to President Wilson.

These Californians wanted drilling in the naval petroleum reserves, especially in Buena Vista Hills. The general argument was that Reserve No. 2 was "checkerboarded" and subject to

---

[17] Robert N. Lynch, vice-president of the San Francisco Chamber of Commerce, to Ira E. Bennett, April 23, 1917, for transmittal to the Secretary of War, Interior Department Records; S. C. Graham to Secretary Lane, May 8, 1918 (copy), Navy Records. See also "Trend Towards Further Regulation," *National Petroleum News*, X (May 22, 1918), 5–7. (Italics mine.)

drainage. It could not be saved by the Navy and ought to be developed for wartime production.

E. L. Doheny, making such assertions, had a considerable influence in government circles. Doheny insisted that Buena Vista Hills must be drilled, that this was the best source for new supply. Any surplus production, he suggested, could be placed in storage tanks for the future requirements of the Navy. Later, in the 1920's, he had a similar plan.

A final, powerful argument from California was forwarded to Washington by Governor Stephens. This was an eleven-page report from the Committee on Petroleum of the California Council of Defense. For the most part, it contained the familiar arguments. The state's fuel oil ran the western United States and much of the Pacific and Latin-American area. Production must be increased by the quickest possible means; that is, by drilling in proven lands. This meant Buena Vista Hills and other withdrawn areas.[18]

The Navy Department did not yield, although Commander Richardson stated that this report was "the most truthful and reliable one" yet presented from California. Richardson, serving at this time on the U.S.S. *Nevada,* read the report and gave the Navy Department his comments. On two important points he agreed with the California interests. First, that a certain large company was holding back and not developing some of its lands, which were expected to be richly productive. Second, that proven lands existed outside the naval reserves, in litigation with the government, and that they ought to be developed by special arrangement, "without prejudice to the government's interests." Richardson concluded that the naval reserves should be developed only as a last resort, and expressed his belief that the oil men, backed "apparently" by the Interior Department, still were

---

[18] J. H. Rosseter of Pacific Mail to President Wilson, June 19–20, 1917, Rosseter (telegram) to Secretary Lane, June 19, 1917, Secretary's File; Kahn to Lane, April 26, 1917, Wilbur to Lane, July 9, 1917, *ibid.;* "Memorandum," June 21, 1917, *ibid.;* Requa to Secretary Daniels, May 21, 1918, Navy Records; Governor's Office, Sacramento, to the Secretary of the Navy, July 7, 1917, forwarding a report of the Committee on Petroleum, *ibid.* See also testimony of Requa, Doheny, Ray Lyman Wilbur, and others in U.S. Congress, Senate, *Leasing of Oil Lands* (1917), *passim;* letter from the "oil desk," Bureau of Engineering (probably Commander Wright), to Landis, June 26, 1917, Navy Records.

thinking primarily of development in disputed lands "for their own benefit." [19]

One side of the oil problem at this time was to produce oil products in unprecedented quantities; the other was to prevent unnecessary consumption. Could fuel oil, gasoline, and other necessities be channeled efficiently into military and defense uses? There was, for example, the automobile and the possibility of its frivolous use. Chairman Bedford of the Petroleum Committee pointed out that from 1910 to 1917 the number of automobiles had increased from 400,000 to 4,000,000. He recommended curtailing their use, but little was ever done.

There was another way to reduce consumption, and possibly to save the naval reserves from drilling. Exports of oil might be reduced, especially those for nonmilitary purposes. Commander Wright reported in September, 1917, that he had recently received this suggestion from "a gentleman" in California: it "would be very advisable" to look into details of the "continuous exports of California fuel oil to South America and other countries." [20]

To look into this question and find the answer was difficult, but as late as 1920 it was still exciting interest. The secretary of a lime and cement company in San Francisco protested to Senator Phelan concerning exports of fuel oil. His company, the secretary said, was being told that they could not buy fuel oil—this in spite of the fact that in the preceding four years they had purchased almost $800,000 worth of this product from the Shell Oil Company. Other places had also claimed they were short of supplies. But a check at the customs house revealed some interesting figures. Exports from San Francisco for January–April, 1920, amounted to 88,242,979 gallons, the largest amount

---

[19] Richardson to Secretary Daniels, July 26, 1917, *ibid.* See also Landis to Richardson, December 12, 1916, Landis to Wright, August 1, 1917, Office of the Twelfth Naval District, quoting Commander Landis, to the Secretary of the Navy, August 2, 1917, *ibid.;* "Governor in Committee Reports Findings," *Oil Age,* XIII (July, 1917), 11–13.

[20] Wright to Senators Paul O. Husting and Claude Swanson, September 25, 1917, Navy Records. Another argument against the alarmists went this way: the shortage, so far as it existed, was due more to a scarcity of oil well supplies and equipment than to a lack of good territory in which to drill. See S. C. Graham to Daniels, February 4, 1918, *ibid.*

going to Canada and the next largest to Chile. Moreover, this oil was being exported at $1.82 a barrel while local purchasers paid $1.85 plus freight.

Would it not be fair, the secretary inquired of Senator Phelan, to prevent "the oil trust" from exporting this oil except "over and above the quantities required for . . . home consumption"? He was ready to make affidavits as to the accuracy of his figures. Senator Phelan, in replying, had no doubt of their accuracy. He would do what he could to rectify the situation. He added that he was communicating with the Secretary of Commerce, and that the Attorney General already had promised an investigation.[21]

Oil men were never able to win "the battle of shortages." The statistics never entirely supported them. For example, Daniels wrote to the President in July, 1918, quoting figures from Timothy Spellacy, a friend of Secretary Lane's and an independent oil man of high standing in Los Angeles: ". . . the production of crude oil in California . . . is some 10,000 barrels a day in excess of consumption. Therefore, the cry of distress of the interests that feared—notwithstanding 30,000,000 barrels in stock —that many necessary commercial interests would be compelled to close down for want of fuel is past."

Another independent from Los Angeles commented: "I cannot help but feel, and I know the feeling of some other oil producers here is the same as my own, that the situation arising out of the war is being taken advantage of by those who disregarded the withdrawal order and entered upon and took possession of the lands in question." [22]

Neither side in the argument could really prevail until 1921 —when curiously California was flooded with an oversupply of

---

[21] W. H. George to Senator Phelan, with enclosure, May 20, 1920, Phelan to George, June 8, 1920, enclosing a copy of a letter to the Secretary of Commerce, June 8, 1920, Secretary's File, Department of the Interior.
[22] Daniels to President Wilson, July 29, 1918, Daniels Papers, Box 14; S. C. Graham to Secretary Lane, May 8, 1918, Navy Records. See also Daniels to Requa, May 18, 1918, Requa to Daniels, May 21, 24, 1918, *ibid.;* Josephus Daniels, *The Wilson Era: Years of War and After, 1917–1923,* Chapel Hill, N.C., 1946, pp. 246–248; Commander Wright to Landis, May 18, 1918, Navy Records. Wright commented: "They are making a big howl about shortage, present and future. A small part of it I think is probably justified but more is propaganda."

oil. In retrospect it was apparent that a dangerous shortage had never materialized. Much of the agitation from California had been correctly labeled as propaganda.

## 5

Regardless of current supply, the men who controlled petroleum production were emerging as a new force in domestic and world affairs. There was a remarkable continuity in this respect from the Wilson to the Harding administration. In the Interior Department, in wartime agencies, and in the State Department the petroleum lobby made itself felt. By 1919, when A. Mitchell Palmer became Attorney General, the Justice Department grew more cordial. This trend was normal, perhaps inevitable. England and other powers were scrambling for oil concessions—it was apparent that the nations which controlled oil supplies might control the postwar world. The United States joined in the scramble; it placated its oil men, and cooperated with them in devising means for economic imperialism.

Mark L. Requa signalized the trend in September, 1918. He wrote on "The World Problem of Raw Materials—as Related to Petroleum." The struggle for petroleum, he said, would be "most intense"; the theory of government regulation and control by "penal statute" must be abandoned; between industry and government there must be "a spirit of mutual confidence and cooperation." Van Manning of the Bureau of Mines declared: ". . . in the future it is going to be necessary for this Government to work with the oil men in encouraging development abroad and in obtaining the needed oil supplies wherever possible. The Government should take all pains to establish just and cordial relations with the oil men and to avoid taking measures during this emergency which will prohibit future cordial relations with the oil industry." [23]

Many others worked toward these nationalistic objectives. Among them were Secretary Lane, Secretary of State Robert Lansing, Norman H. Davis (acting Secretary of State), Secretary

---

[23] Requa, September 30, 1918, Secretary's File, Department of the Interior; Van Manning to Newton D. Baker, undated but early 1920, *ibid*. See also views of Secretary Lane and many other government leaders, *ibid*.; George Otis Smith, "Where the World Gets Its Oil," *National Geographic Magazine*, XXXVII (February, 1920), 201–202 and *passim*.

of State Charles Evans Hughes, Secretary of the Interior Albert
B. Fall, and E. L. Doheny. The climate, as affecting oil operators,
was undergoing a marked change. The Navy, however, did not
abandon its objectives; and there were many who believed that
the government should not compromise itself, or take chances
of doing so, in its relations with the petroleum industry.

# Secretary Daniels and the Deadlock over Legislation

 **CHAPTER VII**

*Thank God, you have got a Secretary of the Navy who has the nerve and the zeal and the patriotism to stand here for the public interest.*
Senator Claude Swanson (Democrat, Virginia), December 17, 1917

*The oil man is a gambler by instinct; otherwise he would not be an oil man; and they have been gambling on legislation as well as on other things.*
Commander Nathaniel H. Wright, U.S. Navy, March 2, 1918

1

In the war and postwar period Josephus Daniels emerged as one of the most powerful and controversial figures in the Wilson administration. The charge was often made that it was Daniels who prevented an early compromise on the oil leasing question. But *The Oil Age,* a responsible California source, unhesitatingly placed much of the blame upon those opposed to Daniels—especially those "oil operators of California and Wyoming" who were interested in protecting their holdings on the public lands, "whether legally or illegally obtained." *The Oil Age* distributed the blame; it believed the Navy and Justice Departments had been unduly severe with these same western claimants.[1]

Certainly the Navy and its allies dealt harshly with those deemed to be trespassers. They exercised a powerful influence both inside and outside the Congress, striving to defeat oil men's "relief" bills. In a sense they played politics with the oil question.

---

[1] "Oil Land Legislation Taken Up," *Oil Age,* XIII (December, 1917), 1. See also "Oil Land Bill Not Yet out of Committee," *ibid.,* XIV (April, 1918), 1, and *passim* in issues of 1917–18.

They had little alternative if the oil lobbyists were to be defeated. But the aftereffects were not always what they desired.

## 2

Possibilities of compromise were never out of the question in spite of disagreements. There were moments when all parties were tempted to yield.

Late in 1915 an exchange of letters occurred within the Navy Department. The Bureau of Engineering (particularly Admiral Griffin and Commander Richardson) prepared for Secretary Daniels an analysis of the situation affecting the naval reserves, in which they attempted to define their best strategy for the future. To them a compromise of some sort seemed politic: "It is believed that it would be unwise for the Navy Department to depend entirely upon the chance of defeating all oil land legislation that would be inimical to the Navy's interests." [2]

But on what basis might they consider a compromise? They thought seriously of sacrificing Buena Vista Hills, if the other two reserves could be saved. Worries remained. Would Elk Hills (Reserve No. 1) be rich enough for the purposes of the Navy? Could they be sure that Teapot Dome had oil in it? Also, could these reserves actually be protected against further inroads of private claimants? The answers seemed to be yes. As of 1915, there were no producing wells in Teapot Dome, and there were none in Elk Hills except in private tracts "checkerboarded" through the reserve. No claimants, it seemed, had a strong enough case to acquire new sections under the Pickett Act. Loss through drainage, the naval men believed, was of no consequence in either of these two reserves.

Therefore, they recommended a course of action having broad implications for the future. The Navy should work hereafter to have Elk Hills and Teapot Dome excluded from any relief legislation and to "place these Reserves directly under the control of the Navy Department." In Buena Vista Hills, however, leases now would be permitted, and new plans must be made for the handling of petroleum products from that area.

In other words, the Navy Department for the first time would

---

[2] Griffin to Daniels, November 26, 1915, Navy Records, National Archives. See also Daniels to E. J. Justice, December 2, 1915, *ibid.*

be given authority to use and manage, as well as to conserve, its petroleum products. Policies should be established for the disposition of royalty oil, acquired by the Navy from its leaseholders. The royalty, paid either in money or oil, ought to be fixed as high as possible on gross production, and it should be assigned to "the exclusive use and benefit" of the Navy. Furthermore, the Navy should receive authority to use extra moneys acquired, for the purpose of creating storage facilities above ground. The Secretary should be empowered to make agreements for exchange of royalty oil received in the field for fuel oil located at points on the coast.

Here were recommendations of which much was to be heard later, especially as interpreted and acted upon by the Republican leaders in 1921–22.

So far as the sacrifice of Buena Vista Hills was concerned, Secretary Daniels showed greater reluctance than did his subordinates. Nevertheless, he wrote to E. J. Justice: "It is possible that the pressure may be so great that this Department will be unable to prevent the passage of the relief bill which certainly will be introduced." Enclosing a copy of Admiral Griffin's letter, he appealed to Justice to consider the matter and give his opinion as to "the desirability and practicability" of Griffin's plan. He also urged secrecy. The effect of Navy opposition to relief legislation "would be weakened if it were known that the terms of a compromise had been decided upon." [3] Thus there is every indication that top naval men, as well as Daniels' friend Justice in California, were seriously contemplating the Griffin proposals.

Just at this time, however, the controversy flared up over the Honolulu case in Buena Vista Hills. Never again would Daniels and his group listen seriously to a plan for the sacrifice of this reserve. Yet in some way the rumor got out. Oil men in December, 1916, agitated for the surrender of Reserve No. 2 in such a manner as to indicate that they had heard of Navy vacillation and entertained some expectation of success.

In Congress the old arguments continued. The bill still pending was that originally introduced by Scott Ferris and passed by the House in January, 1916. It did not pass the Senate. Senator Phelan attached amendments which were so controversial that his name was identified with the bill and it was often called the

---

[3] *Ibid.*

Phelan bill. In March, 1917, it expired with the Sixty-fourth Congress. But in the new Congress another bill, almost identical, was introduced by Scott Ferris. Senator Walsh introduced still another which was to become the Walsh-Pittman bill.

## 3

After the Honolulu episode in 1916 it was accepted as a fact that the Navy Department had a powerful position. It could block legislation considered contrary to its interests and it could thwart certain policies of the Interior Department. Probable sources of support were known: President Wilson, officials of the Justice Department, friends in Congress, some of whom were strategically located on the naval affairs committees of both houses, and progressive leaders who could be rallied to the cause.

In 1916–17 Daniels' opponents frankly admitted his power. On one occasion Senators Pittman, Walsh, and Phelan, and the two oil lobbyists, Louis Titus and James N. Gillett, paid Secretary Daniels a visit. Pittman stated for the group that they could not pass the Phelan bill "or in fact any bill" over Navy Department opposition.[4] The bitterness was apparent on this and other occasions, even amid efforts to maintain cordiality.

The Public Lands Committee of the Senate had a good chance to express its feelings in June, 1917, while holding hearings. Pittman made a declaration: "I want to say that it makes no difference what this committee reports, there is not any chance in God's earth of ever passing a bill for the development of the oil fields until the Secretary of the Navy is willing to meet the Secretary of the Interior in a spirit of compromise in this matter." Pittman also blamed the Interior Department for the bad state of affairs because Secretary Lane had allowed others to meddle in matters properly within his jurisdiction. But the man ultimately responsible was Daniels, and he must be held responsible.

In these hearings there were sharp exchanges between Daniels

---

[4] Commander Richardson to Landis, December 15, 1916, *ibid.* In the Senate Committee on Naval Affairs Secretary Daniels had staunch supporters. Included were old Ben Tillman of South Carolina and Henry Cabot Lodge of Massachusetts. Both took a dim view of oil men's so-called equities in the California fields. See U.S. Congress, Senate, *Oil-Land Leasing Bill*, Hearings Before the Committee on Naval Affairs on "So-called Relief Provisions of the Leasing Bill Relative to the California Naval Petroleum Reserve, 64 Cong., 2 Sess., Washington, 1917, p. 104 and *passim*.

and Senator Walsh. At one point Walsh asked, "Can you offer something that is constructive?" After Daniels had spoken, Walsh declared rather ambiguously that on that statement of the situation they all were guilty of gross neglect.[5]

Six months earlier (January, 1917) Senator Thomas of Colorado actually had threatened on the floor of the Senate to oppose Daniels' entire naval program, in view of the Secretary's obduracy on the leasing question. Though speaking for himself, Thomas believed that some of his senatorial associates had the same attitude. Doubtless he was correct,[6] but the coming of war made this particular brand of pressure on the Navy no longer patriotic or practical.

Inside the Navy Department, Daniels continued to receive strong support. Naval officers and planners were convinced that a dependable supply of fuel oil was a growing necessity. This conviction was never more apparent than in 1916, when the Naval Fuel Oil Board, after lengthy investigation, delivered a report of forty-eight pages on the problem. They took note of international developments and of England's leadership, and, endorsing Daniels' policies, pointed the way to the future.

As to the domestic sources of supply, the Fuel Oil Board had a number of recommendations. Retention of oil in the ground, in its natural reservoir, was desirable, yet other action was required. Naval reserves ought to be close to the coast, as were the two in California, which were excellent and should provide for the demands of the Navy in the Pacific area. Teapot Dome, however, was not a proven reserve. The investigation of other possible sites, as in the Osage lands of Oklahoma, would be desirable. They discussed also the advantages of providing storage facilities above ground for Navy oil. Such facilities would permit, for one thing, the buying of oil when prices were low and storing it for future needs.

Finally, they advised the construction of a naval refining plant at an estimated cost of $300,000, to be located on the lower

---

[5] U.S. Congress, Senate, *Leasing of Oil Lands,* Hearings Before the Committee on Public Lands on S. 45, a "Bill to Encourage and Promote the Mining of Coal, Phosphate, Oil, Gas, Potassium, and Sodium on the Public Domain," 65 Cong., 1 Sess., Washington, 1917, pp. 113, 197. Walsh, it seems clear, was insinuating that Daniels' policy had been at fault.
[6] *Ibid.,* p. 197; *Cong. Record,* 64 Cong., 2 Sess., p. 1048, January 9, 1917.

Teapot Rock, Wyoming.

Josephus Daniels and staff, including behind and to his right Franklin D. Roosevelt; behind and to his left Robert C. Griffin, chief of the Bureau of Engineering.

Incoming Secretary of the Navy Edwin Denby and outgoing Secretary Josephus Daniels. Their relations were none too cordial.

Representative Scott Ferris (Democrat, Oklahoma).

Senator John B. Kendrick (Democrat, Wyoming).

Gifford Pinchot.

Senator Robert M. La Follette.

Senator Key Pittman (Democrat, Nevada).

Senator Thomas J. Walsh (Democrat, Montana).

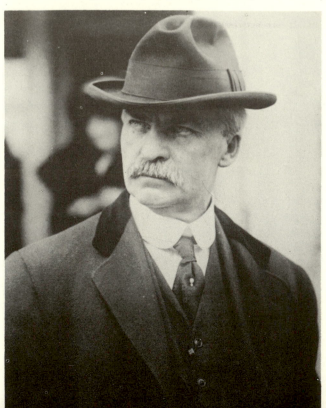

A. Mitchell Palmer.

Secretary of the Interior Franklin K. Lane.

Rear Admiral H. A. Stuart (later photograph).

Captain J. O. Richardson (later photograph).

Gusher in operation, Section 11, Salt Creek, Wyoming.

View from Fourth Street in Taft, California, 1910.

GETTING OUT THE OLD STUFF.

A business conception of reformers and troublemakers. *American Industries*, September, 1918.

THE WILD AND WOOLLY EAST.

From *Tacoma* (Washington) *Ledger*, reproduced in the *Literary Digest*, September 17, 1910.

THE MISFIT.

An example of the abuse to which Josephus Daniels was subjected. *Chicago Tribune*, August 20, 1917.

**GUSHING.**

*St. Louis Post-Dispatch,* February 5, 1924.

Chesapeake Bay. Precedents existed for such a Navy venture, they noted, especially the smokeless powder plant at Indian Head, Maryland. Only by this sort of manufacturing experience could the Navy acquire the knowledge it needed of prices and specifications.

The officers on this Fuel Oil Board showed no sign of timidity or retreat concerning the naval reserve policy. In fact, they referred indignantly to trespassers on the naval lands. As they saw it, the country—and especially the Congress—was being put to a test. Was it possible to protect and reserve these naval areas, or any similar areas in the future, after they had become commercially attractive? [7]

With all of this Secretary Daniels could agree. Yet Daniels, as a politician and a Wilsonian progressive, looked upon the naval reserves somewhat differently than did officers who advised him. They were men of the regular Navy, trained to think of naval needs and problems. Daniels, however, showed almost the same concern for public oil lands everywhere as he did for the naval reserves. Certainly he wished to defeat oil trespassers and exploitative interests everywhere.

Having such an attitude, Daniels was unlikely to compromise. If while clinging to his precious oil reserves he had been willing to give oil men what they wanted outside the reserves, compromise would have been facilitated. But Daniels refused to abandon the Justice Department and congressional progressives and others who were broadly concerned with protection of the public lands. They had a genuine working alliance.

Subterfuge was involved here. Daniels and his allies knew that their opponents were clever and resourceful, and they reacted to successive challenges with equal resourcefulness. Thus Daniels seemed at most times to be interested exclusively in naval reserve lands. But, as necessary or strategically expedient, he extended his interests and helped to defeat a plan designed broadly for the relief of claimants. He usually argued for the naval reserves as a means of preserving petroleum. But he sometimes changed his

[7] "Report of the Naval Fuel Oil Board," December 22, 1916, Navy Records. See also "Naval Board to Investigate Oil Supply," *Oil Age*, XII (June, 1916), 14. The Board consisted of Rear Admiral John R. Edwards (chairman), Lieutenant Commanders J. O. Richardson and John Halligan, Jr., and Paymaster James C. Hilton.

emphasis and said that the Navy in emergencies could produce its own oil. He thought momentarily of surrendering Buena Vista Hills, but later he argued against this on the basis that it was the only reserve yet proven to be genuinely rich and valuable; the Navy could not give it up.

Daniels' arguments necessarily shifted with the changing national and international situation. He unquestionably engaged in much planning and even intrigue to defeat the oil claimants.

Daniels was regarded by his subordinates as an able, stubborn man, with powerful backing from the White House. Thus Commander Wright, at the "oil desk" in Washington, observed in December, 1917: "The oil men seem to be convinced that they can get any bill they want through the Senate and the House but that the President will see that the relief provisions are cut out in conference unless satisfactory to the Navy Department. I am rather inclined to agree with them on this point." The means by which the President and Daniels could, if necessary, exercise their authority in conference was through Scott Ferris, chairman of the House Committee on Public Lands. A loyal administration man, and a moderate, Ferris cooperated closely with the White House.[8] Always, too, there was the ultimate threat of a presidential veto.

Naval officers were occasionally capable of sitting back and viewing the oil disputes with some objectivity. Commander Wright had such a capacity. He often worried over naval policies and the antagonisms they helped to produce. Nevertheless, he, like his chief, was highly suspicious of the oil men and their intentions.

In November, 1917, for example, Wright had a talk with Louis Titus, the oil lobbyist, in Washington. Titus broached the subject of a revised leasing bill which would exclude all the naval

---

[8] Wright to Landis, December 1, 1917, Navy Records; Thomas W. Gregory to President Wilson, December 28, 1917, Thomas W. Gregory Papers, Library of Congress; Ferris to Wilson, April 23, 1918, Navy Records; Wilson to Ferris, May 28, 1918, Woodrow Wilson Papers, File VI, Box 505, Library of Congress. Franklin D. Roosevelt, representing the Navy Department in December, 1916, was asked whether the Navy had an interest in petroleum lands outside the reserves. "Not a bit," he replied. This was incorrect, and it may have been deliberate obfuscation. See U.S. Congress, *General Leasing Bill,* Proceedings of the Special Joint Conference of the Committees on Public Lands and Representatives of the Departments of Justice, Navy, and Interior, on H.R. 406, 64 Cong., 2 Sess., Washington, 1917, p. 101.

reserves from its features. Such an idea left Wright cold, and he informed Titus that the Navy would not think of such a bill unless they were given "full political assurance" that the bill would not be altered in the conference committee so as to include the reserves again.

On another occasion, in 1918, Wright feared that the government was being taken in by the oil men's strategy. They sought temporary contracts (operating agreements) allowing them to continue their development. Even Kearful of the Justice Department was favorably inclined, provided that the net receipts, or profits, were impounded. But Wright informed Landis that such contracts would play into the oil men's hands; temporary relief of this kind was what they wanted. Wright continued: "You know as well as I do that under a normal or intensive drilling program there will be no net receipts for a period of two years, and they feel certain that they can get full relief at a later date." It is abundantly clear that suspicion clouded the eyes even of such moderate and constructive men as Wright.[9]

## 4

Two efforts at compromise in 1917 illustrate the extreme difficulty of arriving at any agreement. The President and his Cabinet were hopeful that they could negotiate a general settlement. For purposes of trying to arrive at a meeting of minds a special commission had been created, consisting of three members of the House Committee on Public Lands, three from the Senate Committee on Public Lands, and representatives from the three executive departments concerned. These men conferred together. Certain senators and oil men also called on Secretary Daniels. President Wilson talked in January with Gregory, Lane, and Daniels.

The result was not a settlement but a serious misunderstanding between Gregory and Lane. Gregory had understood that the President wanted "a joint statement" from the Cabinet members concerned. They were to give their views on pending relief

---

[9] Wright to Landis, November 21, 1917, June 24, 1918, and *passim* in the correspondence of Wright and Landis, Navy Records. Admiral Griffin, chief of the Bureau of Engineering, keenly resented the oil men's demands. See "Memorandum," December 4, 1913, and *passim, ibid.*

measures in the Senate. But within a short time Gregory had received a copy of a report from Lane to the President made independently—a long argument in behalf of relief, which specifically supported the Phelan amendment, and declared that Buena Vista Hills was not and could not be a "real reservoir."

Lane gave the explanation that he had merely put his thoughts of the conference into writing. Of course, he said, he had intended later to participate in a joint report. As it turned out, Daniels and Gregory submitted their report jointly while Lane's went in separately.[10]

President Wilson tried a second possibility. He asked Gregory to investigate the so-called Swanson plan, named after Senator Swanson of Virginia. In the closing weeks of the Sixty-fourth Congress Gregory carried out the President's directions. Writing to Secretary Lane on February 21, 1917, he said that Lane's department and the Navy were principally concerned in this affair, and if they could agree, his department would accept the results. However, Gregory in the circumstances could hardly have expected them to agree.

The Swanson amendment, if accepted, would have been a naval victory. As proposed at this time, it seems to have originated in the hearings held in January before the Naval Affairs Committee of the Senate. Was it possible, Swanson had asked, to have a fair compromise by letting the operators take leases on their existing wells only, paying a royalty of one-eighth? The plan assumed definite shape in February. Operators to qualify for a lease must have entered the lands, or their predecessors in interest must have done so, prior to July 3, 1910. They must have proceeded "honestly and in good faith," commencing discovery work; and if they made discovery of oil or gas, they would be "entitled" to a lease of any such "producing" well, together with the necessary land for operation.

But they would have no right to drill additional wells. A royalty of one-eighth must be paid on oil and gas already produced from the well, with the same royalty applying on subsequent production. Furthermore, where wells were involved in suits brought by the Justice Department, the claimants must

---

[10] Gregory to Lane, January 27, 1917, Lane to Gregory, January 29, 1917, Gregory to Lane, January 30, 1917, Gregory to Daniels, January 30, 1917, *ibid.*

surrender all rights asserted in the particular case, or they could not become eligible for a lease.[11]

Secretary Lane, not taking kindly to this proposal, replied with a counterproposal. He was willing to apply the Swanson plan inside the naval reserves. But outside the reserves, he asserted, the terms ought to be more generous. The purpose of a leasing bill was "to promote the development of these oil lands and their operation under proper regulation." The entire community would receive benefits from this development. As to who ought to do the developing, why not those who already had "invested their money"?

For details Lane referred interested parties to Clay Tallman's suggestions of December, 1916. During a hearing before the public lands committees of both houses, Tallman had advanced a plan surprisingly generous to claimants. He would have permitted any claimant who had successfully developed an oil or gas well to lease the entire mineral location. One condition was that the claimant must enter the land prior to passage of this relief bill, as late as 1916 or 1917. Claimants on Reserve No. 2, as well as the public lands generally, would be eligible. Furthermore, such a claimant might test his right to title before the Land Office. If his claims were too weak and were denied, he still would have ninety days in which to get a lease.[12]

Daniels and Gregory found this unacceptable. Daniels was prepared, however, to accept the Swanson plan for the leasing of wells only. He may have agreed to it knowing that Lane and Tallman would disagree. Nevertheless, as he said, the Swanson policy would represent a departure from his genuine belief that the matter should be settled in the courts, or that private equities in the reserves should be purchased by the Navy.

Daniels continued to insist that trespassers on the petroleum lands after July 2, 1910, should not be rewarded "at the expense of the persons who respected the order, the Navy, and the whole Nation."[13] As for Buena Vista Hills, he pointed out that the

---

[11] Wilson to Gregory, February 19, 1917, Gregory to Lane, February 21, 1917, Wilson Papers, File VI, Box 505; U.S. Congress, Senate, *Oil-Land Leasing Bill*, pp. 56–57; Daniels to Gregory, February 26, 1917, Wilson Papers, File VI, Box 505.

[12] Lane to Gregory, February 24, 1917, *ibid.*; U.S. Congress, *General Leasing Bill*, pp. 103–105.

[13] Daniels to Gregory, February 26, 1917, Wilson Papers, File VI, Box 505.

Justice Department had advised him "there was much reason to expect a favorable outcome"; that is, in pending litigation against the Southern Pacific Railroad and other interests. The government's and the Navy's interests in Buena Vista Hills were "too substantial to be sacrificed." [14]

The efforts of early 1917 came to naught, and Gregory reported to Senator Swanson that his plan had failed. He added that he also was authorized to report for the President, with whom he had discussed the matter, that the Swanson plan was "the limit of liberality to which he [was] willing to go in dealing with these oil claimants." [15]

Eventually, much was to be heard of the plan for leasing wells only, within the naval reserves. But in 1917–18 a legislative compromise, if such was to occur, required a different basis.

# 5

If compromise had been difficult before, it became more so with the outbreak of war in April, 1917. Naval leaders began to think seriously of gaining genuine control over the petroleum reserves. Oil claimants, at the same time, had rising expectations.

A "grand shift" in the oil men's strategy became apparent.[16] They had been accustomed to argue that claimants should be given their land out of simple right and justice, but from 1917 to 1920 they changed the emphasis. Claimants should be given the same land, on the basis of patriotism and national need. Those who opposed them were held to be unwise, unpatriotic, or both.

This pressure, or propaganda, was deeply resented by Daniels, Gregory, and their allies. They regarded themselves as defenders of the public interest. They thought of oil men and their friends as being selfishly or politically motivated. Daniels once commented, in words that were none too tactful: "Perhaps, if I lived in California, my vision would be limited by California. Of

---

[14] Daniels to Senator Pittman, December 23, 1916, quoted in U.S. Congress, *General Leasing Bill*, pp. 103–105.
[15] Gregory to Swanson, February 26, 1917, Wilson Papers, File VI, Box 505.
[16] Unsigned copy of letter, probably by Wright, to Landis, June 26, 1917, Navy Records.

course, environment has some effect upon the views of all of us." [17]

It is clear, also, that many progressives in the war period were determined to carry their principles forward. In a real sense the Progressive Movement continued. The issues were often the same; only the emphasis was different in an atmosphere of war-making. Daniels, Gregory, Senator Husting of Wisconsin, and other Democrats seem to have been spurred on in their progressivism by a determination to show that the war was not, or need not be, a mistake. Progressives in the Republican party, such as La Follette, wished in their way to democratize the war effort.

New, bitter disagreements occurred. In the California and Wyoming oil fields drilling and marketing activities were stepped up. As the threat to public lands increased, so did protective action in the Navy and Justice Departments. New evidence was discovered in the summer of 1917 that the Honolulu Oil Company had fraudulently claimed its locations in Naval Reserve No. 2. This case was never settled; it lay festering, with periodic flare-ups.

Far more serious in 1917 was a threat from the Southern Pacific Railroad. Its leaders planned an extensive drilling campaign in Reserve No. 2, where they controlled all the odd-numbered sections. They already had protective line wells. They now proposed to drill far back into the interior of their holdings—second and third line wells—which hardly seemed justifiable merely for protective purposes. These particular lands were under supervision of the federal court, pending conclusion of the government's cases against the railroad. The court's policy had been conservationist. If the court now gave permission for new drilling, this would be a green light. The Honolulu Company, Standard of California, and other companies on adjacent sections would claim that they also must engage in "protective" drilling. Soon No. 2 would be destroyed as a reserve for future needs of the Navy.

E. J. Justice feared for the future. Although Judge Benjamin

---

[17] See, for example, Gregory to President Wilson, March 28, 1918, Gregory Papers; Daniels' testimony in U.S. Congress, Senate, *Leasing of Oil Lands*, p. 178 (June 23, 1917).

Bledsoe denied the railroad's application, in April of 1917, he seemed to be retreating somewhat from his conservationist views. This was the trend. It was easy to see that the arguments for production, as the war continued, would be difficult to resist.

Moreover, Justice strongly suspected collusion between the railroad company and major purchasing and pipeline companies "to create a situation" by which the naval reserves would be opened up. These major companies, he charged, controlled the price of petroleum in California. They probably had agreed among themselves that the Southern Pacific would be unable to "buy fuel oil on the market." Thus it would be given the excuse to go to the court protesting its shortage of fuel oil. As it got permission to drill, all of the major companies could expect commensurate benefits.[18]

Daniels, Gregory, Commander Landis, and others were deeply disturbed over the threat, immediate and potential. In May the Attorney General and President Wilson made a strong statement upholding the policy of naval petroleum reserves, which was used with good effect upon Judge Bledsoe.

In spite of all that could be done, the railroad obtained permission for drilling some first and second line wells. Commander Landis, in San Francisco, gave a good idea of what the government was up against: "The Southern Pacific is constantly insisting at every opportunity that the withdrawn lands in general and the Naval Reserves in particular must be thrown open to operators in order to relieve [the] shortage." [19] Moreover, "all the operators" hammered on the idea that the shortage could be relieved only by opening the reserves. The statement was "repeatedly" made that drainage from the reserves was so serious that drilling might as well be permitted.[20]

The greatest blow to the Navy and Justice Departments occurred in July, 1917. E. J. Justice died suddenly at his desk in

---

[18] Justice to Daniels, April 27, 1917, Navy Records. See also Justice to Landis, March 20, 1917, Landis to Justice, March 27, 1917, Daniels to Justice, April 7, 1917, *ibid.* For a defense of large unit production in California see "Waking Up to Facts," *Standard Oil Bulletin,* II (March, 1915), 1–2.
[19] Landis to Wright, June 28, 1917, Navy Records. See "Promoting a Crisis," a sweeping indictment of the Navy and governmental policy, in *Standard Oil Bulletin,* V (May, 1917), 1–2.
[20] Landis to Wright, June 14, 1917, Navy Records.

San Francisco. He had been working long hours, particularly on the Southern Pacific cases. Commander Landis expressed his shock: "In my relations with Mr. Justice I have found him always fair, courteous and conscientious and I feel that no one could have better served the Government's interests. His death is a great loss." The effect of Justice's death was calculated by an engineer, a civilian who had assisted Landis and Justice in the oil work: "With Mr. Justice gone it seems to be the feeling that the governments [*sic*] case has lost much, more because he had so much of it in his own hands and head, and the enormity of the case is a handicap to a new mans [*sic*] picking up its multitudinous details in any limited time."

For Secretary Daniels the death meant a personal loss. Justice, he declared, had given his life in the cause: he had worked to the end against defiant lawbreakers. Daniels and others showed increasing determination not to give in to the California petroleum interests.[21]

Justice's successor was Henry F. May, who came to believe no less passionately than Justice had in the rightness of their cause. He continued the assignment of supervising litigation in California and trying to prevent second and third line drilling.

Inevitably he conflicted with the Honolulu and other companies. In the summer of 1918 the government receiver in the Honolulu case, on application to Judge Frank Rudkin of the District Court, authorized new drilling by the Honolulu Company 600 feet within the lines of the particular section. Henry May had not been notified, and he fairly exploded: "This conduct on your part makes it more than ever necessary to resist that part of the order that you recently obtained, which, in effect, places the drilling in the hands of the Honolulu Company, subject only to the check of your permission, which is no check." [22]

That a trend had set in against the Navy and its allies seemed apparent. They could gain some encouragement from the fact

---

[21] Landis to Wright, August 1, 1917, J. H. G. Wolf to Wright, August –, 1917, *ibid.;* unsigned letter, probably by Wright, to Landis, August 8, 1917, *ibid.;* Josephus Daniels, *The Wilson Era: Years of Peace, 1910–1917*, Chapel Hill, N.C., 1944, pp. 372–373.

[22] May to Gratz Helm, July 18, 1918, Navy Records. See also May to A. C. Diericx, president of the Honolulu Oil Company, July 18, 1918, Wright to Landis, August 14, 1918, *ibid.*

that President Wilson was firmly on their side. Early in 1918 he told Colonel House that Secretary Lane was not carrying out the presidential policy for western petroleum lands, that rather he was willing to lease the lands or to tie them up in such a way that heavy loss of oil would occur before legal action could be brought to a conclusion. The President also said that Lane had "stood still." In 1913 he was considered a progressive, but now he had become a conservative, and most of his friends were conservatives.[23]

Josephus Daniels had only begun to fight. He would not surrender his reserves. He would not consent to any leasing bill that treated claimants liberally. Before 1917 was over, he seized the offensive, invoked his wartime authority to thwart oil men's claims, and advanced alternative plans for naval control over supplies of petroleum. For better or worse, Daniels had elected to fight this matter through to the end.

[23] Entry of January 9, 1918, in Diary of Edward M. House, vol. 13, Yale University Library, New Haven, Conn. Courtesy of Richard Lowitt.

# The Debate over Wartime Controls

**CHAPTER VIII**

*Everyone knows that the sensible and sure way to increase the output of oil is to restore the withdrawn lands to public entry and to remove the clammy, oppressive hand of the government. . . . Government is not an exotic growth and a democracy is not a hothouse plant.*
**Senator William H. King (Democrat, Utah), December, 1917**

1

Congressional personalities were to figure dramatically in the petroleum fight of 1917–19: Walsh of Montana, Pittman of Nevada, Phelan of California, Kendrick of Wyoming, Swanson of Virginia, La Follette and Husting of Wisconsin, Ferris of Oklahoma. But there were many more, some showing a genuine interest in the petroleum question for the first time.

There was Albert B. Fall of New Mexico. Since his arrival in the Senate in 1912, Fall had said little on this issue. In 1916, however, the Interior Department sent him detailed information concerning the withdrawn oil lands. The picture they painted was an inviting one of precious though idle lands waiting for development, and Fall's interest may have been sharpened. As to how western development should occur, there was no doubt in Fall's mind. On several occasions he stated that he hoped for the day when Congress could abolish the Department of the Interior for the lack of any work for it to do.[1]

Walsh and Pittman were not so easily classified as Fall. They

---

[1] *Cong. Record*, 62 Cong., 2 Sess., p. 6495, May 15, 1912. See also *ibid.*, p. 6561, May 16, 1912; Fall to Walter L. Fisher, Secretary of the Interior, August 21, 1912, Albert B. Fall Papers, Huntington Library, San Marino, Calif.; David H. Stratton, "Albert B. Fall and the Teapot Dome Affair,"

did become, however, the most vigorous senatorial sponsors of leasing legislation. Walsh had arrived in the Senate in 1913 as a progressive, Wilsonian Democrat. Gifted as a lawyer, ambitious and energetic in his committee assignments and on the Senate floor, the Montanan quickly assumed his place as an administration leader. He took a keen interest in Wilsonian reforms, as well as in politics and national political campaigns, in 1916 managing the Democratic campaign in the West. Walsh was sensitive to the economic demands of the western states and threw himself into the movement for legislative solution of western resource problems. He regarded himself as a key supporter of Secretary Lane, and attempted to convert to leasing those western men still dedicated to the old system of alienation. Particularly in the war years, Walsh emerged as a powerful figure, introducing leasing bills of major importance, using his influence with the administration, arguing in congressional hearings and in the Senate.

Harry Slattery was impressed, though skeptical of what Walsh was about. Writing to Pinchot, Slattery said: "In the whole public land question here lately . . . Walsh has clearly put himself forward as the real public land leader in the Senate and spokesman for the Administration upon this subject. I think he has assumed the place but he is so able on public land matters that he is getting away with it in fine shape. He doesn't belong on the Public Lands Committee, but seems to be able with the assistance of Phelan, Pittman, Shaffroth [sic] and Jones, together with side-door assistance from Smoot and Fall, to dominate the situation." [2]

The major leasing bill with which Walsh was identified also gained Pittman's vigorous support. This was the so-called Walsh-Pittman bill—center of legislative conflict in the Sixty-fifth Congress. Walsh introduced the bill, but when he suffered a breakdown in 1917 following the death of his wife, Pittman assumed sponsorship, and the bill came to represent Pittman's views more closely than Walsh's.

Key Pittman seems to have been authentically a product of the

---

unpublished Ph.D. dissertation, University of Colorado, Boulder, 1955, pp. 1–79, for Fall's career previous to the Harding administration.

[2] Slattery to Pinchot, August 2, 1917, Gifford Pinchot Papers, Box 1838, Library of Congress. See also J. Leonard Bates, "Senator Walsh of Montana, 1918 to 1924," unpublished Ph.D. dissertation, University of North Carolina, Chapel Hill, 1952, *passim*.

mining frontier. Born in Vicksburg, Mississippi, of well-to-do parents, he was educated by private tutors and at Southwestern Presbyterian University (Tennessee). At the age of eighteen he went west, and soon was hunting elk in the Cascade range of Washington and having other adventures. He settled down temporarily to the study of law in the Seattle office of James Hamilton Lewis (later a United States senator from Illinois).

After 1897 Pittman combined an interest in law and mining. He joined the rush to Alaska, working for two years as a miner, and opened a law office in Nome. In 1902 he went to Tonopah, Nevada, where silver had just been discovered. Pittman achieved distinction in the next decade as a lawyer and a specialist in mining law. Active also in the Democratic party, he was elected to the Senate in 1913, where he remained until his death in 1940. For obvious reasons this "lean, lanky, blue-eyed Senator from Nevada" was interested in western resources, in development, in miners and claimants, and in protecting their interests.[3]

Pittman deserved to be classed, as he sometimes was, as an "oil Senator." From 1917 to 1919 he was in very close communication with oil operators and attorneys. They were "taking up all of . . . [his] time," he once remarked.[4] Pittman was himself an aspiring oil man. Excited by news of a discovery in Nevada, on the public lands, he directed his brother in Tonopah to get in on the ground floor and to take as "many leases as possible." His brother was to use family names, but not the senator's. Pittman gave detailed information as to how to proceed. This land had not yet been withdrawn from private entry, and Pittman promised that he would "keep in touch with the situation" in Washington, so that any executive withdrawal could be anticipated, if possible.

Pittman was a close personal friend of James N. Gillett and Louis Titus, the California oil lobbyists. He was engaged with them in oil ventures, and they had passed on to him information about the Nevada oil strike mentioned above.[5] Meanwhile Pitt-

---

[3] See Joseph H. Baird, "Key Pittman: Frontier Statesman," *American Mercury*, L (July, 1940), 306–313; George Creel, "Daniel of the Gold Fields," *Collier's*, XCVII (April 25, 1936), 25; Senator Walsh to Pittman, June 30, 1917, Key Pittman Papers, Box 92, Library of Congress.

[4] Pittman to Joseph Scott, San Francisco, January 31, 1917, *ibid.*, Box 9.

[5] Pittman (telegram) to Vail Pittman, undated but about July 20, 1917, Pittman (telegram) to Vail Pittman, July 21, 1917, *ibid.*, Box 10; Pittman to

man in the Senate was pressing for passage of his leasing bill
tailored to the wishes of oil men. His conduct, to say the least,
was questionable. Yet Pittman also had won a reputation as a
strong Democrat and administration man. To oppose President
Wilson and certain party associates on this oil question was an
unpleasant necessity.

Differing sharply with Pittman were Democratic Senators
Claude Swanson and Paul O. Husting. They worked as closely
with the Navy Department and the National Conservation Association as Pittman did with oil lobbyists. Swanson, a party
wheelhorse from Virginia, held a strategic position on the Senate
Naval Affairs Committee, and through him Daniels endeavored
to protect the Navy's interests. In 1918 their principal object was
to win support for the "commandeering" bill.

Husting, a militant Democratic reformer from Wisconsin, came
to the front in 1917 in the petroleum controversy. He powerfully
aided the Navy's cause. As district attorney in Dodge County,
Wisconsin, and as a state senator from 1907 to 1913, he had grown
up with La Follette's "Wisconsin idea." He worked for a state
income tax, the national income tax amendment, labor laws, the
regulation of utilities, corrupt practices legislation, but most of
all for the conservation of natural resources.

According to La Follette, Husting had the "call of the wild"
in his veins. When elected to the United States Senate in 1914
—with backing from La Follette—it was natural for Husting
to broaden his efforts for conservation. He immediately plunged
into a fight against the Shields water power bill. By 1917, oc-
cupying a seat on the Public Lands Committee, he was regarded
by naval men as one of their few genuine friends. Indeed, in a
moment of discouragement, Commander Wright referred to
Husting as "about our only friend in the Senate."

In the same period Harry Slattery had only one real criticism

Vail Pittman, July 26, 1917, *ibid.*, Box 46. See also Pittman to Mrs. Louis
Titus, August 21, 1916, *ibid.*, Box 10; Pittman to John Bass, Jr., August 14,
1917, *ibid.*, Box 46; Oil Industry Association of California (for James N.
Gillett) to Pittman, July 20, 1917, Gillett to Pittman, September 24, 1918,
*ibid.*, Box 46. Pittman exclaimed to his brother in the letter of July 26: "Oil
is now attracting more attention than any other mineral, and I believe that
[in] the next two or three years there will be a tremendous oil demand in
the United States. Fortunes have been made everywhere and will be made
in oil. It is worth watching."

of Husting: his tendency to "put great reliance in the President"; to believe that eventually with Wilson's help they would get good legislation.[6] Husting was a loyal Wilson man, while La Follette and innumerable Wisconsinites and liberals turned against Wilson in the war period.

Husting was almost a minority of one in the Public Lands Committee of the Senate. Hearings were conducted in June, 1917, on a leasing bill (one of several introduced by Senator Walsh), to which amendments for relief were soon added. Slattery commented: "Our few friends in the Public Lands Committee were bowled over in good fashion." Commander Wright believed that the new bill contained provisions "as objectionable as ever," under which the Navy would certainly lose all of Reserve No. 2; the lobby had been working very hard and had been quite successful. Only Senator Husting, he said, had really stood by the Navy.[7]

Working through Husting, the Navy Department and conservationists decided to effect an exposé of the new bill, which would be in the form of Husting's minority report and a substitute bill. Apparently Slattery and Wells did most of the work. Slattery commented (to Pinchot) that the senator was exceedingly pleased with the report and believed that it would be "most useful as a basis for holding up the raiding crowd." [8]

Husting's report of 1917 reflected the changed conditions of wartime. The majority of the Public Lands Committee, he said, would turn Reserve No. 2 over to "private exploitation," for the benefit of "defiant lawbreakers." These men claimed that production was imperative, that there was no time to wait for

---

[6] Slattery to Gifford Pinchot, August 2, 1917, Pinchot Papers, Box 1838; unsigned copy of letter, probably by Wright, to Commander Landis, August 8, 1917, Navy Records, National Archives; Robert M. La Follette, "Husting's Death Is Loss to People," *La Follette's Magazine*, IX (November, 1917), 1. See also Belle C. and Fola La Follette, *Robert M. La Follette*, 2 vols., New York, 1953, I, 506–509.

[7] U.S. Congress, Senate, *Leasing of Oil Lands*, Hearings Before the Committee on Public Lands on S. 45, a "Bill to Encourage and Promote the Mining of Coal, Phosphate, Oil, Gas, Potassium, and Sodium on the Public Domain," 65 Cong., 1 Sess., Washington, 1917, p. 218; Slattery to Pinchot, August 2, 1917, Pinchot Papers, Box 1838; unsigned letter, probably by Wright, to Landis, August 25, 1917, Navy Records; unsigned letter, probably by Wright, to Landis, October 1, 1917, *ibid*.

[8] Slattery to Pinchot, September 24, 1917, Pinchot Papers, Box 1838.

ordinary legal procedures. His answer was, the Navy should immediately take over its reserves and drill and "do every other thing necessary" to insure supplies of oil. As to the public lands, generally, Husting declared, the "public interest" demanded a "high degree of public control." The government should assume such powers as restriction over exports, control of production, fixing of prices, prevention of waste, and insurance of good conditions for employees. The "vices of private ownership" had been exhibited at their worst in the oil industry.

Husting went ahead to a point-by-point indictment of the oil claimants and those who had befriended them. With "sincere regret" he evaluated the record of Secretary Lane, who had been "very tender" toward the oil trespassers when the record called for "justice upon them and not mercy." Husting declared: "These men and corporations are defiant plunderers of public property if ever men or corporations were, and the property they would seize is absolutely necessary for the National Defense." Running to some forty pages of typescript, this was the frankest and probably the most powerful argument ever put together against the oil men's claims. Among the naval men and progressives, it had a notable influence.

However, the report was never published. Husting went to Wisconsin on a hunting trip, where he was accidentally shot and killed by his brother. Since he had not signed the document, it could not be published as a minority report.[9] Husting's death, coming only a few months after that of E. J. Justice, was a serious blow to the conservationist group.

## 2

A new session of Congress convened in December, 1917, and a full-scale debate occurred over the problem of mineral lands legislation. In the Senate it was the Walsh-Pittman bill which received consideration. Kendrick of Wyoming emphasized the great value of the oil lands: "Mr. President, I feel perfectly free in saying that we are not dealing with the fragments of the public estate. We are dealing with the treasures of an empire." Passage

---

[9] Husting's Minority Report on S. 2812, unpublished, 1917, copy in Harry A. Slattery Papers, Duke University Library, Durham, N.C.; Wright to Landis, November 21, 1917, Navy Records.

of the Senate bill for the development of these resources, he argued, was necessary for the successful prosecution of the war. "In my judgment it . . . will direct the future growth and happiness of this Republic to a greater and more favorable degree than many of us imagine." [10]

Pittman and Swanson led the opposing forces, with Swanson aiming particularly at protection of the naval reserves, and they arrived at a temporary understanding. Much of the debate concerned this. Swanson held in readiness the naval bill for commandeering, with Pittman's knowledge and approval. The two men further agreed that the leasing bill might be passed, omitting the naval reserves. Pittman said to the Senate that he accepted such an arrangement only to get the leasing bill passed.

Pittman used the late Senator's Husting's name in a way that some considered questionable. Arguing for passage of the bill, he said that Husting had been interested mainly in the naval reserves. If they were omitted from terms of the bill, that feature of the controversy would be eliminated.[11]

In the Senate debate there were numerous protests, sometimes in the most bitter vein, against the idea of government operation. Phelan asserted that if the Navy successfully operated Reserve No. 2 it would only be because oil "pioneers" already had proven the richness of the area. It would be "nothing less than burglary," unless compensation were promptly made. The oil men, he said, were anxious for the government to have the supplies it needed, but they knew that they could produce and supply oil better than the Navy could. Moreover, the Navy's plans for Buena Vista Hills were unrealistic. Because of continuing drainage, this area could not be maintained as a reserve.

As to the Pittman-Swanson agreement, Phelan did not like it; he thought it an injustice. But the California oil companies, except the Honolulu Company, were willing to have it. He would accept it also—solely as a means of passing the general provisions.[12]

Senator Smoot bluntly called names and went to the heart of

---

[10] *Cong. Record*, 65 Cong., 2 Sess., pp. 388–391, December 17, 1917.
[11] *Ibid.*, pp. 287–288, December 14, 1917; Gregory to President Wilson, December 28, 1917, Thomas W. Gregory Papers, Library of Congress; Husting's Minority Report on S. 2812.
[12] *Cong. Record*, 65 Cong., 2 Sess., pp. 395–399, December 17, 1917.

the matter. He had seen the Navy plan, he said, for purchase of all claims in the reserves. They thus proposed to clear the way for government operation. They could not even estimate the cost, which he believed must run close to $200,000,000. He raised other troublesome points. There was especially the Honolulu case and the unwillingness of the Navy Department to allow adjudication by the Interior Department. In contrast to Senator Phelan, he said he had received a number of protests against the Navy's plans for commandeering. It was not the Honolulu people alone.

Smoot turned to the Navy and its friends and their interference with the legislative process. He declared that the Secretary of the Navy, on this very day, had sent word to the Senate that the bill could not pass as it had come from the Public Lands Committee. Smoot was indignant. He also singled out the National Conservation Association as having "a great influence with members of Congress." He said that he would agree, under protest, to the elimination of the naval reserves from application of the bill.[13]

The longest and most vigorous protest was that of Senator King. Was he to understand, he asked at one point, that "the Navy Department, or some executive of the Government," was standing "with a bludgeon threatening Congress," preventing the passage of legislation which the Congress believed to be "just and fair and right"?[14] King soon launched into a speech running more than ten pages, without interruption. A Spencerian in point of view, he opposed the principles of federal conservation and leasing, as well as the details of the legislation under discussion. He opposed the Navy Department and its plans. The facts, he believed, called for "a stern rebuke" of its "unprecedented and unwarranted usurpations." He deprecated the idea that this legislation was necessary to win the war: "Everyone knows that the sensible and sure way to increase the output of oil is to restore the withdrawn lands to public entry and to remove the clammy, oppressive hand of the government."

Senator King was joined by a few others in opposing federal leasing and regulation, as a matter of principle. It was Senator

---

[13] *Ibid.*, p. 288, December 14, 1917; *ibid.*, pp. 398–399, 413–414, December 17, 1917.
[14] *Ibid.*, p. 395, December 17, 1917.

Pittman who tried to bring them back to reality: "It is either a bill of this character or none." [15] Of all the senators, only Swanson defended Josephus Daniels and the Navy. Speaking with vehemence and apparent sincerity, he seems to have impressed the Senate.

Nothing had been settled, although things had been "popping," as Commander Wright said. The Senate now recessed for Christmas, with the understanding that the bill would be voted on in January, as Swanson and Pittman had arranged. [16]

In January the debate continued. The question of monopoly was now uppermost. Would the leasing system under the pending bill afford sufficient safeguards? Curiously, those who said no were, on the one hand, diehard advocates of private ownership and development like Senator King; on the other, they were those who believed in genuine governmental control, or operation. Both extremes opposed the leasing compromisers in the middle. Senator King continued his former line of argument, maintaining that the leasing plan was a "delusion and a snare": it would strangle competition, rather than enhance it. [17]

The Midwest Company's monopoly in Wyoming came in for much attention. Kendrick of Wyoming, apparently persuaded that nothing could be done to reduce Midwest's power, at least not without hurting the state's economy, was anxious to see the leasing bill go through. Borah, Smoot, and others raised the question whether the Midwest Company was controlled by Standard Oil. Pittman said it was not, and reported a conversation with the vice-president of Midwest (probably a business associate of his). [18] Thomas also reported that he was told by his friends in Denver, officers of Midwest, that they had no connection with Standard. Borah remained unconvinced. He believed that the Senate had not received enough intelligence on the Wyoming situation.

---

[15] *Ibid.*, pp. 402–404, 413, and *passim,* December 17, 1917.

[16] Wright to Landis, December 21, 1917, Navy Records.

[17] *Cong. Record,* 65 Cong., 2 Sess., p. 652, January 7, 1918.

[18] James N. Gillett, writing to Pittman on September 24, 1918, discussed the division of stock in an oil company in which they were associated. Among the other stockholders were Harry Blackmer and L. L. Aitken of the Midwest Oil group, Denver. Pittman Papers, Box 46. Blackmer soon was to be involved in the notorious Continental Oil deal, along with Harry Sinclair and others.

A high point of this debate was an announcement from Borah. He had been converted to a belief in public control of natural resources: "I shall never again vote for a bill which has the effect of conveying even by lease these natural resources. I am in favor from this time on of city, state, or Government ownership and operation of the natural resources, such as oil and power in our Western States . . . these great oil, coal, and power possessions now belonging to the Government should be held and operated by the public for the public."

Even Pittman, in reference to this, said that as between private monopoly and public monopoly, he preferred the latter. But privately he deeply regretted that "so staunch a supporter of the West" as Borah "should have been converted to government operation of our western resources." [19]

The Walsh-Pittman bill—with naval reserves excluded—finally passed the Senate on January 7, 1918. The vote was 37 to 32. Among those voting nay were Borah, Norris, La Follette, and Swanson. They thought the bill too lenient and full of loopholes. Also among the opposition were King and similar believers in private control, who doubtless resented, in part, the fact that the Navy had won its point by getting the reserves excluded from this bill.

Senator King soon renewed his attack on the executive departments. They were "chloroforming" the Congress, he said. Whereupon Swanson eloquently defended Daniels and Attorney General Gregory. These men were public servants whose only mistake—if any—had been that they were "too zealous" in their defense of "the interests and rights of the Government." Senator King, speaking in a milder tone, paid tribute to Daniels as a "strong and able" Secretary, who had brought the Navy to a peak of efficiency. But there had been "usurpations."

He went ahead to criticize tellingly the plans for naval operation of its own petroleum reserves. The expenses would be "staggering." Many obstacles and complications, not anticipated, would appear. He suggested that Swanson and the Navy give further consideration to their plans. King's discernment is perhaps indicated by the fact that at this very time within the Navy

---

[19] Pittman to Robert N. Bell, March 7, 1918, *ibid.*, Box 92; *Cong. Record*, 65 Cong., 2 Sess., pp. 648, 653, January 7, 1918. See also *ibid.*, p. 569, January 4, 1918; *ibid.*, pp. 642–646, January 7, 1918.

Department Commander Wright was worried over the complexities of Navy operation, should it come to pass.[20]

## 3

Naval leaders pressed on with their ideas of government operation. Daniels had written to the President on January 3, saying that the situation concerning the oil reserves called for "a plan." A bill had been drawn up, he said, providing for commandeering of the reserves and for operation by the Navy; there would be an equitable adjustment of claims. Senator Swanson, Attorney General Gregory, and he had conferred on the subject. They agreed that commandeering was the "best solution," and they requested a conference with the President for further discussion.[21]

On January 15 Swanson introduced his bill, to "provide for the common defense and general welfare of the United States with respect to the production, use, and conservation of oil and gas in naval petroleum reserves, and for other purposes." He asked that it be referred to the Committee on Naval Affairs.

Smoot was ready with a substitute proposal—that the bill be referred to the Committee on Public Lands. A sharp clash occurred. The Public Lands Committee, said Swanson, was unfriendly toward this bill, and it should not have jurisdiction. Thomas of Colorado passionately made reply. He thanked God that there was one committee of the Senate which was "still friendly and tolerant of that spirit which settled the West and which, if left untrammeled," would provide for the Nation's resource needs. Members of this committee knew that private operation and development would supply all the petroleum required. Anyway, Thomas charged, the Navy had no intention of producing oil on its reserves.[22]

This argument was jurisdictional and sectional. As a number of western senators spoke, Swanson grew impatient. He could

---

[20] *Ibid.*, pp. 572–575, January 4, 1918; unsigned letter, probably by Wright, to Landis, January 11, 1918, Navy Records. See also *Cong. Record*, 65 Cong., 2 Sess., p. 662, January 7, 1918.
[21] Daniels to Wilson, January 3, 1918, Navy Department, memorandum for the Secretary, January 8, 1918, Josephus Daniels Papers, Box 14, Library of Congress.
[22] *Cong. Record*, 65 Cong., 2 Sess., pp. 872–875, January 15, 1918; *ibid.*, pp. 894–896, January 16, 1918; *ibid.*, pp. 922–925, January 17, 1918.

not understand, he said, this effort to deprive his committee of jurisdiction and give it to another committee "that has never had anything to do with naval matters." Senator Phelan undertook to enlighten him. This dispute, he reminded the Senate, went back to the Honolulu case and to the question of who controlled the public lands. In the Honolulu dispute, executive pressure had forced the Secretary of the Interior to yield. But the fight had continued. The Secretary still retained jurisdiction over these naval reserves, and he was trying to uphold the "integrity of his department" under the laws of the United States. The Senate should help him. It should "preserve the integrity of its rules" by referring this bill to the Committee on Public Lands.[23]

By a vote of 40 to 15, the Senate supported Swanson. The bill therefore went to the Naval Affairs Committee. Commander Wright in Washington and Landis in California were now giving serious thought to matters of personnel and procedure, in the event they took over the reserves. Harry Slattery's optimistic mood showed the trend of thinking among the pro-Navy men. He commented to Philip Wells that Swanson's bill was "in a large part" the same measure that Wells had drafted for Senator Husting. It was to be "keenly regretted" that Husting was not present to observe the progress that their bill was making.[24]

# 4

Actually the barriers to operation of the reserves by the Navy continued to be formidable, if not insurmountable. Past differences were far from reconciled. Much depended, too, upon what happened in the war. Military successes or failures, production of petroleum and the increased demand for it, attitudes of officials in powerful wartime jobs, the degree of responsibility shown by private industry—these would strongly affect any decision of the Congress.

Action was centered in two places: in the House of Representatives, where the Senate bills, or alternative House bills, must receive consideration; and in the executive departments, including now the wartime agencies.

---

[23] *Ibid.,* pp. 1008–09, January 18, 1918.
[24] *Ibid.;* unsigned letter, probably by Wright, to Landis, January 21, 1918, Navy Records; Slattery to Wells, February 19, 1918, Pinchot Papers, Box 1838.

In January, 1918, Mark L. Requa assumed his post as petroleum administrator. Holding such a position, his influence in the petroleum controversies was potentially great. He urged increased production and efficiency, and appointed men of like views as his assistants. Quickly it was recognized by many oil men that Requa was on their side and that they faced a common enemy on the home front. Their enemy was the critic of business, the government agent and investigator, and—Josephus Daniels. He was anyone who gave aid or comfort to Daniels' ideas. One journal, referring to Swanson's commandeering bill, had this to say: "It is a remarkable bill, not merely in that it proposes to put the navy into the oil business, but in the scant courtesy it pays to the rights of private citizens in the oil fields." [25]

Many saw the Federal Trade Commission as a foe of legitimate business. It was a federal interloper, endeavoring to frustrate Requa's well-conceived plans for the oil industry. In 1917 George Otis Smith, of the Geological Survey, had warned Secretary Lane of certain activities of the FTC: the commissioners, he believed, were thinking of petroleum price-fixing, or perhaps of commandeering certain fields. There could be no doubt that the FTC was critical of certain oil companies. In April, 1918, it charged the Standard Oil Company of Indiana with unfair practices and "profiteering." Oil men sprang to the defense. Speaking undoubtedly for much of the industry, the *National Petroleum News* bluntly classified the FTC as an enemy: "It is well known that the Commission has harbored a feeling of antagonism against the general oil industry for some time. . . . It is also well known to some of the industry that the Commission is in favor of the government's taking the industry over entirely." Requa, they continued, not the FTC, must be left in control of the industry. The object of administrators should be to win the war, not to maintain competition—as the FTC desired.[26]

[25] "Navy May Become an Oil Operator," *National Petroleum News,* X (January 30, 1918), 13. See also "Oil Land Bill Not Yet out of Committee," *Oil Age,* XIV (April, 1918), 1; "The Navy's Oil Supply—A Protest," *Standard Oil Bulletin,* VII (August, 1919), 1–2.

[26] Smith to Lane, September 4, 1917, Secretary's File, Department of the Interior, National Archives; "Trade Commission Charges Profiteering by Oil Trade," *National Petroleum News,* X (May 1, 1918), 1. See also "Commission Must Not Disturb Requa's Control," *ibid.,* X (May 15, 1918), 11; "For a Common-Sense Policy," *Standard Oil Bulletin,* V (March, 1918), 1–2; "Oil Land Bill Not Yet out of Committee," p. 1.

For reasons not altogether clear, a new crisis over petroleum production occurred in the spring of 1918. Public lands remained unopened, as leasing bills were stalled in the House of Representatives. Scott Ferris, chairman of the Committee on Public Lands, was very active and did apparently all that he could do. He made detailed inquiries on the troublesome matter of claimants, their rights, and alleged rights. His committee conducted hearings. Efforts were made once again to get the heads of Interior, Justice, and Navy to agree on the terms of a compromise. Efforts were also made to hold the oil men to reasonable demands.

According to Harry Slattery, however, there was "much bitterness" in Ferris' committee. Ferris had become convinced that the oil men wanted too much. When they appeared before the committee in the number of fifty or sixty, they presented amendments for relief which were wholly unacceptable to administration leaders. Ferris reported to the President that he was opposing the majority of his own committee in this matter; that it was "in the interest of common justice that these lands be not grabbed up by a lot of oil claimants and speculators." The Justice and Navy Departments added their protests.[27]

Thus the old stalemate persisted. At this juncture Requa decided on drastic action. He would obtain the production that he believed was so badly needed. Why not bring all pressure to bear on Bernard Baruch, the President, Daniels, Gregory, and others including the oil men? Why not compel some form of compromise?

On two points Requa was vehement. First, Naval Reserve No. 2, "the richest known proved oil area in the United States," must be opened to development. Second, "the integrity of the Mexican source of supply" must be guaranteed as a "war measure." On April 20 he wrote to Bernard Baruch to this effect. He also commented in some detail on the precarious shortages of the West Coast and the "mistaken policy" of the Navy.[28]

---

[27] Ferris to Wilson, April 23, 1918 (copy), Navy Records. See also Ferris to Secretary Lane, January 14, 1918, and additional correspondence, Secretary's File; U.S. Congress, House, *Oil Leasing Lands,* Hearings Before the Committee on Public Lands on H.R. 3232, to "Authorize Exploration for and Disposition of Coal, Phosphate, Oil, Gas, Potassium or Sodium," and S. 2812, to "Encourage and Promote Mining of Coal, Phosphate, Oil, Gas, and Sodium on the Public Domain," 65 Cong., 2 Sess., Washington, 1918, p. 1220 and *passim.*
[28] Requa to Baruch, April 20, 1918, Navy Records.

Toward the end of April matters came to a climax. A delegation of publishers and editors from western states converged on Washington. The shortage of fuel oil was so critical, they maintained, that paper mills, newspaper plants, and other businesses might have to close down. They demanded action.

One of these editors, V. S. McClatchy of the *Sacramento Bee,* described something of what happened in Washington. Requa, Baruch, Daniels, the publishers, the oil claimants (represented by Gillett and Titus), and others were involved in numerous conferences. On the demand of the West Coast group, Secretary Daniels agreed to the opening of the naval reserve "under control of the President." Oil claimants would be reimbursed for their equities. But the oil claimants had "rather demurred" at this solution. As McClatchy understood things (he left Washington early), Requa, Daniels, and the publishers were now putting pressure on the oil men to accept this scheme of commandeering.

On the day that McClatchy wrote, newspapers carried a later story. Requa had served an ultimatum on the oil claimants. Either they must agree with the government within two weeks on a bill for immediate production in the naval reserves or Requa "would recommend to the President to commandeer the land and have the litigation settled later." Baruch went even further, it was reported. If commandeering became necessary he would recommend that the entire fuel oil business of the West Coast "be taken over by the Government." [29]

All of this signified a temporary victory for the Daniels point of view. If emergency production occurred, it would be mostly on his terms. The oil men apparently had overplayed their hand, while Daniels had won Baruch, the President, and others to his side.

There was no immediate development of Naval Reserve No. 2, as Requa had desired. Nor was there, of course, a declaration of war against Mexico or other action to guarantee the Mexican supply.

A Daniels victory is also suggested by developments in Congress. Last efforts were made, for this session, to arrange a com-

---

[29] McClatchy to Lane, April 28, 1918, Secretary's File; "May Seize Rich Oil Lands," *New York Times,* April 28, 1918. See also "Seek Development of Coast Reserve," *National Petroleum News,* X (May 8, 1918), 38.

promise, and at least in a procedural sense the Daniels forces had the upper hand. Scott Ferris gained full control in the House Committee on Public Lands. The leasing bill reported out was, as Commander Wright saw it, "about as good" as the Navy could "reasonably expect" to get. It was much tougher on claimants than two leasing bills passed in previous years by the House.[30]

Representatives from western states were relatively acquiescent. In effect, the same thing happened in the House as had happened in the Senate. Those who wanted relief, and who objected bitterly to plans for commandeering, would go along for the moment with a stringent administration bill. Later, in the conference committee of senators and representatives, they expected a liberalization.

Mondell of Wyoming could not restrain himself entirely. He said the bill proposed relief "so ridiculously inadequate that one not familiar with the conflicting influences that have brought about the change would be sorely puzzled to know how it happened." After raising many objections and proposing amendment on amendment, he burst out with the statement that his section of the country was being badly treated. If this bill became law, "millions of acres of the most valuable lands in various Western States" would be partially lost as a source of revenue, that is, through permanent federal ownership.

Shouting insults at each other, Ferris and Mondell revealed more than they had intended to. Ferris said that Mondell's criticisms were as "remarkable" as they were "monstrous." Speaking as chairman of the Public Lands Committee and as a Democrat, he would not tolerate Mondell's "self-assertive motives" and his "politics" and "propaganda." The western members of the committee had been true to their constituents, true to the public. They had obtained the best bill they could. Mondell retorted that Ferris' remarks were "abusive." He hinted at executive influence and intrigue in the management of the bill: "There are things that could be said about this bill that I do not want to say, but that I am tempted to say."[31]

Mondell then settled down to see what would happen. This

---

[30] Wright to Landis, May 13, 1918, Navy Records.
[31] *Cong. Record*, 65 Cong., 2 Sess., p. 6993, May 23, 1918; *ibid.*, pp. 7102–03, May 25, 1918. See also Representative Edward T. Taylor to Woodrow Wilson, Wilson Papers, File VI, Box 505, Library of Congress.

wartime bill had a production motif, which helps to explain its passage. Claimants were permitted to lease their producing wells and the hope was held out that later they might receive presidential permission to drill and lease additional wells. The Daniels group was satisfied since commandeering of petroleum land was specifically authorized. When the vote occurred on May 25, westerners were cooperative. The bill passed without a roll call.[32]

For a brief time, the passage of the bill seemed an important step ahead. Ferris reported the good news to the President and received in turn his thanks and congratulations.[33] From this point on, the administration plans went awry. The House bill went to the Senate, and Pittman got the Senate to disagree. In the conference committee, now appointed, things were hopeless. The House appointed Ferris, Taylor, Raker, William La Follette, and Nicholas J. Sinnott. The Senate conferees were Pittman, Phelan, Shafroth, Smoot, and Fall. As Commander Wright saw it, this meant probably "a fight between Ferris and the other nine." Since Ferris had behind him the power of the administration, the end result was another stalemate. The leasing bill was now bottled up and was not heard from again on the floor of Congress until February of 1919.[34]

## 5

In 1918 the need for action was all-apparent, and the general weal superseded the demands of private interests. Not too surprisingly, therefore, the cry of *Commandeering!* was often heard.

In the summer of 1918 a unique case arose concerning the Salt Creek field of Wyoming. Should this rich area of public lands, controlled by the Midwest Oil Company, be taken over by the government? Senator Kendrick of Wyoming said yes, and he won wide support. The whole affair was precipitated when Kendrick wrote to the President in June, suggesting an immediate investigation into the means by which private interests had se-

---

[32] *Cong. Record,* 65 Cong., 2 Sess., pp. 6984–87, 6995, May 23, 1918; *ibid.,* pp. 7091, 7103, 7108, May 25, 1918.

[33] Ferris to Wilson, May 27, 1918, Wilson to Ferris, May 28, 1918, Wilson Papers, File VI, Box 505.

[34] Wright to Landis, June 13, 1918, Navy Records; *Cong. Record,* 65 Cong., 2 Sess., p. 7111, May 27, 1918; *ibid.,* pp. 7164–65, May 28, 1918.

cured control of public lands in the Salt Creek field. On the basis
of this information, he suggested, the President would be able
to determine whether he should commandeer the field, using his
authority under the Lever Act.

There was no doubt about Kendrick's feelings. He had changed
considerably since 1917. For six and a half pages he reviewed
what he regarded as fraudulent and antipublic activities of Midwest's interests. He claimed that they were currently engaged in
sinking new wells surreptitiously on public lands "as rapidly as
they can be sunk." Of the pending suits involving claims of Midwest, he said: "It is my conviction that the contentions of the
Government may easily be sustained and that neither the Midwest Company nor its predecessors has an honest title to any of
the land upon which it is now operating." He criticized the
operating agreements, under the act of 1914, by which the Midwest Company was allowed to continue operations. They took
seven-eighths of the production, although they did not have
title and the government had a very strong case against them.
He noted that the Justice Department believed "a considerably
larger amount of the entire product should be held in escrow to
protect the rights of the Government."

Kendrick's language seems to reveal a wartime solicitude for
the public interest. This oil in Salt Creek belonged to the American people. Midwest's interests had taken it by "unblushing
fraud," as was well known to those acquainted with the area.
"The leaders among them [Midwest] have become millionaires
through the sale of oil which is not owned by them but by the
people of the United States." If the facts were known, public
opinion would block the exploiters: "Nothing is clearer than
that public sentiment during the past decade has undergone a
very great change and that the country is now practically unani-
mous in the belief that the great resources on the public domain
should be held for the benefit of the many rather than sequested
[sic] by a few for the benefit of a few."

Kendrick had a proposal, based on the country's wartime need
for oil. He offered no comfort to the oil men. Preferably, the
government should now assert its title by commandeering the
Salt Creek field and continuing production through government
operation. If that were impossible, the least the government could
do would be to increase the royalty to 50 per cent; and this

royalty "should be based, not upon the sale price as fixed by the operator, who is also the refiner [Midwest], but upon the value of the oil in the open market." [35]

President Wilson forwarded Kendrick's letter to Attorney General Gregory, requesting his advice. He added: "I have learned to think Senator Kendrick a very sincere and disinterested public servant." Solicitor General John W. Davis replied for Gregory. After carefully considering Kendrick's statements, he said, he had concluded that they were "quite conservative." So far as the rectitude of the situation went, Midwest should not even obtain the 50 per cent which Kendrick would allow them to have. They were producing oil at a cost of eight cents per barrel, while the market price was $1.85 per barrel. The government had the authority to step in. The Secretary of the Interior could increase the amount to be impounded, and, though there were technical difficulties, commandeering could occur. Like everybody else, Davis recommended policies to increase production. If private operators, working under the operating agreements, did not cooperate they would have to surrender possession. [36]

These recommendations were accepted by the President. The next difficulty was in gaining support from the Interior Department. Presidential orders went out, first, for impounding a larger amount of production; second, for examining with utmost care and seriousness the possibility of commandeering the Salt Creek field. At every step this policy was opposed by Secretary Lane and Commissioner Tallman. While expressing their willingness to carry out the presidential orders, they submitted various objections.

Tallman made a long defense of the Interior Department's policy because, as he said, he was "largely responsible" for what the Department had done in this oil land matter. He denied Kendrick's charge that Midwest was secretly putting down new wells. He objected to a 50 per cent royalty basis as being impracticable. He argued that it was wrong to impound so much of the operators' oil as the Justice Department wished to. Oil men's

---

[35] Kendrick to Wilson, June 19, 1918, Records of the Department of Justice, National Archives. See also "Wyoming's Pioneer Field," *Curb News* (New York), October 22, 1917.

[36] Wilson to Gregory, July 3, 1918, Davis to Wilson, July 18, 1918, Records of the Department of Justice.

incentive would be lessened. How about taxes they paid, how about maintenance and other expenses?

He mentioned as an alternative a plan offered by L. L. Aitken, representing Midwest and other companies. They would drill new wells "as rapidly as possible on a basis of reimbursement only for the cost of drilling the wells and the cost of operation." Tallman really proposed, however, "a good stiff royalty, say onefourth, for drilling and operating these proven lands." [37]

In spite of the Interior Department, the new policy went into effect. Orders were issued to tighten control and impound the net proceeds of operations, under agreements made with claimants.

Then the Justice Department made a discovery: the Midwest Refining Company had a curious method of keeping its books. It had previously been surrendering not one-eighth of net proceeds but rather one-sixteenth. Under the new policy they had begun to surrender not all proceeds, but rather about one-half. This figure had been approved by the Interior Department—apparently with full knowledge of the facts.

The basis of such an arrangement went back to 1913. At that time the Midwest Oil Company and contending parties in the Salt Creek field had settled their claims and differences to mutual advantage. The Midwest Refining Company was created to conduct all the physical operations of drilling, refining, and marketing. For its services it took one-half of the net profits and paid the other half to claimant companies (with which it was allied). In some manner, then, Midwest Refining was able to conclude that only one-half of their production was subject to a government royalty, or claim.

The Justice Department charged deliberate misrepresentation and falsification of records. Assistant Attorney General Francis J. Kearful was especially vehement. But Gregory and John W. Davis also believed that the President's order was being circumvented. Tallman and Lane angrily denied these charges. The records had always been available for investigation, they said.

In the meantime, problems of commandeering were found to be insurmountable. Oil men, as well as a few government officials,

---

[37] President Wilson to Lane, July 12, 1918, Lane to Wilson, July 17, 1918, enclosing Tallman to Lane, July 15, 1918 (copies), *ibid.* See also Lane (telegram) to Wilson, August 16, 1918, Wilson Papers, File VI, Box 505.

stubbornly objected. When Wilson went to Paris, late in 1918, the matter was still unsolved.[38]

## 6

In one notable instance, oil men were compelled to yield to government demands. The Navy Department, acting under its wartime authority, fixed a price on fuel oil and required delivery at the established figure. That is, it refused to buy at the market price and fixed what was determined to be a "just and reasonable price," allowing a fair profit. Under this order fuel oil had to be delivered at San Francisco for $1.08 a barrel in the fiscal year 1917–18 (about thirty-seven cents below the market) and for $1.47 a barrel the next year. According to the Navy, this was a necessary action: market prices had not been established by genuine competition, and too many businessmen were "ready to capitalize the war demands to their benefit"; [39] the Navy had a responsibility to receive "full value for every dollar expended." [40]

Initially the oil companies accepted Navy prices without much complaint. But increasingly in 1918–19 they grew bitter. This policy was nothing less than confiscation, they charged, as well as being one more evidence of Secretary Daniels' animosity toward private business, and an insult to oil men patriotically doing their part in the war emergency.[41] When price-fixing con-

---

[38] Kearful, memorandum for the Attorney General (marked "confidential"), August 7, 1918, Records of the Department of Justice; John W. Davis, memorandum for the Attorney General, August 15, 1918, *ibid.*; Gregory to Lane, August 25, 1918, Lane to Gregory, September 13, 1918, Assistant Attorney General (probably Kearful) to Henry F. May, November 16, 1918, Wilson to Gregory, October 2, 10, 1918, Wilson to Lane, January 7, 1919, and miscellaneous, *ibid.* See also Harold D. Roberts, *Salt Creek Wyoming: The Story of a Great Oil Field*, Denver, Colo., 1956, pp. 87–100 and *passim*.

[39] Bureau of Supply and Accounts in *Annual Report of the Navy Department, 1918*, Washington, 1918, pp. 602–603, 635–636, and *passim*. See also "Oil Industry Faces Government Regulation," *National Petroleum News*, IX (July, 1917), 8; "Business's Big Bit," *Standard Oil Bulletin*, V (July, 1917), 1.

[40] Secretary of the Navy in *Annual Report of the Navy Department, 1918*, pp. 97–98.

[41] Speech by Thomas A. O'Donnell, quoted in "Produce More Oil," *Standard Oil Bulletin*, VI (May, 1918), 1–2; "The Navy's Oil Supply—A Protest," *ibid.*, VII (August, 1919), 1–2; "The Navy and Its Oil Supply," *ibid.*, VIII (August, 1920), 1–2. See also an attack on Daniels and his attitude toward business in "To Challenge Its Loyalty Unfair: Business, Which Must Pay for and Conduct the War, Gives No Cause for Such Remarks as Came from President," *National Petroleum News*, IX (July, 1917), 7.

tinued, even in 1920, the Navy was quite susceptible to accusa-
tions of unfairness.

Everything considered, the Navy and Justice Departments
succeeded remarkably well in holding the line against private
claimants on the public lands and in battling oil companies and
their friends in public office. To a limited extent they fixed oil
prices, and they threatened to do so on a broader basis; they
prepared measures for commandeering of the naval reserves and
gave serious consideration to commandeering all of Salt Creek;
they attempted to win support for operation of California lands
under the supervision of a government receiver.[42] They could
rightfully claim also that, despite the everlasting fears of an oil
shortage and of governmental interference with private business, the war was won with adequate supplies.

Nevertheless, the consequences of their policies, negatively
speaking, might be momentous. They had not furthered a leasing program. Nor had they won friends among oil executives
and western politicians. Political tides, meanwhile, were beginning to run against them.

---

[42] Wright to Landis, May 28, 1918, Navy Records; Gregory to Lane, June
14, 1918, Alexander Vogelsang, acting Secretary of the Interior, to Gregory,
June 17, 1918, Secretary's File; William Kent to Woodrow Wilson, June 17,
1918, Wilson to Kent, June 19, 1918, Wilson Papers, File VI, Box 505.

# Harassed Wilsonians Appeasing the West, 1918–19

**CHAPTER IX**

*My trouble is that the party is in very great need of assistance of every sort in regaining the confidence of public opinion. . . .*
Woodrow Wilson, Paris, to Attorney General Gregory, January 31, 1919

1

By 1918 the Democratic party was in serious trouble. If this seemed true in the late summer, it became glaringly apparent after the elections in November, when the Democrats lost control of Congress. At least, their control would end after the "lame duck" session of the Sixty-fifth Congress, in March, 1919. Party leaders were hard-pressed. In some manner they needed to regain the country's confidence.

Woodrow Wilson, continuing as President, was increasingly occupied with problems of winning the peace. At the same time Wilson was aware of widespread dissatisfaction within his party, and notably in the western United States. Western leaders bombarded him with appeals to support their development bills. There was, for example, the Walsh-Pittman oil leasing bill, still tied up in the conference committee.

As always, the President had to keep in mind not one but many contending groups and economic interests, and he faced a rising opposition. Progressives of the Republican party, such as Pinchot, La Follette, and George Norris, turned against him. La Follette emerged as the arresting figure in the petroleum fight, while the President, it seemed, might be giving up his role as a champion of conservation.

## 2

It is a curious fact that at the height of Wilsonian internationalism there should have been a resurgence of American sectionalism. Woodrow Wilson, the southerner and the partisan Democrat, was the butt of many attacks. His party, it was charged, was a pro-southern party which had failed to interest itself in all areas of the Union. This charge had a corollary: Wilson was the powerful executive, thwarting the will of the whole people, as expressed in their legislatures and in the Congress.

The petroleum controversy lent itself to sectional arguments against the President. His most trusted advisers in the matter had been southern men—Daniels, Gregory, McReynolds, E. J. Justice, John W. Davis, Claude Swanson; while the advice of Lane, Tallman, and other westerners often had been disregarded. Moreover, the executive branch in this instance had played an unusual role. It could be charged with overriding the wishes of western people. Through 1918 a chorus of criticism came from western politicians, with Democrats speaking almost as freely at times as Republicans.

In June, Senator Fall wrote with apparent sincerity about his disappointment in the Wilson administration:

Much to my disappointment Lane, as Secretary of the Interior, has displayed a woeful lack of understanding of the needs of the west and, even when grasping any part of such needs, has then been hampered with interference from some other member of the Cabinet.

I found that there had developed under this administration that spirit of bureaucratism which had been developing for so many years under previous administrations; and I found the Democratic Congress absolutely determined, apparently, not only to obey every command, but to yield to every indication of desire communicated to them, either directly or indirectly from any department of the government. . . .[1]

Senate debates of September 19, 1918, further showed the trend. Thomas and Pittman (Democrats) and Smoot, Fall, and Albert B. Cummins of Iowa (Republicans) joined in an attack on administration policies. The Senate had been discussing a water power bill, but was diverted by Thomas to the petroleum shortage. Here, he said, was a subject "far more vital than water

---

[1] Fall to *Albuquerque Evening Herald,* June 14, 1918, Albert B. Fall Papers, Huntington Library, San Marino, Calif.

power at this time." He proceeded to review the oil fight from 1909 to 1918. Immediate passage of the Senate oil bill was his aim, and he proposed to attach it as an amendment to the water power bill.

Thomas had little mercy on those responsible for what he considered a deplorable stalemate in oil production. He referred to officials of the Navy and Justice Departments.

Key Pittman, chairman of the conference committee, gave his version of why the Senate and House conferees could not agree. It was the chronic complaint of executive interference: "The conferees on behalf of the House have indicated very clearly that nothing will be agreed to by the House that is not approved in toto by these [executive] departments, and that if we agree to anything else it will be a useless act and a waste of time. I am inclined to believe they are right."

Secretary Lane, he asserted, had been willing to confer, willing to cooperate. This was not true of the Attorney General or the Secretary of the Navy. As to the disastrous consequences, he did not spare these two officials. The Department of Justice had "laid a blanket protest over every great known oil field" in the public land areas. There had been, as a result, a "depreciation of the oil production." He brought up the matter of operating agreements and described how the Attorney General had recently gone "even so far" as to compel the Secretary of the Interior to impound the entire production. The result had been that most of the private operators had "abandoned their contracts."

Pittman also raised the specter of government operation. If private operators were not permitted to do the job, the government must step in.[2]

Senator Cummins did not believe that Cabinet officers "ought to have anything to do with legislation." All of this was "very deplorable." Senator Smoot concurred. But, Cummins continued, Cabinet officers already were interfering; perhaps the solution was to take the matter to "the one man" who could settle the affair. This was logical, thought Senator Fall: "If we are going to be governed by Executive orders in our legislation, we certainly should go to headquarters."

Senator Thomas turned again to the conflict among Cabinet

---

[2] *Cong. Record,* 65 Cong., 2 Sess., pp. 10485–86, 10490–93, September 19, 1918.

members. In his experience, he said, the situation was unique: "It is a humiliating fact that the Secretary of the Interior, so far as we can judge from this condition, does not control the department over which he has been appointed to preside, but the subject matter of his jurisdiction is within the control and subject to the absolute domination of the Secretary of the Navy and the Attorney General of the United States." [3]

Thomas and other senators joined in a denunciation of the Department of Justice. The senators were aware, or they correctly surmised, that relations between the Justice Department and Interior Department had reached the breaking point. Thomas was particularly interested in Assistant Attorney General Francis J. Kearful.

The so-called Kearful affair reached its climax in 1918. Testifying in February, before the House Committee on Public Lands, Kearful had been questioned and led on to say frankly what he thought. What were his views on cases of fraud, as handled by the Interior Department? Surely he did not believe that Secretary Lane would permit leases where fraud had been proven? Yes he did; at least in cases "where charges of fraud had been made and without [further] investigation."

Thomas, as he reviewed the affair, put the worst aspect upon Kearful's remarks: "Mr. President, the serious aspect of these statements lies in the official character of the men who make them. As the representative of the Department of Justice, Mr. Kearful virtually declares that the Secretary of the Interior is a dishonest man, and that, in the event of the enactment of the Senate oil bill, he will so administer it as to commit a fraud and an injustice upon the rights of the people of the United States." Thomas went on to say that he had "waited long and patiently" for the Attorney General to repudiate this point of view; but he had waited in vain. [4]

Speeches such as these were not calculated to weld the Demo-

---

[3] *Ibid.*, pp. 10492–93, September 19, 1918.

[4] *Ibid.*, pp. 10486–88, September 19, 1918; U.S. Congress, House, *Oil Leasing Lands,* Hearings Before the Committee on Public Lands on H.R. 3232, to "Authorize Exploration for and Disposition of Coal, Phosphate, Oil, Gas, Potassium or Sodium," and S. 2812, to "Encourage and Promote Mining of Coal, Phosphate, Oil, Gas, and Sodium on the Public Domain," 65 Cong., 2 Sess., Washington, 1918, pp. 979–983 and *passim.* Kearful made a cogent defense of policies pursued by the Justice Department.

cratic party together. Attorney General Gregory, for example, was not in a compromising mood, and continued to give full support to Kearful. Western "propaganda," he believed, had caused the attacks on his assistant. Gregory became bitterly critical of the Senate bill and of Pittman's allegations that in this bill the main objections of the late Senator Husting had been met. There were other things to irritate him, such as the much-maligned policy of impounding net production.

On September 24, after the Senate debates described above, Gregory wrote to Senator Pittman, taking issue with some of what the Nevadan had said on the Senate floor. In the strongest terms, though officially correct, he specified how Pittman had misinterpreted his position. A copy of this letter was sent to Senator Swanson, with a covering letter. Gregory referred to Pittman's "very palpable errors," saying that if Pittman did not correct them, he hoped very much that Swanson would set the record straight. Writing privately about the same time, Pittman referred to his "unpleasant relations with the Attorney General." [5]

Western Democratic leaders in 1918 were aware of widespread discontent at the grass roots. They shared in some of it. They knew that the party's position had weakened since 1916, yet there was little to do but press on toward the same goals. If they could pass their leasing bills, if they could win the sympathetic attention of the administration, they could face the voters back home with confidence. Otherwise they were in deep trouble.[6] There was another possibility—painful to contemplate. Should the

---

[5] Woodrow Wilson to Gregory, March 21, 1918, enclosing a copy of a telegram from the San Francisco Chamber of Commerce, Gregory to Wilson, March 28, 1918, Thomas W. Gregory Papers, Library of Congress; Gregory to Pittman, September 24, 1918, Gregory to Swanson, September 24, 1918, *ibid.; Cong. Record*, 65 Cong., 2 Sess., pp. 10488–90, September 19, 1918; Pittman to H. H. Schwartz, October 7, 1918, Key Pittman Papers, Box 92, Library of Congress.

[6] E. S. Bonfils to Pittman, January 28, 1918, enclosing a clipping of January 27 from the *Denver Post, ibid.* See also Frank G. Curtis to Pittman, May 2, 1918, *ibid.;* Representative Edward T. Taylor (Colorado) to Woodrow Wilson, April 27, 1918, Woodrow Wilson Papers, File VI, Box 505, Library of Congress; Pittman to Wilson, September 7, 1918, *ibid.,* File II, Box 148; Lane (telegram) to Wilson, August 16, 1918, *ibid.,* File VI, Box 505; H. Alan Rispin to Lane, May 7, 1918, Secretary's File, Department of the Interior, National Archives; Seward W. Livermore, "The Sectional Issue in the 1918 Congressional Elections," *Mississippi Valley Historical Review,* XXXV (June, 1948), *passim.*

Democrats lose, eastern leaders of the party might finally wake up; might finally realize that hope had been "too long deferred" in the public land states.

That the Democrats should meet defeat in these off-year elections was not surprising. Even in 1916, with a relatively harmonious party, they had carried the country by a close vote. Heaviest losses in 1918 occurred in western and middle western states. In the Senate races, for example, the Democrats gained a seat only in Massachusetts, and lost seats in Illinois, Missouri, Kansas, and Colorado, as well as in Delaware and New Hampshire. Senator Shafroth lost his seat in Colorado. In the closest of contests, Senator Walsh in Montana managed to hang on to his. Losses in the Senate gave the Republicans control by 49 to 47— provided that La Follette cooperated for the purposes of organization, as he did.[7]

Surveying the wreckage of Democratic hopes, Senator Walsh concluded that sectionalism was primarily responsible. The public had been receptive to the argument that the South was "running the government, and running it selfishly," and that the remedy lay in giving power to the Republicans. It had been plausibly argued that the administration's economic policies discriminated in favor of the South.[8] Wilson's appointment policy, according to Walsh, had been partial to the South, and he cited the recent appointment of a new Solicitor General. The man was a Georgian of only local reputation, said Walsh. It would have been easy to suggest "half a dozen abler lawyers north of Mason and Dixon's line." [9]

Thus Walsh, and other administration supporters in the West, voiced criticisms similar to those of Republicans, and made clear the dilemma of their party.

## 3

Democrats did not lose hope. Until March 4, they had an excellent chance to obtain final passage of the Walsh-Pittman bill. In

---

[7] *Ibid.*, p. 58. J. Leonard Bates, "Senator Walsh of Montana, 1918–1924," unpublished Ph.D. dissertation, University of North Carolina, Chapel Hill, 1952, pp. 80–83, 89–90.

[8] Walsh to W. M. Johnston, November 12, 1918, Thomas J. Walsh Papers, Library of Congress.

[9] Walsh to C. F. Morris, November 19, 1918, *ibid.* See also Homer S. Cum-

that success they might also gain some political capital. The burning question remained, what would the President do? And what would his subordinates do? Could the President be induced to use his powerful influence in favor of the leasing bill?

In late November, Senator Shafroth sent an appeal to the President via Postmaster General Burleson. Shafroth had been defeated in the recent election, and for that reason his words may have gained poignancy. He said that in view of election results in the western states, he felt he should again call the President's attention to the leasing bill, which was still tied up in conference. He had in mind the welfare of his party and the nation, and the fact that citizens of public land states undoubtedly felt they had been treated unjustly. Delay in passage of the pending bill had "much to do" with this feeling.

He proposed, therefore, that the President send "a word . . . to the Departments interested in these matters." What he meant in plain language was that if Daniels, Gregory, and company could be persuaded to cooperate, the bill might be passed.[10]

The burden was now upon President Wilson. Should he adopt the suggested policy of placating the West? In doing so, there would be considerable risk. He might expose himself to the bitterest of attacks by conservationists like Pinchot and La Follette. And the bill might not pass, even with his support.

There is considerable evidence as to Wilson's trend of thought. He had misgivings, as in the past, about the oil leasing bill. He tended to agree with Daniels, Gregory, and others who were suspicious of the oil claimants, but at the same time he was primarily concerned in 1918–19 with his world responsibilities, with the Paris Peace Conference, and with winning support at home for the treaty that would be negotiated. The political defeats of November, 1918, had shocked the President. He was ready, in spite of his doubts, to compromise with intraparty critics.

Wilson's awareness of the new situation was vividly expressed in a letter of January 31, 1919, written from Paris. The problem

mings to Wilson, November 7, 1918, Wilson Papers, File II, Box 155; Daniel C. Roper to Wilson, March 3, 1919, *ibid.*, File VIII–A, Box 22; Livermore, "The Sectional Issue in the 1918 Congressional Elections," *passim.*
[10] Shafroth to Burleson, November 25, 1918, Wilson to Burleson, November 27, 1918, Albert S. Burleson Papers, vol. 22, Library of Congress.

of the moment was a successor to Gregory in the Justice Department, who had decided to resign and strongly recommended Assistant Attorney General G. Carroll Todd as his replacement. The President replied: "My feeling towards Todd is most warm and I admire everything I hear about him. My trouble is that the party is in very great need of assistance of every sort in regaining the confidence of public opinion, and the mere fact that Todd was born in Virginia, though he lived there only nine years, would certainly be seized upon to deepen the impression that ours was only a Southern party, and that disturbs me greatly. I would love to honor Todd, and yet we must strengthen the party." [11] The man subsequently decided upon—against Gregory's recommendation—was A. Mitchell Palmer of Pennsylvania.

In February, the President made another fateful decision. He sent "the word" that Senator Shafroth had requested to the executive departments. This was in the form of a cablegram from Paris to Tumulty in the White House: "For Attorney General Gregory. Understand that the conferees on the oil leasing bill have come to an agreement and think it unwise in the circumstances to attempt further guidance in the matter. To insist upon alteration now would throw the matter into the next Congress where much less favorable action would be certain with perhaps serious consequences to the country." Thus the Wilson men in Washington received their instructions. They should cease opposition to what was widely considered a giveaway bill.[12]

A turning point had come. Ostensibly, at least, Wilson's supporters in Congress assumed an anticonservationist position, and a fight with progressives and conservationists of the Republican party was now inevitable. Managing the leasing bill were Scott Ferris in the House and Pittman in the Senate. "Fighting Bob" La Follette assumed leadership of the opposition.

On February 18, 1919, Scott Ferris called up the conference report on the leasing bill for immediate action. He proposed to read a short statement on the report, rather than the full document; only two hours were allotted for debate. James R. Mann, however, insisted that the report be read.

Some of Ferris' remarks on the relief situation were in

[11] Wilson to Gregory, January 31, 1919, Gregory Papers.
[12] Wilson to Tumulty, February 5, 1919, Wilson Papers, File VIII–A, Box 18.

startling contrast to those he had expressed in 1918. His whole attitude now had become that this bill ought to be passed; this "long-drawn-out matter" should be brought to a conclusion. The conference bill, he said, was "substantially" the same as the bill that had passed the House three times in the past. Of the government suits against oil claimants he said: ". . . the Government has held them up and impounded $15,000,000 of their money." This litigation would now be settled under the conference bill, and these "oil pioneers" would receive leases on their property.

"Politics!" charged Representative James A. Frear of Wisconsin. Other representatives joined in sharp criticism of Ferris and his attempt to push this bill through.[13]

The leasing bill was not an easy thing to defend. It was comprehensive and detailed. In its provisions were included public lands containing coal, sodium, phosphate, and gas—as well as the controversial petroleum areas. This was not entirely a leasing bill but rather would continue, to a considerable extent, the alienation of public lands. Prospectors seeking to discover oil in new territory would be permitted to acquire a combination of patent and leasing rights.

The naval reserves were brought under the bill. Producing wells would be leased to claimants (under a modified Swanson plan), and at the discretion of the President such claimants would also be permitted to drill additional wells. The Navy was not given control over its lands, such as it had hoped to achieve. Oil claimants, on the whole, seemed to be treated quite generously. Surprisingly also the national forest areas, the Grand Canyon National Park, and the Mt. Olympus National Monument would be opened to prospecting under the terms of the bill.[14]

Democrats failed to close ranks in support of this bill. Daniels and Gregory withheld an endorsement, although at the same time they did not oppose the bill with any vigor. They had

---

[13] *Cong. Record*, 65 Cong., 3 Sess., pp. 3690, 3698–3701, 3705–06, and *passim*, February 18, 1919. Senator La Follette and others correctly surmised that the President had sent instructions to pass the oil leasing bill. See *ibid.*, pp. 4713–16, March 1, 1919. Philip Wells expressed his belief that E. L. Doheny or George Creel may have influenced the President while they were in Paris. Wells to Pinchot, December 6, 1919, Gifford Pinchot Papers, Box 1700, Library of Congress. Creel, it was true, entered the employ of Doheny in 1919; this was brought out in the Teapot Dome hearings of 1924.

[14] *Cong. Record*, 65 Cong., 3 Sess., pp. 4696–97, March 1, 1919.

"waived much of their contentions," as Senator Walsh described it. In private they continued to disapprove; in public they discreetly withheld comment. Finally, in response to appeals to state their position, they did so. Gregory simply said, in a few words, that he had "declined to advocate" the passage of the conference bill. In a longer letter, Daniels was rather ambiguous, mildly stating some objections. He favored the leasing bill but was not satisfied with the provision concerning the naval reserves; he did not approve the bill as it stood.[15]

## 4

It was clear that if the bill were to be defeated, the Democratic administration would no longer do the job; it must be by opposition of the Pinchot group, of progressive Republicans in Congress, and of certain organization Republicans for whatever reasons they might have in mind.

Harry Slattery was back at work for the National Conservation Association early in 1919. Having completed a temporary assignment with Secretary Lane, he now followed closely the work of Congress and its conference committee on the oil leasing bill, and did much to organize the opposition. Philip Wells came down from his home in Connecticut, and the two of them were as if "on a treadmill for long hours at a time," analyzing bills and reports and preparing ammunition for their allies in Congress.[16]

Gifford Pinchot remained in Philadelphia, but, exceedingly anxious about the oil bill, he sent communications to prominent leaders throwing his influence against it. He urged Slattery to keep him fully informed. Slattery reported on February 17 that a recent letter of Pinchot's protesting against the conference bill already had produced good effects on Capitol Hill. Congress needed to be awakened on this thing.

---

[15] Senator Walsh in *ibid.*, p. 4042, February 22, 1918; Gifford Pinchot (telegram) to Gregory, February 26, 1919, Gregory to Pinchot, February 26, 1919, quoted in *ibid.*, p. 4492; Daniels to Swanson, February 27, 1919, quoted in *ibid.*, p. 4396. See also Gregory to President Wilson, February 5, 1919, Gregory Papers.

[16] Slattery to Pinchot, March 4, 1919, Pinchot Papers, Box 1842. See also Slattery to Pinchot, February 4, 1919, *ibid.*; Wells to Stephen W. Phillips, March 7, 1919 (marked "not sent"), *ibid.*, Box 1676; Slattery to John J. Hannan (La Follette's secretary), February 19, 1919, Harry A. Slattery Papers, Duke University Library, Durham, N.C.

Another idea occurred to Slattery. After a long talk with several of his progressive friends he proposed that they should "immediately" proceed to "tie" this leasing bill to the President, and he attached a tentative statement for a cable to President Wilson. Democratic vulnerability, from the political standpoint, was thus sensed by the Pinchot group and also by Representative Frear of Wisconsin, Senator La Follette, and others in Congress.[17]

As the debate occurred in the House and Senate, alternating with speeches against the League of Nations, and with consideration of critical appropriation bills, charges of politics were freely made. Feelings were bitter on both sides of the aisle.

Philip Wells commented of this dying session:

I have never seen such bitterness and extreme hatred toward any President as is now shown in Congress. It is largely a personal matter due to the fact that the progressive Republicans feel that they have been swindled by the President as to domestic measures, and to the feeling that Wilson is "not a good sport" as Roosevelt was—not willing to accept the blows that come to him under the rules of the game; also to a feeling that the Senate has been contemptuously overridden as to the treaty. One of the Progressives said to me that he would rather see [Boies] Penrose President than Wilson because in Penrose he would have an open enemy instead of a secret one.[18]

Republican leaders had determined on a strategy for keeping the President and his peace plans under surveillance. Still the minority, they would delay, and filibuster if need be, in order to prevent passage of appropriation bills. The President would be compelled, therefore, to call a special session of the new Congress, controlled by the Republicans. In this atmosphere of politics, hatred, and suspicion—mixed with high principle—the oil leasing bill fitted perfectly.

In the House on February 18, the steamroller was at work. The leasing bill passed quickly in spite of spirited opposition from James R. Mann and others, by a vote of 233 to 109.[19] Chances of stopping the bill in the Senate seemed rather remote at this time.

---

[17] Pinchot to Slattery, March 1 (telegram), 2 (letter), 1919, Slattery to Pinchot, February 17, March 4, 1919, Pinchot Papers, Box 1842; Frear in *Cong. Record*, 65 Cong., 3 Sess., p. 3706, February 18, 1919; La Follette in *ibid.*, p. 4713, March 1, 1919.

[18] Wells to Stephen W. Phillips, March 7, 1919 (marked "not sent"), Pinchot Papers, Box 1676.

[19] *Cong. Record*, 65 Cong., 3 Sess., pp. 3707–10 and *passim*, February 18, 1919.

Only Senator La Follette, it seems, had the ability, parliamentary skill, and audacity to fill the breach. Bold tactics were required, based on the rush of business at the end of the session. A limited amount of time could be given to the leasing bill, hence parliamentary delay or filibustering could defeat it. La Follette was willing, but he believed this to be a thankless task, to override the hopes of western representatives and senators and the wishes of the Democratic majority.

La Follette was subject, moreover, to "personal considerations" which made his task painful. He referred probably to the fact that his cousin, William La Follette of the state of Washington, was one of the five conferees from the House, and was intensely interested in the passage of the bill.[20]

The first step in La Follette's strategy was, if possible, to get the bill recommitted to conference. But how? Someone discovered that contrary to the rules the conferees had inserted new material in their version; that is, material found in neither the Senate nor the House bills. This gave La Follette the desperately needed possibility for carrying a point of order.

On February 22, the Senate resumed consideration of the leasing bill. Pittman as manager was in a violent mood; he suspected a covert attempt by "one or two Senators" to "contravene" the majority will of the Senate. This was all right, this was legal, but he was going to force them to show their hand. Moreover, he threatened: "I want to tell you that if the report of this committee, which was appointed by this body, is not considered and this bill fails by reason of it, those who are responsible for it will have a burden to bear which is possibly far greater than they at present realize."

Pittman called names and hinted broadly at others. He was exasperated with Reed Smoot because Smoot, although one of the five Senate conferees, was not supporting the bill. Pittman doubtless suspected political motives; in the next Congress Smoot would be chairman of the Committee on Public Lands. Pittman also complained about people making speeches on the League of Nations when this subject was not before the Senate.[21]

---

[20] *Ibid.*, p. 4714, March 1, 1919.
[21] *Ibid.*, pp. 4023–24, February 22, 1919. See also *ibid.*, pp. 3824–29, February 20, 1919; Belle C. and Fola La Follette, *Robert M. La Follette*, 2 vols., New York, 1953, II, 941–948.

Resenting Pinchot's opposition to the bill, Pittman referred to him as "a fraud." [22]

Finally La Follette had his chance. Shafroth, Walsh, and Thomas pleaded for passage of the bill. Pittman called for a vote. But the presiding officer (William F. Kirby of Arkansas, a southern radical) recognized La Follette for a point of order, over Shafroth's objections. La Follette got the floor and retained it, declaring that he would not yield until he had finished his statement. He showed that neither the House nor the Senate bill had provided for the leasing of coal lands in Alaska. Here in the conference bill was the "rankest violation of the rule which could be conceived," for it "absolutely and actually reversed the action of both Houses." Though this point seemed incontrovertible, Pittman, Walsh, and Shafroth refused to give up the fight. Shafroth, seemingly the most desperate, tried to argue that La Follette had made his point of order too late, and he cited a rule to prove it. But, George Norris asked, was that not a House rather than a Senate rule?

Waiting impatiently in the chair, Kirby sustained La Follette's point of order, and the bill was recommitted to the conference committee.[23] Soon it was returned to the House, where for the second time it passed, with the necessary changes. Still it had not passed the Senate. Time was running out for the friends of the bill.

La Follette's second tactic was filibuster. On Saturday, March 1, four hours were allotted for consideration of the leasing bill. La Follette got the floor and spoke almost entirely to the subject, well armed with material from Slattery, Wells, and company.

Without going exhaustively into details of the bill, he nevertheless made a powerful case against it. Pile everything together, he said: the long delay of the conferees in coming to agreement; the insertion of new matter, contrary to the Senate rules; the attempt to shove this bill through at the last minute, after more or less coercing the conferees into agreement—like a "jury which has been locked up for six months on bread and water"; the opposition of both the Navy and Justice Departments over a period of many years and, moreover, their present opposition although senators had been told that they favored the bill.

---

[22] *Cong. Record*, 65 Cong., 3 Sess., p. 3826, February 20, 1919.
[23] *Ibid.*, pp. 4044–48, February 22, 1919.

Why, said La Follette, one fact alone ought to persuade the senators not to enact this measure in the last seventy-two hours of the life of a Congress. The record showed that the Attorney General of the United States had fought this legislation step by step; he had fought all the way through the courts "to protect the public rights against the encroachment of men who are to-day represented in the lobbies about the Congress of the United States, seeking to secure this legislation, men who have been seeking to get confirmed by legislation rights which the courts have denied to them." [24]

At points in his speech La Follette was conciliatory toward the West. He explained his personal interest in conservation and his experience with monopoly in Wisconsin, which he hoped to avert in other parts of the country. He intended, he said, to impugn no man's motive. He must go his way, while other men no less good must go theirs.

But when La Follette clashed with administration leaders he was tough. There was no doubt that he believed passionately that this was the worst kind of measure. He talked out the time and killed the bill.[25]

## 5

Among contemporaries, the oil leasing fight in the closing weeks of the Sixty-fifth Congress was a memorable one. According to the Pinchot group, the bill they had defeated was deplorably bad. They identified it as a Democratic, Wilsonian bill. La Follette's filibuster, in the judgment of these men, was a heroic episode in the long struggle against exploiters of the public domain. Six years later Philip Wells paid tribute to La Follette: "He

---

[24] *Ibid.*, pp. 4713–14 and *passim*, March 1, 1919. See also La Follette, *Robert M. La Follette*, II, 942–947; Philip Wells to Stephen W. Phillips, March 7, 1919 (marked "not sent"), Pinchot Papers, Box 1676; Senator Walsh to J. S. Warner, March 5, 1919, Walsh Papers; National Conservation Association, "News Letter on Conservation," March, 1919, copy in Pinchot Papers, Box 1842.

[25] *Cong. Record*, 65 Cong., 3 Sess., pp. 4709–15, March 1, 1919; *San Francisco Chronicle*, March 1, 2, 3, 1919; La Follette, *Robert M. La Follette*, II, 943–947. La Follette continued to participate in the filibuster until noon of March 4. If it had collapsed there was still a chance that the leasing bill might pass. See *Cong. Record*, 65 Cong., 3 Sess., pp. 4980–91, March 4, 1919.

stood by and saved this cause for us in Congress when all others forsook it and fled." [26]

Many Democrats were bitter. They had worked and fought for this bill. Shafroth said on the floor, at the conclusion of La Follette's speech, that it was "an outrage on the people of the West"; "there is a rule of the Senate that is far more pernicious than any other—that is the rule permitting one Senator to defeat a measure by unlimited debate, even if three-fourths of the Senators are in favor of the legislation."

Senator Walsh felt almost as strongly. He wrote to one constituent on March 11 that the filibuster which beat the oil leasing bill was "a rather expensive piece of partisan politics for Montana." To another he said he was sorry to report that this bill, on which he had worked for four years, had been "talked . . . to death" by Senator La Follette. [27]

Thus the Democrats' efforts were all in vain. They had failed to pass the bill they wanted and to satisfy western demands, and they also were attacked as anticonservationists for having made the attempt. The charges against them were not altogether true or just; nevertheless, before the end of 1919 there were further indications that the Wilson administration was retreating from its previous conservation policy.

---

[26] Wells to Robert M. La Follette, Jr., June 19, 1925, Pinchot Papers, Box 1676.

[27] *Cong. Record*, 65 Cong., 3 Sess., pp. 4716–17, March 1, 1919; Walsh to J. E. Logan, March 11, 1919, Walsh to J. S. Warner, March 5, 1919, Walsh Papers.

# A. Mitchell Palmer and the "Celebrated Billion-Dollar" Case

CHAPTER X

*I think that the Southern Pacific getting this oil land [1919] on the ground that it was not mineral land was the greatest crime I ever heard of and ought to be remedied.*

Josephus Daniels to Senator Thomas J. Walsh, May 20, 1924

1

Throughout the oil land controversy, it had been recognized that the Southern Pacific cases were crucial. In the naval reserves alone, the railroad had patent to almost every other section. If those patents were sustained in court, the Navy lands would be checker-boarded, drainage into Southern Pacific and other private holdings would be heavy, and particularly in the case of Buena Vista Hills (No. 2) the reserve would be destroyed. If, however, the government could win, the Navy would have "a splendid property," as Commissioner Tallman observed. It was this hope above all others that buoyed up Josephus Daniels and his assistants. Nor is there any question that, whether they could win or not, they were passionately convinced that the Southern Pacific was guilty of fraud, and did not deserve the fabulously rich sections involved. One-half billion to a billion dollars was the valuation placed upon them.[1]

[1] Tallman in U.S. Congress, *General Leasing Bill,* Proceedings of the Special Joint Conference of the Committees on Public Lands and Representatives of the Departments of Justice, Navy, and Interior on H.R. 406, 64 Cong., 2 Sess., Washington, 1917, p. 118; Commander Irvin Landis to Secretary Daniels, January 21, 1916, Navy Records, National Archives; Daniels to Attorney General Palmer, December 6, 1919, *ibid.*

## 2

This area had been obtained by the railroad under its land grant of 1866. Included were the odd-numbered sections for twenty miles on each side of the track (or substitute selections). The act specified that mineral lands, except iron and coal, were excluded. Therefore, when the railroad filed its selections with the Land Office from 1894 to 1904 it had to submit affidavits and attest to the non-mineral character of the land. The principal question came to be, were these affidavits fraudulent?

The Taft administration believed they were, and initiated proceedings to invalidate the Southern Pacific patents. In his annual report of 1912 Attorney General George W. Wickersham described two classes of litigation against the Southern Pacific Railroad, one already in process, another soon to begin. First, there was the so-called Elk Hills suit, affecting about 6,000 acres of land valued at $18,000,000. This area, located entirely in Naval Reserve No. 1, had been selected in 1904, under the act of 1866, which excluded mineral land. But the patents when issued did not exclude such lands. One fact of importance was that the government started proceedings in 1910 before the statute of limitations had run.

A second group of suits was finally consolidated into one. This concerned lands selected from 1894 to 1902 and included about 165,000 acres, immensely valuable for petroleum. In this case, both the act of 1866 and the patents when issued had excluded mineral land. Yet it could be alleged by the railroad that most of the selections antedated major discoveries of oil in the area; therefore the railroad had no knowledge of hidden wealth. Also, the courts might hold that the statute of limitations had run. This would depend upon the scope of the fraud, if such were established.

Of this total area (in the consolidated suit) about 20,000 acres lay in Naval Reserves No. 1 and No. 2. Every alternate section in Buena Vista Hills (No. 2) was involved. The remainder of the 165,000 acres surrounded the reserves, running from south of Maricopa, in a northwest direction beyond Coalinga.[2]

---

[2] *Annual Report of the Attorney General, 1912,* Washington, 1912, pp. 40–41; *Annual Report of the Attorney General, 1915,* Washington, 1915, pp. 37–38:

When the Wilson administration came into power, its legal officers believed the Southern Pacific was guilty, and the suits were continued. E. J. Justice bore the main responsibility until his death in 1917. Justice once said "the story of the fraud and methods employed by the Southern Pacific Railroad Company to acquire these lands is as interesting as a novel." His general point of view concerning the Southern Pacific and the "Big Four" was similar to that of most historians: that the Southern Pacific had dominated California, employing chicanery, outright bribery and fraud, or even force, to have its way.

One historian of the Southern Pacific condemned the railroad's malpractices in these words: "One rises from the study of the political activities of the owners of the Central Pacific [and Southern Pacific] with a feeling of indignation at the selfishness of these men, their indifference to all save considerations of private gain, and their readiness to use any and all methods which would advance their financial interests."

For the Southern Pacific to ignore rich petroleum lands, which it might obtain merely by a subterfuge, seemed out of character. Undoubtedly, Justice and others were prejudiced against the Southern Pacific; they were ready to believe the worst. They also had some solid evidence. Where they lacked it, or where it was weak, they believed the railroad had shrewdly covered its tracks.[3]

*Burke* v. *Southern Pacific Railroad Company,* a private suit which reached the United States Supreme Court in 1914, helped to establish the ground upon which the government must argue its cases. Burke and others claimed five sections of land in the Coalinga field, under the placer law. This land, they argued, could not be legally acquired by the railroad under terms of its grant or its patents. Agreeing with their contention, the Department of Justice filed a brief in the case.

Justice Van Devanter delivered the opinion of the court, hold-

---

*U.S., Appt.,* v. *Southern Pacific Company et al.,* 64 Law. Ed., 251 U.S. 97 (Elk Hills, 1919); Daniels to Palmer, December 6, 1919, Navy Records; Slattery, memorandum, January 4, 1920, Harry A. Slattery Papers, Duke University Library, Durham, N.C.

[3] E. J. Justice, memorandum on Southern Pacific cases, September 29, 1916, Navy Records; Stuart Daggett, *Chapters on the History of the Southern Pacific,* New York, 1922, p. 220 and *passim;* George E. Mowry, "The Southern Pacific's California," in *The California Progressives,* Berkeley, Calif., 1951, pp. 1–22.

ing for the railroad. The patents, he showed, had been issued some fourteen years before Burke filed his suit in 1910, and the statute of limitations had run. Moreover, the Land Office had approved the grants. Whether its procedure was or was not correct, its action was final—barring the discovery of fraud.[4]

E. J. Justice was not dismayed. He commented on the day of this decision that the question of fraud and that of the statute of limitations—in connection with fraud—"were not decided by the Supreme Court." The court had not heard as yet what the government's contentions were.

The Southern Pacific's leading attorney, C. R. Lewers, was pleased with his victory and he expressed himself candidly about the forthcoming contests with the government. It would be contended against them, he said, in the larger case, "that the statute of limitations did not run, because the lands were obtained by fraud and because this fraud was concealed until recently." This contention could not be sustained. "There was no fraud and there was no concealment." He showed less confidence about the smaller Elk Hills suit. It came within the statute of limitations and was "a direct attack on the ground that the patent was obtained by fraud."[5]

The Southern Pacific now attempted to get the consolidated suit thrown out of court, primarily on the basis of the statute of limitations, but the government was able to defeat this maneuver. Judge Bledsoe of the District Court in Southern California held, as Justice had argued, that if there were fraud in the issuance of patents, and concealment, the statute of limitations could not bar the suits.[6]

Thus from 1910 into the late Wilson period these Southern Pacific patents were under attack. Although the railroad was the main defendant, there were several hundred defendants in all, largely due to the fact that the railroad had sold some 20 per cent of its selections. From the beginning, the big suits (or consolidated suit) were before Judge Bledsoe of the District Court. Evidence was taken in Los Angeles, San Francisco, Chicago, New

---

[4] *Burke v. Southern Pacific Railroad Company*, 58 Law. Ed., 234 U.S. 1527 (1914). See also "Southern Pacific Wins First Round," *Oil Age*, IX (June 26, 1914), 8–9.
[5] *Ibid.*
[6] *Annual Report of the Attorney General, 1915*, pp. 37–38.

York, and Washington. As *The Oil Age* commented: "A half-dozen assistants to the Attorney-General" appeared, during the Taft and Wilson administrations. The attorneys for the railroad and other parties would "make a battalion." "The records, maps and exhibits in the case would fill a freight car." E. J. Justice said in 1916 that he had 6,000 pages of testimony showing fraud on the part of the railroad.[7]

As the cases ground on, resentments accumulated. A critical question in the war years was the drilling of new wells, which, with the attendant dangers, Navy Department officials and their friends in the Justice Department attempted to prevent.

Highly important in the ultimate outcome was the chronology of court decisions. The big consolidated suit was not decided until 1919. In the meantime, the Elk Hills suit had gone to the District Court in 1915 (Judge Bean of Oregon presiding), and in 1918 it went to the Circuit Court. These two suits, while in some respects dissimilar, might influence one another: they both turned upon the interpretation of fraud.

Judge Bean's decision of 1915 was a victory for the government. It mentioned damning revelations about the Southern Pacific's land policy. The railroad's land agent, one Eberlein, Julius Kruttschnitt, a vice-president, and other high officials were culpable, for they had conspired to obtain these lands in Elk Hills, knowing the probable oil content.

The proof was documentary: various letters of the officials involved were introduced into evidence. Most interesting were quotations showing that the railroad was managing its oil properties on certain even-numbered sections, while simultaneously claiming the adjacent odd-numbered sections as non-mineral. It took precautions that these facts were not publicized. Moreover, the tone of the correspondence indicated that this was routine procedure for the railroad.

Judge Bean indicated that he was bothered by only one point in arriving at his decision for the government. In 1904, the date of patent, oil had not actually been discovered in Elk Hills, although discoveries nearby had occurred. He concluded that the probable oil content was known and that the railroad officials

---

[7] "Southern Pacific Wins," *Oil Age*, XV (September, 1919), 12–14; E. J. Justice, memorandum, September 29, 1916, Navy Records. See also Harry Slattery, memorandum, January 4, 1920, Slattery Papers.

bore responsibility for the making of fraudulent affidavits. Their patents were canceled, subject to review by higher courts.[8]

Then came an unexpected blow. In May of 1918 the Circuit Court of Appeals reversed Judge Bean's decision, one judge dissenting. The government's failure at this point may have occurred because E. J. Justice died in the preceding year and his valuable services had not been available. The defeat was a little hard to believe. Commander Wright commented from his Washington desk that he had always thought this case was "cut and dried," while he knew that the consolidated suit was more difficult. In California, Commander Landis expressed his surprise. He heard that "the Southern Pacific authorities were greatly surprised too." [9]

This case remained to be taken to the Supreme Court. In the meantime, Judge Bledsoe was nearing a decision in the tremendously important consolidated suit. How, if at all, might he be affected by the government's recent defeat in the smaller Elk Hills suit?

## 3

Just at this time A. Mitchell Palmer became Attorney General. The oil suits, predicted Harry Slattery, would now "go by the board." [10]

Sometimes known as the "Fighting Quaker," Palmer had been one of the original Wilson supporters in 1912, and from 1909 to 1915 served as a representative from Pennsylvania. In 1915 he was offered the post of Secretary of War, but is said to have declined because of his religion. He resumed a lucrative law practice, and in 1917 became alien property custodian. In the war

[8] Judge Bean's decision, quoted in R. G. Tracie, senior petroleum engineer, Navy Department, "History of the Naval Petroleum Reserves," unpublished manuscript, compiled in 1937, copy in Josephus Daniels Papers, Box 264, Library of Congress. See also *Southern Pac. Co. et al.* v. *United States*, 249 Fed. Rep. 785 (1918); *U.S., Appt.,* v. *Southern Pacific Company et al.,* 64 Law. Ed., 251 U.S. 97 (Elk Hills, 1919); Daggett, *History of the Southern Pacific,* pp. 444–446.

[9] Wright to Landis, May 13, 1918, Landis to Wright, May 21, 1918, Navy Records.

[10] Slattery to Gifford Pinchot, June 25, 1919, Gifford Pinchot Papers, Box 1842, Library of Congress. See also Woodrow Wilson to Thomas W. Gregory, January 31, February 26, 1919, Thomas W. Gregory Papers, Library of Congress.

period Palmer established large business connections, including some with oil companies, and he gave indications of superpatriotism and of rising political ambitions.[11]

These may have been the "matters" which Gregory raised with President Wilson when he objected to Palmer's appointment as his successor, but Gregory was in a minority. Most Democratic leaders, including Josephus Daniels, favored the appointment. Palmer was forceful, personable, and politically an apparent asset to the declining Democratic organization.[12]

Almost immediately the new Attorney General moved toward abandonment of his predecessor's oil policy. The tip-off was his attitude toward Francis J. Kearful. Would Palmer retain the services of such a controversial figure? In June of 1919 an announcement was made that Frank K. Nebeker of Salt Lake City, formerly a Democratic national committeeman, had been selected as Kearful's replacement.[13] Kearful was being pushed out for reasons that he believed were political, and he was probably right. Later he wrote to President Wilson of how he had been grossly abused by western senators, who demanded his resignation.

It may be imagined that pressure to eliminate Kearful from the Department of Justice was intensified when Palmer became Attorney General; Palmer was more susceptible to such pressures than Gregory had been. There is also some evidence that Secretary Lane contributed to the movement against Kearful.[14]

Meanwhile, Palmer adopted a conciliatory policy toward oil claimants. This was particularly true in the case of Wyoming. In the spring of 1919 Kearful was preparing cases against Mid-

[11] Robert D. Warth, "The Palmer Raids," *South Atlantic Quarterly*, XLVIII (January, 1949), 1–2 and *passim;* Arthur Wallace Dunn, "The New Attorney General," *American Review of Reviews*, LIX (April, 1919), 374–375; Harry Slattery to Senator George Norris, July 19, 1919, George W. Norris Papers, Box 1841, Library of Congress.

[12] Woodrow Wilson to Gregory, February 26, 1919, Gregory Papers; Jonathan Daniels, *The End of Innocence*, Philadelphia, 1954, pp. 289–290; John M. Blum, *Joe Tumulty and the Wilson Era*, Boston, 1951, pp. 187–188.

[13] Slattery to Pinchot, June 25, 1919, Pinchot Papers, Box 1842. See also Kearful to Palmer, June 13, 1919, enclosing "Memorandum by the Attorney General," February 27, 1919, Records of the Department of Justice, National Archives.

[14] Kearful to Wilson, June 28, 1920 (copy), *ibid.;* Daniels, *End of Innocence*, pp. 289–290; *Cong. Record*, 65 Cong., 2 Sess., pp. 10486–88, September 19, 1918; Slattery to Pinchot, June 25, 1919, Pinchot Papers, Box 1842.

west's interests in Wyoming. These had grown out of the controversy in the preceding year which involved Senator Kendrick and others and led to the threat of commandeering the Salt Creek field. Everyone who looked into the situation in Wyoming agreed that the Midwest Company had a monopoly. Various representatives of the Department of Justice over a period of years were convinced that Midwest's operations had been characterized by a succession of frauds. Nevertheless, when the president of the Midwest Company wrote to Palmer, asking a settlement out of court, Palmer was receptive. What harm could it do, he wrote to Kearful in Cheyenne, to delay court action and try for a settlement? [15]

Midwest's interests argued as follows: Congress was moving toward passage of a leasing bill, through which disputes over the public lands would be amicably settled. Why not in their case? Furthermore, if the suits were brought and there were a tendency to discredit the company, "serious losses" would be suffered by thousands of innocent stockholders. The states of Wyoming and Colorado—so heavily dependent upon the petroleum industry —would be injured "greatly." [16]

The proposed suits were dropped, in spite of Kearful's opposition. Midwest's interests proceeded in 1920 with the approval of Attorney General Palmer, Franklin K. Lane, Clay Tallman, and others to obtain leasing privileges on their claims under the new leasing law. This was in the face of an antifraud provision and

[15] L. L. Aitken to Palmer, March 26, 1919, Palmer to Kearful, April 3, 1919, R. C. Bell to the Attorney General, January 19, 1921, enclosing "Memorandum, Leasing Salt Creek Field," January 18, 1921, Records of the Department of Justice. In a preface to his memorandum, Bell, who was a special assistant to the Attorney General, said that no attempt had been made to specify "all the various acts of fraud" but enough to show that the situation demanded a special proceeding. In a long memorandum to the Secretary of the Interior, January 15, 1921, Bell and A. B. Bouton said they were trying to prevent the "giving away" of "millions of dollars in government property to those who have so long and so successfully defied the law and the government." *Ibid*. See miscellaneous in *ibid*. and a letter to Congress from the Federal Trade Commission on the oil industry of Wyoming, January 3, 1921, quoted in *Cong. Record*, 66 Cong., 3 Sess., pp. 994–995, January 5, 1921. For a persuasive interpretation, stressing the advantages of "unit control" in Salt Creek, see Harold D. Roberts, *Salt Creek Wyoming: The Story of a Great Oil Field*, Denver, Colo., 1956, chap. ix and *passim*.

[16] D. D. C. (probably David D. Caldwell), "Memorandum Relative to the Wyoming Oil Land Situation," December 20, 1919, Records of the Department of Justice.

in spite of many continuing criticisms of the Wyoming situation.

The Kearful affair was not soon to be forgotten. In August, 1919, shortly before Kearful's resignation became effective, Harry Slattery went to see him and took him to Senator La Follette's office. There Kearful "had a talk with Senator La Follette and other Senators regarding the whole situation." It was not a "very wholesome story," Slattery wrote to Pinchot. The President knew of it, and the senators hoped that by discussion on the floor they might embarrass the President and even prevent Palmer's confirmation.[17] This proved to be a forlorn hope.

## 4

The final evidence of Palmer's attitude was yet to come. It was to be found in his conduct of the Southern Pacific cases. Neither the Elk Hills suit nor the consolidated suit had been brought to a final conclusion.

In September, 1919, *The Oil Age* proclaimed over a feature story: "Southern Pacific Wins." Judge Bledsoe had just handed down his decision in the big consolidated suit. The fact that the railroad had won was not surprising, but some of the judge's language was. One point took on added significance a few months later. This litigation, he said, "in its general aspect" was "parallel" to that in the Elk Hills suit, recently decided in favor of the Southern Pacific. Thus the Elk Hills decision in the Circuit Court seems to have influenced the judge.

The judge sounded at times like a son of the Golden West. "Stripped to the core," he said, the government was trying to prove that the " 'Big Four' of the Central and Southern Pacific Companies, the original initiators of that great unified enterprise (Stanford, Crocker, Huntington, and Hopkins), together with several lesser lights . . . were all parties to a deliberate, long-enduring, and wide-embracing scheme to acquire from the government wrongfully vast areas lying on the west side of the San Joaquin Valley, involving some of the richest oil lands that the world has ever known. . . ." To the judge's mind, this contention—against "some of the most prominent, most forceful, most

---

[17] Slattery to Pinchot, August 27, 1919, Pinchot Papers, Box 1842. See also Slattery to Pinchot, June 25, 1919, *ibid.*; Slattery, memorandum on A. Mitchell Palmer, September 2, 1919, Slattery Papers.

far-seeing men" ever produced by the state—was beyond the "realm of possibility."

In any event, Judge Bledsoe was convinced that fraudulent intent had not been proven. Within the area under suit, there had been no commercially successful development antedating the company's patents. Moreover, the company, having acquired the land, repeatedly put it up for sale at nominal prices as agricultural or grazing land. The judge asked: would men have perjured themselves to get land they then were ready to sell? He refused to accept as credible the testimony of government witnesses concerning conversations with Southern Pacific officials now deceased; this was weak evidence. He refused to accept a definition of "mineral lands" which might have led to the conclusion that seepages on the surface and sporadic discoveries had indicated this semidesert area was most valuable for its mineral content. Such was the testimony of a distinguished geologist, Dr. John Casper Branner, of Stanford University. In conclusion the judge again alluded to the Elk Hills decision. He said that even in that case—where the evidence of fraud was strongest—the government had lost its contention.[18]

Ironically, only two months later, this Elk Hills decision was reversed by the Supreme Court. The government had finally won. Justice Van Devanter, delivering the opinion, pointed out that the land was "unfit for cultivation" and had "little value for grazing," yet company officials had been exceedingly anxious to get it. Citing the documentary evidence concerning Eberlein, Kruttschnitt, and others, Van Devanter concluded that fraud was "proved so well" that it was "beyond dispute." [19]

In this Elk Hills suit the government undoubtedly had a stronger argument than in the consolidated suit. Yet when Supreme Court justices found a company guilty of fraud revolving around activities in 1902, and the same company, including some of the same officials, were accused of a similar fraud a few years earlier, there might be a predisposition to find them guilty. Perhaps the Supreme Court would not be awed by the "Big

---

[18] *United States* v. *Southern Pac. Co.,* 260 Fed. Rep. 511 (1919). See also "Southern Pacific Wins," pp. 12–14.

[19] *U.S., Appt.,* v. *Southern Pacific Company et al.,* 64 Law. Ed., 251 U.S. 97 (Elk Hills, 1919). See also "Southern Pacific Loses Elk Hills Land," *Oil Age,* XV (December, 1919), 1.

Four," as was Judge Bledsoe. The definition of mineral lands was a crucial point. The activities of Southern Pacific geologists in the 1880's and 1890's was another. Justice Van Devanter's opinion referred to "a corps" of company geologists at work in 1902, and obviously this work had started earlier.

There were many points in the consolidated suit about which lawyers might ponder. It would seem that the government had a chance to win an appeal. Gifford Pinchot argued this way: Judge Bledsoe in the District Court had decided the consolidated suit "upon the authority of the like decision by the Circuit Court of Appeals in the Elk Hills case." This being true, when that decision was reversed in favor of the government the consolidated suit might also be reversed, following the later ruling. *The Oil Age* and various others assumed there would be an appeal. The report of the Attorney General for 1919 announced that the government was "perfecting an appeal." [20]

Nevertheless, on December 5, 1919, A. Mitchell Palmer announced there would be no appeal. Perhaps most significant of all, in perspective, he took this action without even conferring with the Navy Department.

Josephus Daniels immediately protested. He had discovered in the newspapers, he said, that the Department of Justice was "considering abandoning" its Southern Pacific suits, and reminded the Attorney General of what the Navy had at stake. These lands comprised "every alternate section" in Reserve No. 2 and seven and a half sections in Reserve No. 1. "You will see that the dismissal of this suit involves the practical abandonment of the Naval Reserve Policy, a policy in which the President of the United States has taken the greatest personal interest." Daniels went on at some length. He had conferred in the past with Palmer's predecessors and with lawyers in the Justice Department, "some" of whom had believed that the government had enough evidence to win and "all" of whom "believed the Gov-

---

[20] *Ibid.;* E. J. Justice, memorandum on Southern Pacific cases, September 29, 1916, Navy Records; Slattery, memorandum, January 4, 1920, Slattery Papers; *Annual Report of the Attorney General, 1919,* Washington, 1919, p. 93; M. K. Miller to Josephus Daniels, November 25, 1920, Daniels to Miller, November 29, 1920, Daniels to the Attorney General, December 15, 1920, Daniels to Nicholas J. Sinnott of the House Committee on Public Lands, January 7, 1921, Navy Records; Slattery to Pinchot, January 4, 1921, Pinchot Papers, Box 1846.

ernment ought to win." They had believed there was fraud, and the Elk Hills case proved it. Judge Bledsoe's decision in the other case was by no means conclusive. He hoped to discuss the matter with Palmer before a final decision was made.

Palmer, however, had made his final decision. He replied that in "deciding the purely legal questions involved" he had not underestimated the importance of this case. He had thoroughly canvassed the matter with his special assistant, the same assistant who had won the Elk Hills suit in the Supreme Court. They had agreed that "the controlling facts" in that case "were entirely dissimilar to those in the other cases." If he thought there was "even a remote chance of success on appeal" he would have appealed, but he did not, and though he would be glad to confer with Daniels he did not see how "any possible exigencies of policy" would change the result.[21]

## 5

The progressive-conservationist group would never accept Palmer's interpretation. On the day of Daniels' protest to the Attorney General, Philip Wells also read the newspapers. He was shocked by Palmer's announcement and shocked even more by its effects on the stock market. Wells concluded on the basis of stock quotations and newspaper articles that "Wall Street was astonished by Palmer's surrender to the oil interests."

According to the *New York Sun,* the news of Southern Pacific overshadowed important domestic and foreign news: "Seldom in the history of trading in Wall Street has there been a wider or a wilder opening than that in Southern Pacific yesterday morning. The Street had believed that any announcement about the oil case was at least a year away. It had expected that the case would be appealed and that no immediate effect was to be anticipated." And the *Sun* article continued to say that, led by Southern Pacific, which advanced some twelve points, other petroleum stocks also shot up. The *Sun* concluded that the broad

---

[21] Daniels to Palmer, December 6, 1919, Palmer to Daniels, December 9, 1919, Navy Records. It seems significant that Judge Bledsoe had argued, contrary to Palmer, that the cases were similar in their "general and controlling features." Certainly the facts indicate that this was true. See Bledsoe's decision, 260 Fed. Rep. 511 (1919); also Gifford Pinchot to R. W. Borough, Los Angeles, April 16, 1925, Pinchot Papers, Box 1676.

aspect of this case was the "friendliness of the Government toward big business in general."

Wells believed that the Wilson administration had now come under the influence of petroleum. Writing to Pinchot, he cited the activities of Palmer, Lane, George Creel, E. L. Doheny, and the senatorial bloc. He also reviewed the long fight conducted by Gregory, Kearful, La Follette, and others to protect the public interest. Wells was ready to fight. He urged Pinchot to give thought immediately to what action they might take in view of "Palmer's surrender." [22]

Harry Slattery in the meantime was preparing material for Pinchot's use. On January 9 Pinchot addressed a letter to the Attorney General—which was never answered. In early February Pinchot then wrote to President Wilson, an invalid since his collapse the previous fall. The letter was received in the White House by Joseph Tumulty, who immediately forwarded it to Mrs. Wilson. Here, he said, was a letter "so vitally important" that she might read it to the President when she thought fit. Whether she read it or not, there was no formal reply to Pinchot.[23]

The Pinchot group was emotional; their letters were strident about this affair. If Palmer did not appeal by February 29, it would probably be too late. They attempted, therefore, to exert pressure through the President, compelling action by the Department of Justice. They called upon their friends in Congress. Senator Gronna introduced into the *Record* Pinchot's letters to Palmer and the President. Representative Edward E. Browne of Wisconsin took up the fight in the House, proposing to show that the government's case was a strong one and that Palmer ought to appeal.[24]

---

[22] Wells to Pinchot, December 6, 1919, enclosing clippings from the *New York Sun,* December 6, 1919, *ibid.,* Box 1700. See also *New York Times,* December 6, 1919.

[23] Slattery, memorandum, January 4, 1920, Slattery Papers; Pinchot to Palmer, January 9, 1920, quoted in *Cong. Record,* 66 Cong., 2 Sess., p. 3382, February 24, 1920; Pinchot to Woodrow Wilson, February 3, 1920, Pinchot Papers, Box 1843; Slattery's secretary to Philip Wells, February 11, 1920, *ibid.;* Tumulty to Mrs. Wilson, enclosing Pinchot's letter of February 3, 1920, Woodrow Wilson Papers, File II, Box 167, Library of Congress.

[24] *Cong. Record,* 66 Cong., 2 Sess., p. 3382, February 24, 1920; *Wall Street Journal,* February 14, 1920, clipping in Pinchot Papers, Box 1700; a proposed joint resolution, "instructing the Attorney General to institute certain suits," undated, Slattery Papers.

Palmer was finally goaded into saying something. He told the newspapers that Pinchot's criticisms had been "cowardly and contemptible," and he reviewed the case, attempting to show that any appeal would fail. He said in conclusion: "There is abundant evidence to sustain the findings, and it is settled law that in such a case an appellate court will follow the findings of the trial court." [25]

The case was never appealed, but it was never forgotten. Californians such as William Kent, or Timothy Spellacy the oil man, or oil workers in the California fields, expressed their indignation. Harry Slattery could scarcely find words to express his contempt for A. Mitchell Palmer. There were many who felt the same.

The Navy Department continued its efforts meanwhile, in conjunction with congressmen and others, to find some means of retaining the Southern Pacific tracts. As late as 1924 Josephus Daniels could say: "I think that the Southern Pacific getting this oil land on the ground that it was not mineral land was the greatest crime I ever heard of and ought to be remedied." It was too late, however.[26]

## 6

The Southern Pacific cases, small and large, symbolized the drift of things in 1919. The small case was won by the government; and, as a matter of fact, Elk Hills, or Naval Reserve No. 1, turned out to be far richer than suspected. But, most important, the loss of the big case virtually destroyed Buena Vista Hills as a genuine reserve. It took from government control a portion of Elk Hills, as well as many thousands of acres of surrounding petroleum land. All in all, the outcome was a major setback for

[25] *Washington Post*, February 9, 1920, *Washington Herald*, February 9, 1920, clippings in Pinchot Papers, Box 1860.
[26] Kent to Josephus Daniels, March 3, 1920, enclosing a clipping from the *Los Angeles Record*, March 2, 1920, Daniels Papers, Box 235; Timothy Spellacy to Daniels, June 10, 1920, *ibid.*, Box 239; telegram to Daniels from H. V. Johnson, secretary of the Oil Workers Union, Lost Hills Local No. 1, February 10, 1920, *ibid.*, Box 235; telegram to Daniels from Local 18, Oil Field, Gas Well and Refinery Workers of America, February 11, 1920, *ibid.*, Box 236; Slattery to Pinchot, August 26, November 3, 1920, Pinchot Papers, Box 1841; miscellaneous, 1920–21, Navy Records; Daniels to Senator Thomas J. Walsh, May 20, 1924, Walsh to Daniels, May 24, 1924, Thomas J. Walsh Papers, Library of Congress.

the policy of public control. In the same year the suits in Wyoming against Midwest's interests were compromised, and the Interior Department attempted to give the Honolulu Company its claims. Here in these executive actions of the Wilson administration was a precedent for later decisions sympathetic toward private claimants. Here also was one of many bases for political attack on the tragically deteriorating Democratic party.

# After "10 Long Years," a Leasing Law

## CHAPTER XI

*As a matter of plain public right and justice the trespassers were entitled to no consideration but when such matters are settled by legislation compromise is almost always resorted to.*

Philip P. Wells, memorandum in the
Gifford Pinchot Papers, February, 1920

1

In the new Congress meeting in May of 1919, the Republican party had control, with the League of Nations the great issue. Perhaps the very fact that the energies of legislators were devoted so much to wrangling over the League accentuated a desire for constructive action on other matters, including petroleum. The new Republican leaders wished to achieve something of a constructive record, while Democratic sponsors of leasing bills, having labored so many years, were anxious to press on to a conclusion. Even the progressives saw reasons for a settlement. With such a willingness to act, the leasing bill finally passed. Proof of the new law, however, lay in its administration, first by Democrats and soon by Harding Republicans.

2

In many ways the fight over the new oil bill in 1919–20 was a continuation of that in the closing days of the Sixty-fifth Congress. In other ways it was quite different. Republican control of Congress, the change of committee chairmanships, the inability of President Wilson to influence Congress as he had in the past, the international rivalry for oil supplies—these and other factors helped to create a new atmosphere. However, the combatant groups remained basically the same.

La Follette in the Senate continued to hold the center of the stage. At one point in the debates Reed Smoot, who had now become chairman of the Public Lands Committee, attested to La Follette's influence. When the Wisconsin senator was off the floor momentarily, Smoot, referring to his absence and to the dozen or so amendments he had prepared, said they might as well wait until he returned. La Follette had maintained his intense interest in petroleum matters during the recess. Harry Slattery reported that the senator had "talked with quite a few men on both sides of the house since the session ended." He had come to believe that "a constructive program should be introduced immediately," otherwise the western group might be able to claim there was "no alternative" to their own plan.[1]

Western Democrats were unhappy over the new Congress. Key Pittman apparently believed that with the Republicans in power and Reed Smoot as chairman of the Public Lands Committee, the forthcoming legislation would be less sympathetic toward oil men. He wrote to one of his disgruntled constituents: "We were four years getting as favorable a bill as we did get agreed upon between the two Houses [the Sixty-fifth Congress]. I am very fearful that the bill that will be finally passed will not be so favorable." He wrote later when the bill was about to pass the Senate: "It is not a question of what we want but what we can get." [2] Charles S. Thomas, James D. Phelan, Walsh of Montana, and other Democrats were now in the minority.

These westerners seem to have feared in all sincerity a plan for government operation. They believed that if oil men were too demanding, and if the leasing bill failed again, the result could be government operation; the victory would go to La Follette's crowd. Partly for this reason, many Democrats would cooperate with the Republican organization to pass a leasing bill. However, a few Democratic senators, including John F.

---

[1] *Cong. Record*, 66 Cong., 1 Sess., p. 4619, September 2, 1919; Slattery to Gifford Pinchot, March 21, 1919, Gifford Pinchot Papers, Box 1842, Library of Congress.

[2] Pittman to James D. Finch, May 23, September 1, 1919, Key Pittman Papers, Box 92, Library of Congress.

Nugent of Idaho, William F. Kirby of Arkansas, and David Walsh of Massachusetts, showed a strong tendency to line up with La Follette and the Republican insurgents.

The Republican party seemed to be more liberal than the Democratic on conservation matters. It contained its share of states' rights extremists and haters of government control—including the increasingly vocal Albert B. Fall of New Mexico. However, the power which they could exercise was still unclear in 1919 and early 1920.

The mood of oil men, as suggested by that of their spokesman Pittman, was not pleasant. Their expectations had risen in 1918–19 with the advance of the Walsh-Pittman bill, but had been dashed at the last moment by La Follette's filibuster. Now the interminable delays of the politicos must be endured again. The traditional impatience of practical men of affairs with theorists and political meddlers approached the boiling point. To an extent the very successes which they achieved in the federal courts helped to convince them that they had been right in the first place, that the many years of litigation and lobbying should never have been necessary.

Oil men continued in their efforts to produce a friendly attitude in the government. James N. Gillett of California, the Midwest Company officials of Wyoming, and others were actively lobbying in 1919–20. Harold D. Roberts describes in *Salt Creek* how the oil executives and their lawyers repeatedly took the long, tiring train trip from Denver, or Casper, to Washington. Midwest's interests established an office in the Munsey Building in Washington, D.C., and maintained it for a period of two years.[3] It appears, however, that oil lobbyists were disconcerted and weakened in 1919 by the change to Republican control of Congress and by the activities of the militant band of senators led by La Follette.

If they lost influence in Congress, oil men had greater success elsewhere. Necessarily, leaders in the government and leaders of the petroleum industry were drawn together, searching for an effective oil policy. The world situation continued to affect

---

[3] Harold D. Roberts, *Salt Creek Wyoming: The Story of a Great Oil Field*, Denver, Colo., 1956, pp. 135–140, 155, and *passim*; James N. Gillett, New Willard Hotel, Washington, to Pittman, November 8, 1919, Pittman Papers, Box 92.

what was done on the domestic scene. Senator Phelan remarked in the debates of August, 1919: "I do not think the Senate is fully informed on the world movement in oil. It is the greatest thing that is now happening in the economic life of the world." Senator Lenroot expressed a conviction that became almost commonplace: "The nation that controls the oil supply of the future controls the commerce of the future. . . ." Harry Slattery observed, in a slightly different vein, as the Congress was getting organized: "It is perfectly clear that . . . oil is going to be the great fight in this Congress, because of the enormous speculative value of oil." And again he noted: "The whole question of oil has shared with the Peace Treaty the debate in Congress." [4] Oil had become an international prize and a temptation; concessions in the Near East or in Latin America were well worth scrambling for. At the same time, the question arose, should the United States ban foreigners from its own public lands? These were among the problems that Congress had to consider in far-ranging debates of 1919.

The Pinchot group organized for the fight they saw coming. Slattery, Philip Wells, and George W. Woodruff worked closely with Senator La Follette. They loaded him with "ammunition" and assisted him in the drafting of legislation. But they also wished to preserve their own identity and to function through Lenroot or others as necessary. Philip Wells remarked in one letter that they must take care not to "get the wires crossed" between La Follette and Lenroot; [5] the antagonism between these two must not be allowed to interfere with the work in which both could give their assistance.

This problem of personal relationships was satisfactorily solved. Slattery conferred frequently with La Follette and his assistant, Colonel John J. Hannan, a legislative expert. Arrangements were made for Philip Wells to bear the principal burden of drafting a leasing bill, and the efforts of Wells, the La Follette office force, and Lenroot were to some extent correlated. When Wells suffered a breakdown, he turned over the responsibility to George W. Woodruff. Slattery meanwhile kept in close touch

---

[4] *Cong. Record,* 66 Cong., 1 Sess., p. 4170, August 22, 1919; Lenroot in *ibid.,* p. 4167, August 22, 1919; Slattery to Pinchot, July 1, August 27, 1919, Pinchot Papers, Box 1842.

[5] Wells to Woodruff, May 22, 1919, *ibid.,* Box 1700.

with these men and with many others on Capitol Hill, looking toward concert of action by a liberal bloc.[6]

## 3

In June, Senator Smoot introduced his mineral leasing bill; this was promptly referred to the Senate Public Lands Committee. The House committee took up consideration of a similar bill under the direction of Nicholas J. Sinnott of Oregon, who had replaced Ferris as chairman.

As the bills went to committee, the situation looked "bad" to Harry Slattery. The Republicans were doing "some very strange things," and "most peculiar" were their actions regarding conservation. He urged Pinchot in Philadelphia to come to Washington and talk with Smoot, Henry Cabot Lodge, Frederick H. Gillett of Massachusetts (the new Speaker), and other Republican leaders and show them how their policy would be "unprofitable to them in the long run."

Pinchot did come to Washington, and apparently had a very satisfactory round of conferences with Senator Smoot. He wrote on July 16 "pursuant to . . . [their] conversation," proposing a number of changes in the Smoot bill. In one major respect this bill was already considered superior to the Walsh-Pittman bill; it provided for straight leasing, rather than a combination of patent and leasing. As La Follette observed, much of the criticism from the previous Congress was thereby "disarmed."[7]

On the other hand La Follette, Pinchot, Wells, and company had amassed a number of objections, some of which were reasonable and convincing. Grand Canyon and Mt. Olympus, they argued, should not be included in the area subject to coal leases. The maximum royalty prescribed for oil was 25 per cent of the value of what was extracted; this royalty, they maintained, was considerably under that paid by some operators on private land, who also occasionally gave a cash bonus for the privilege of leas-

---

[6] See Slattery to Pinchot, March 21, 1919, Pinchot to Slattery, March 23, 1919, *ibid.*, Box 1842; John J. Hannan to Wells, March 24, 1919, Wells to Lenroot, May 21, 1919, Wells to Hannan, August 20, 1919, *ibid.*, Box 1700; Slattery to Pinchot, August 14, 23, 1919, *ibid.*, Box 1842.

[7] Slattery to Pinchot, June 25, 1919, *ibid.*; Pinchot to Smoot, July 16, 1919, Harry A. Slattery Papers, Duke University Library, Durham, N.C.; La Follette in *Cong. Record*, 66 Cong., 1 Sess., p. 4742, September 3, 1919.

ing. Why have a maximum? Why not leave the Secretary of the Interior with discretion, in the case of very rich wells, to require more than a 25 per cent royalty? They objected to the fraud provision, according to which no fraudulent claimant could obtain a lease but a successor in interest could do so if he had allegedly been given no notice of fraud. No more "prolific source of perjury" could be found, Pinchot wrote; an "innocent" purchaser could simply buy the rights of fraudulent claimants.

Pinchot argued that all of the relief section ought to be omitted. Provisions affecting the naval reserves would open the way to their destruction, he said. "Either the claimant who might be favored . . . has rights or he has not. If he has rights, they will either be admitted by the Land Department after consultation with the Navy Department, or the claimant can have his usual recourse to the courts. At any rate, the Naval Oil Reserves should be protected just as far as is legally possible."

Pinchot was not adamant on all points. Proposing amendments, he indicated that there might be compromise.[8] His relations with conservative Republican leaders were no doubt improved in this period by a readiness to attack Wilson in public addresses and to consider, like other Republicans, means of uniting the party for the approaching presidential contest.[9]

Concurrently, Pinchot moved to arouse Democratic leaders, whom he felt could improve the pending bill. The day after writing to Smoot he wrote to Josephus Daniels. Daniels, he said, had earned, "or ought to have earned," the gratitude of every public-spirited citizen for his defense of the naval petroleum reserves. In reference to the Smoot mineral leasing bill, Pinchot declared that the bill would permit the issuance of leases to all trespassers in the reserves if they had flowing wells. But "one more vigorous protest" would "save the Petroleum Reserves for the Navy and the Nation." He was sure that the friends of conservation could count upon Daniels.

An immediate response from Daniels and others in the Navy Department was gratifying. The bipartisan "alliance" for protection of the reserves was continued.[10]

---

[8] Pinchot to Smoot, July 16, 1919, Slattery Papers.
[9] Pinchot, quoted in *Christian Science Monitor*, June 14, 1919, clipping in Pinchot Papers, Box 1842.
[10] Pinchot to Daniels, July 17, 1919, *ibid.;* Slattery to Pinchot, July 24, August 23, 1919, Pinchot to Slattery, July 29, 1919, *ibid.*

Meanwhile, in the Senate Committee on Public Lands, Lenroot was doing what he could. He had surprising success in his advocacy of the Conservation Association's amendments. Smoot, he reported, was "in a very compromising mood and was very anxious to avoid anything that looked like a fight." [11] Lenroot's work in committee was highly important; and while La Follette, not being a member, bided his time, waiting for the fight on the floor, his assistants continued with the necessary preparations.

## 4

In August Senator Smoot brought his bill, now much amended and renumbered, to the Senate floor. He wanted quick action. When Nugent of Idaho proposed a more detailed examination of certain points, Smoot exclaimed: "I wish to say to the Senator from Idaho that I can take him over to the Public Lands Committee and show him not one ton but tons of documents in the way of hearings upon a leasing bill. Report after report has been made. For 10 long years this subject has been before Congress." [12]

The Senate proceeded, in spite of his protest, to give the bill detailed consideration. One of the first problems concerned the international rivalry for oil. Should aliens be permitted to acquire leases on the public lands? If they were barred from this country would their governments (notably England and Mexico) retaliate against citizens of the United States?

The prevailing atmosphere was one of economic nationalism, and senators agreed almost unanimously that safeguards must be erected against foreigners. Leases, or investment in such leases, would be permitted to foreigners, but only under a stipulation that the President at his discretion might take over their properties; the production from their lands, if needed, must be sold in the United States. Senator Phelan was unsuccessful in his efforts to ban aliens absolutely from the public lands.[13]

The senators turned next to something closer to their hearts and far more controversial—the principles of public land policy. Senator Smoot said that he had "lived with this legislation" for almost ten years. He had opposed leasing and he still opposed it.

[11] Slattery to Pinchot, August 14, 1919, *ibid.;* La Follette in *Cong. Record,* 66 Cong., 1 Sess., pp. 4754–55, September 3, 1919.
[12] *Ibid.,* p. 4248, August 23, 1919.
[13] *Ibid.,* pp. 4160–71, August 22, 1919

Nevertheless, leasing now afforded the only possibility for development. When his colleague from Utah, Senator King, objected to the evils of paternalism, Smoot rejoined with a solemn warning: there was a growing sentiment for government operation; they had better take leasing as the lesser of two evils. Senator Thomas of Colorado concurred.[14]

Senator Fall also supported the bill. He explained why, directing his remarks to Senator Walsh of Massachusetts.

I will tell the Senator frankly that the people of the West who believe in building up the States never would have consented to such a bill had it not been provided that a portion of the proceeds of these royalties should go directly to the States, 45 per cent of it, because of the fact that you are taking away from them their sovereign power of taxation, through which they must sustain themselves as sovereign States on an equality with the State of Massachusetts. But in view of the fact that finally, after seven years' hard fight, we have engrafted in this proposed legislation the proposition that the States themselves shall be given a portion of the proceeds of the lease, we have agreed to it, and in [going] that far we have followed the policy of the conservationists of the East.[15]

Thomas the Democrat and Fall the Republican gave a bipartisan demonstration of states' rights extremism. At the same time they favored the bill. In response to a question as to who was behind this bill, Fall replied: first of all, the people of the West whose resources lay undeveloped. But he went on to say that the bill by no means wholly coincided with western beliefs. ". . . we believe in the old Anglo-Saxon doctrine that a man's house is his castle, and, built upon that, we believe in individual initiative and not in Government ownership or operation of anything. That we have understood to be the Anglo-Saxon heritage of our people in this country." [16]

Fall and Thomas agreed that bureaucratic administration of the law would probably ruin it, and they cited the awful example of Attorney General Gregory and Secretary Daniels. Thomas then proclaimed: "There must be a change in these conditions; otherwise we will be compelled, or our posterity will be compelled, to conclude that this last war was fought to make the world safe for bureaucracy." [17]

---

[14] Ibid., pp. 4111–12, August 21, 1919.
[15] Ibid., p. 4172, August 22, 1919; Fall to E. S. Raffety, September 8, 1919, Albert B. Fall Papers, Huntington Library, San Marino, Calif.
[16] Cong. Record, 66 Cong., 1 Sess., p. 4284, August 25, 1919.
[17] Ibid., p. 4257, August 23, 1919.

Senator Henry Ashurst (Democrat of Arizona) also let loose a blast at the leasing principle and the "false conservationists" who had stirred up so much trouble. Senator Walsh of Montana, however, took care to explain that he supported the bill on principle and felt no apologies were necessary in the matter. Senator King summed up the western senators' viewpoint rather accurately, stating that most of them did not want a leasing bill but would support it, not because they approved of it but because it was better than the present "iniquitous" and "intolerable" policy.[18]

# 5

Senator La Follette also turned to general principles in discussing the bill. The problem of resources and their utilization led him to speculate about the kind of government necessary to achieve democratic ends. La Follette, like many senators, stood as if on a plateau, knowing this legislation would probably pass, looking back and reviewing with a keen sense of history its relation to the events and failures of the preceding generation. He also looked hopefully to the future.

There had been, in La Follette's opinion, only "one great issue in all the history of the world": the issue "between labor and those who would control, through slavery in one form or another, the laborers." Perhaps it was "an inexorable law of evolution" that the United States, like other nations, would be destroyed in its struggle against privilege and monopoly. But he had hoped to the contrary. No nation ever had had such an opportunity as this: the "virgin soil," the "new material" from the old world, the desire for "more liberty and democracy." He had "inherited, as it were, the belief and the hope that this was the place for the consummation and the working out of the most perfect Government on earth, the most perfect Government attainable."

What should be done about privilege and monopoly? La Follette seemed to say that the free play of the economy, or industrial freedom, was his basic objective. Senator King could hardly believe his ears and had to ask: had he correctly interpreted the senator? Did he believe that "if we would enforce the laws against trusts and monopolies and allow the free play of the law

---

[18] *Ibid.*, pp. 4250–51, 4258, August 23, 1919.

of supply and demand and the economic forces of the country, we should have nothing to fear with respect to the industrial freedom of the American people or the progress and growth and development of our country?"

La Follette then revealed how tough he would like to be. If he had his way, he would begin with the United States Steel Trust, evaluate their property, and publish a list of reasonable prices. Failure to adjust their price levels would lead to more drastic measures. As to primary resources, iron ore, coal, and the like, he would have the government take back its title. He would "maintain . . . an absolute control of the production and the prices of those basic products, either by a strict leasing system or by actual Government operation, or both." He believed it would be necessary to have "a limited amount of Government operation in various lines of production, to the end that we might have a measure, a standard, of fair production cost and fair selling price." [19]

Notwithstanding his fundamental beliefs, La Follette was willing to compromise on the oil leasing bill. It was, he asserted, an immense improvement over previous measures. He felt "gratified" at the changes made, for they constituted a repudiation of the bill against which he had filibustered in the previous session of Congress. He seems to have won his point. Neither Pittman nor any other senator stepped forward to defend the Walsh-Pittman bill by contrast with the new measure under consideration.[20]

La Follette's influence had made itself felt before he said a word in Senate debate. In March he had filibustered out of existence the Walsh-Pittman bill. The knowledge that he and his allies could do the same to the current bill had indeed encouraged a number of improvements. Largely, they were those actually proposed by Pinchot in his letter to Senator Smoot.

Further improvements were effected as the debate continued and various amendments received consideration. Much that was said also had historic importance.

La Follette recounted the long fight against oil lobbyists. He eulogized such men as Daniels, Gregory, E. J. Justice, his former colleague Senator Husting, and Gifford Pinchot for their efforts

---

[19] *Ibid.*, pp. 4755–58, September 3, 1919.
[20] See *ibid.*, pp. 4622–23, September 2, 1919; *ibid.*, pp. 4742–44 and *passim*, September 3, 1919.

to save the naval reserves and protect the public interest. Observing that oil lobbyists were strangely inactive at this time, he asked whether this indicated they were quite satisfied with the bill. He charged that this was a Standard Oil measure, at least in its ultimate effects. Walsh of Montana spoke up, denying the charge and giving his own version of the "genesis" of the bill, dating back to 1914. As Slattery observed, La Follette was making a good many senators angry. Meanwhile he made progress with his amendments.[21]

The omnipresent question of drainage in the naval reserves flared up, in a manner having historic interest. La Follette and Walsh took different sides of this question; each offered an expert in support of his contention. They were to learn the dangers of "expert" opinion—La Follette immediately, Walsh later in the 1920's.

La Follette opened this discussion by proposing that the naval reserve section of the bill be eliminated. Thus, he said, the reserves would not be leased; government control could be maintained over this basic resource, needed by ships of the Navy. The theory that drainage out of the reserves was destroying them and that therefore they might as well be leased was wholly unacceptable to La Follette. He noted the opinion of a certain expert, stressing drainage. In La Follette's opinion the man was probably a Standard Oil lobbyist, and he urged the Senate to be guided by the advice of Secretary Daniels, or by the recommendations of E. B. Latham, a highly trained geologist who had supported the naval arguments and whose independence of judgment was unquestioned.

Senator Walsh challenged these remarks. He showed with documentary evidence that, as a matter of fact, La Follette's own "expert," Latham, had been employed by the Southern Pacific interests.

Walsh might have stopped there, but he went ahead to quote his favorite expert—E. L. Doheny. The California oil man had testified that the naval reserves were subject to serious drainage and therefore should be leased. Walsh commented: "However it may be regarded by anyone else, I attach very great importance

---

[21] Slattery to Pinchot, September 3, 1919, Pinchot Papers, Box 1842; *Cong. Record*, 66 Cong., 1 Sess., pp. 4742–43, September 3, 1919.

to the testimony of Mr. A. [*sic*] L. Doheny . . . it occurs to me that the committee have acted wisely in providing that the wells already upon the reserves should be leased and that the President should have the authority to direct the drilling of other wells whenever, in his judgment, it became necessary to subserve the public interests. I do not believe, therefore, that those provisions of the bill are open to any serious objection." [22]

La Follette continued to disagree. He offered an amendment to except the naval reserves from leasing, but it was rejected without a roll call.

The respective arguments of the two senators from Wisconsin, Lenroot and La Follette, were interesting and significant in the light of later history. Both were in the confidence of the National Conservation Association. Both were relatively disinterested in their quest for a good bill. Lenroot, however, was the more conservative, a "semi-conservative," as Slattery described him.[23] Yet Lenroot had worked intimately on this particular conservation issue, as was well known. He was more of a senatorial expert on this measure, extremely influential in bringing it to a vote. It appeared at times as if certain senators needled La Follette by implying that it was not he but his junior colleague from Wisconsin who really knew what he was talking about.[24]

With undoubted authority Lenroot traced the history of leasing legislation and defended the latest provisions for relief, arguing that the bill was easily the best to come before the Senate. He was willing to be lenient toward those "trespassers" who had doubted the validity of the presidential withdrawal in 1909 but had committed no fraudulent act. To give them a preferential lease was, in his opinion, perfectly all right. He denied that claimants having equities could be provided for in the courts; the remedy had to be a legislative one, he said, because under the law as written claimants were inadequately protected and the courts could do little about it. He denied that the bill would give any particular advantage to Standard Oil, and introduced documents purporting to show that the Midwest Oil Company was not Standard-controlled.

---

[22] *Ibid.*, pp. 4750, 4754–55, 4759, 4770, September 3, 1919.
[23] Slattery to Pinchot, August 21, 1919, Pinchot Papers, Box 1842.
[24] See, for example, Walsh of Montana in *Cong. Record*, 66 Cong., 1 Sess., p. 4742, September 3, 1919.

Turning to the naval reserves, he noted the recent decision in the big Southern Pacific case. The chances of recovering No. 2 for the Navy were "very small indeed." Why not go ahead and make the best of the situation, as provided in the bill, letting the producing wells be leased?

Lenroot was the compromiser par excellence. He was able at points to defend the Standard Oil Company, the big companies, and many claimants while also praising the Justice Department for merely trying to do its duty in prosecuting claimants. And he eulogized the conservation group for its wonderful work: "Mr. President, if it had not been for Gifford Pinchot and Theodore Roosevelt, if it had not been for these conservationists, who are sneered at by some of the people of the West, these very lands that are now the subject matter of this bill would have been in private ownership and under the control of monopoly." [25]

On a number of specific proposals and amendments Lenroot and La Follette clashed. For example, La Follette offered an amendment under terms of which the government reserved price-fixing powers over all petroleum products derived from the areas under lease. Lenroot and Smoot argued that this was impractical, and would militate unfairly against the lessees as compared to operators on private lands. As a matter of fact, they said, it would play into the hands of Standard Oil. La Follette replied that the land in question was the public's; it contained the public's oil, and the government had every right to set the price. Moreover, if a standard price, a fair price, on a portion of the national production were maintained this would have a tendency to compel fair prices in the entire petroleum industry. On a roll call vote, La Follette's amendment was defeated 48 to 10. La Follette, however, was able to gain acceptance of an amendment to the effect that "lessees must at all times furnish their products to the United States and to the public at reasonable prices." [26]

Before this protracted debate of September 3 had come to a close almost every point of view had found expression. In the final phases the two extreme positions were again made apparent. Senator King delivered a long speech, calling for an amendment in the nature of a substitute, a proposal to cede the public

---

[25] *Ibid.*, pp. 4761 ff., September 3, 1919.
[26] *Ibid.*, pp. 4733–36, 4773, September 3, 1919.

lands to the states. Against his better judgment, he added the provision that the states should not dispose of this land to corporations nor grant more than 2,500 acres to any single person.

Senator Kirby of Arkansas, with the support of La Follette, offered his amendment in the nature of a substitute, which provided for governmental control and operation of coal, oil, and gas lands. Both amendments were rejected without a roll call.

As the debate continued, senators shouted for a vote. Finally at 10:40 P.M. on September 3, after some twelve hours of discussion and argument, the leasing bill was passed by the Senate.[27]

## 6

Shortly after the bill went through the Senate, Harry Slattery visited Pinchot in Pennsylvania. They concurred in a general satisfaction with its provisions, but maintained a determination to improve it as much as possible in the House. As to this they were optimistic, thinking that the oil men and their friends in Congress were prone to compromise in the belief that this was the best they could get. Slattery wrote, immediately after his return from Pennsylvania: "Coming down on the train yesterday I met one of the oil attorneys who was frank enough to say that he thought all the interest people would now be anxious to force some legislation—even leasing—for fear they might get something worse later on." [28]

As the House of Representatives took the bill under consideration, Slattery made his contacts with John M. Baer, a Nonpartisan Leaguer from North Dakota, and others on the Public Lands Committee. Materials prepared for La Follette but not used and various amendments offered unsuccessfully in the Senate were readied for use in the lower house. The Navy Department made its wishes known; likewise the oil men.[29] In contrast to the Senate the fight occurred mostly in committee.

The House maintained its reputation for being somewhat less

---

[27] *Ibid.*, pp. 4774–89, September 3, 1919.
[28] Slattery to Pinchot, September 8, 1919, Pinchot Papers, Box 1842.
[29] Slattery to Pinchot, October 15, 1919, *ibid.*; Franklin D. Roosevelt to Josephus Daniels, September 13[?], 1919, Roosevelt to Sinnott, September 18, 1919, Navy Records, National Archives; Warwick M. Downing to Key Pittman, November 7, 1919, James N. Gillett to Pittman, November 8, 1919, Pittman Papers, Box 92.

responsive to special interests than the Senate was. In a few important respects the bill was made tougher on oil claimants: notably, there was no ceiling on the royalty that must be paid.

Sinnott, Ferris, and Mondell—the incumbent chairman and two ex-chairmen of the Public Lands Committee—all spoke in the bill's behalf, and its early passage was assured. Nevertheless, there were sharp exchanges on the floor as several representatives assumed a position similar to La Follette's in the Senate. Anthony J. Griffin, a Democrat of New York City, and Sidney Anderson, a Republican from Minnesota, endeavored strenuously to win approval for an antimonopoly amendment. It was aimed by implication at units derived from the Standard Oil Trust. Griffin declared: "We may assume, I say, that those who will stand ready to grasp these lands and leases as soon as the barriers are thrown down will be the component parts of this Standard Oil Trust." Their efforts were futile. They also endeavored to get the bill recommitted and had the satisfaction of obtaining 44 votes, as against 201. On October 30, 1919, the bill was passed.[30]

There still remained the necessity of a conference. When the conferees got into a row, it appeared for a time as if the measure once again would fail to become law. However, Slattery reported in January that the oil men had become "anxious to take the House Bill"; they wanted a compromise and pressured Smoot, Pittman, and the other senators into reopening the conference. The House conferees thereupon won almost all of their points,[31] and a conference report was prepared. By February of 1920 there was one big question. Would the President sign the bill?

7

Last-minute maneuvering occurred; there was still considerable opposition to the bill.

On February 24 Key Pittman wired to Senator Claude Swanson in Daytona, Florida: "Am afraid Gregory may influence veto

---

[30] *Cong. Record*, 66 Cong., 1 Sess., pp. 7786–91, October 30, 1919. See Frank Mondell's interpretation of the monopoly charge, *ibid.*, p. 7526, October 25, 1919. If this measure was monopolistic, he said, all the reformers and conservationists had been "wrong from the beginning."
[31] Slattery to Pinchot, January 31, February 7, 1920, Pinchot Papers, Box 1841. See also John Ise, *The United States Oil Policy*, New Haven, Conn., 1926, pp. 350–351.

of bill. Such act may bring about legislative, political and economic chaos in many quarters. Please wire President particularly with regard naval provisions and remedial legislation. Your plan adopted relative naval reserves." [32] Pittman—who had bitterly disagreed with Gregory for many years—had reason to fear his influence.

At this very time Gregory was communicating his views to the President via Josephus Daniels. Gregory restricted himself to the relief features of the bill, which he regarded as not a compromise but a surrender. Claimants who had entered the withdrawn lands after the executive withdrawal of September 27, 1909, but before July 3, 1910, and who had done so "in good faith" on the assumption that the placer law still applied, could now qualify for relief. Actually, however, "not even good faith compliance" under the old law was required. A claimant who proceeded ultimately to sink a well, a producing well, any time up to the date of the new act could be rewarded with a lease of his claim. Gregory also insisted that the royalty terms of the leases would be too liberal. Many of the richer tracts which certain operators had been exploiting for years would normally "command a royalty of one-fourth or more with large bonuses."

Noting the receivership cases and the temporary operating arrangements in effect since 1914, Gregory commented bitterly: "This bill would turn over all the millions so impounded to the favored claimants, except the one-eighth back royalty provided for." Section 19, moreover, granted either a lease or a prospecting permit on "every claim initiated while such lands were not withdrawn"; "every claim" would include paper locations and seemed intended to insure "against the possible retention of any tract of withdrawn public oil land for the public benefit or public participation."

He noted the naval reserve features. Only the producing wells would be leased, unless on special permission of the President. The same provisions ought to apply, he asserted, on public lands outside the reserves. This did not mean he was complacent about the naval reserves. Operation of certain wells as allowed would intensify drainage and would lead to the drilling of additional

---

[32] Pittman to Swanson, February 24, 1920, Pittman Papers, Box 92.

wells. "Inevitably and quickly" the "best" of the reserves must be destroyed.[33]

Gregory's analysis was unacceptable from a political standpoint. Founded perhaps on righteous indignation and on well-grounded suspicions of many oil men, it was legally and technically close to the mark, yet it was an extreme interpretation. If embodied in law his ideas would have resulted in some injustices.

Others attempted to persuade the President that he should not sign. Representative Griffin and Senator Nugent communicated to the President their grounds of opposition. From an oil man in Denver came a denunciation of the bill. The Midwest Company and other trespassers, he said, would now be confirmed in that which they had always "wrongfully held"; and the result would be "the most gigantic fraud ever attempted upon any government." Senator Nugent, in closing his letter, remarked upon an attached clipping: Secretary of the Interior Lane was leaving the government to take a position with the Doheny interests at an announced salary of $50,000 annually.[34] His implication was clear.

However, the weight of informed opinion was in favor of this bill. Pinchot sent his congratulations to Sinnott, and this letter was printed in the *Record*. Philip Wells, looking out his window in Middletown, Connecticut, through a driving snowstorm, wrote to Harry Slattery in Summerville, South Carolina. It was a notable victory that Slattery had won. The National Conservation Association was "entitled to congratulate itself on the outcome of this long fight."

Wells went on to express his misgivings. The relief sections condoned the activities of trespassers; certain phraseology was loose and ambiguous; careless administration might result in "immense damage." In the naval reserves "about the least harmful *compromise*" had been obtained. He concluded: "As a matter of plain public right and justice the trespassers were entitled to

---

[33] Gregory to Daniels, February 23, 1920, enclosing memorandum on S. 2775, Thomas W. Gregory Papers, Library of Congress.

[34] Anthony J. Griffin to Wilson, February 18, 1920, John F. Nugent to Wilson, February 18, 1920, J. A. Owenby to Wilson, February 24, 1920, Woodrow Wilson Papers, File VI, Box 505, Library of Congress.

no consideration but when such matters are settled by legislation compromise is almost always resorted to." [35]

Administration leaders wanted the bill passed. Scott Ferris, Josephus Daniels, Franklin K. Lane, and his successor John Barton Payne were among those advising acceptance.[36] On February 25, 1920, President Wilson signed it into law. Thus, with the general minerals leasing bill, the long fight over petroleum lands seemed to come to an end.

## 8

Who had won? The act was long and complicated. It applied to coal, phosphate, and sodium lands, as well as to oil and gas. It contained provisions for prospecting on unproven lands, for preferential leases to claimants, for compromise of cases in litigation, and royalty payments to the government. Each state, as finally decided, was to receive 37½ per cent of all royalties accruing within its borders. This was less than the states had hoped for. Furthermore they would get nothing in federal royalties from the naval reserves. Claimants in the reserves could surrender their alleged patent rights and lease their producing wells only, unless the President, at his discretion, authorized the leasing of larger tracts.

Implicitly in the new system there was federal supervision and continuing public responsibility. Acreage limitations and anti-monopoly safeguards indicated a determination to maintain a competitive system. The urge to reduce waste was here and there apparent, and the Secretary of the Interior was given authority to prepare regulations for that purpose. In February, 1920, it seemed that conservation leaders had framed an excellent law. Indeed, it was a good law, a successful law, which has continued to the present day, although with many amendments.[37]

[35] *Cong. Record,* 66 Cong., 2 Sess., p. 2709, February 10, 1920; Wells to Slattery, February 19, 1920, Wells, memorandum on S. 2775, February 19, 1920, Pinchot Papers, Box 1700. See also Pinchot to Slattery, February 24, March 13, 1920, *ibid.,* Box 1841.

[36] Josephus Daniels commented that the bill was far from what he had desired but that "all things considered it was wisest for the President to have signed it." Daniels to Timothy Spellacy, April 12, 1920, Josephus Daniels Papers, Box 239, Library of Congress.

[37] *Oil Land Leasing Act of 1920 with Amendments and Other Laws Relating to Mineral Lands,* compiled by Elmer A. Lewis, Washington, 1952; Lewis

Troubles that might arise had been suggested by the debates of 1919–20. These debates were of lasting significance. La Follette, Smoot, Lenroot, Fall, Pittman, Walsh of Montana—these and others would be heard from again. Their ideas, embodied in the leasing law, were not to be forgotten. In many respects, they were immediately put to the test. Was it possible, for example, that all of the efforts by La Follette and others to prevent monopoly and unfair practices would go for naught? Had they placed too much discretionary power in the hands of the Secretary of the Interior and the President? Had trespassers and corruptionists actually carried the day, in spite of their vigilance? Along with the unfolding events of 1920, there was cause for such questions, and for not a little disillusionment.

---

Edwin Hoffman, *Oil and Gas Leasing on the Public Domain*, Denver, Colo., 1951, with a Foreword by Marion Clawson, Bureau of Land Management; Ise, *United States Oil Policy*, pp. 342–343, 351–352, and *passim;* Roberts, *Salt Creek*, pp. 135–137.

# The Compromise of 1920

**CHAPTER XII**

*Senator Harding was not made to my order, but he is by no means
the Reactionary I thought him. . . . Under him, there will be no one-
man rule at Washington, Congress will represent not the President but
the people, and the government will be American again.*

Gifford Pinchot, statement for Republican newspapers, October 2, 1920

1

A recent scholar has referred to the election of 1920 as the "debacle" of progressivism.[1] His description is peculiarly apt for
conservation policy and the oil question. Yet the leasing law of
February serves as an illustration of reform ideas which could not
be canceled by the politics of the year. A second law (June, 1920)
seemingly gave the Navy what it had long sought—genuine control for conservation purposes over its petroleum reserves. However, by this time the extent and content of the reserves had been
sharply reduced and the effects of the law remained to be seen.
In the administrative decisions concerning petroleum a number
of important precedents were established while the Democrats
still remained in office. The various happenings in 1920, some
public and some *sub rosa*, were so intricate—and sometimes so
mysterious or conspiratorial—that they will never be fully understood.

---

[1] Wesley M. Bagby, "Progressivism's Debacle: The Election of 1920," unpublished Ph.D. dissertation, Columbia University, New York, 1954. See
also his articles: "The 'Smoke-Filled Room' and the Nomination of Warren
G. Harding," *Mississippi Valley Historical Review*, XLI (March, 1955),

## 2

Franklin K. Lane had the satisfaction of offering his resignation in January, 1920, when the leasing bill seemed almost assured of passage. He had the further satisfaction, upon retirement, of a number of panegyrics upon his career. *The Outlook,* for example, while noting that Lane had not belonged to the "inner circle" of the Wilson administration, declared that he was of "truly Presidential fiber" and "a great conservationist in the broadest use of that word." Lane said with greater modesty, in offering his resignation to the President: "The program of administration and legislation looking to the development of our resources, which I have suggested from time to time, is now in large part in effect, or soon will come into effect through the action of Congress." [2]

The most accurate, and the saddest, commentary upon Secretary Lane was the man himself speaking through his letters at the close of his public career. He did not believe, in spite of his earlier progressivism, that the world would be changed "much for the good out of any materialistic philosophy or by any shifting of economic affairs." To his "amazement" the recent war had made the world less secure. What was needed now was a religious revival, but personally he had no faith to save himself from his afflictions, only a "sinking of the heart." He envied his friends, to whom he wrote with touching warmth, their capacity for religious belief.[3]

In his insecurity and disillusionment, Lane turned increasingly to the leadership of great capitalistic figures. To Van Manning of the Bureau of Mines he wrote: "It is quite manifest now that private enterprise must stand in the forefront in the development of this [petroleum] industry, and that what the government can do will be supplemental and suggestive. . . . I have the belief that whatever the body of oil men would agree upon

658–671; "Woodrow Wilson, a Third Term, and the Solemn Referendum," *American Historical Review,* LX (April, 1955), 567–575.

[2] "A Great Public Servant," *Outlook,* CXXIV (February 18, 1920), 268; Lane to Woodrow Wilson, February 5, 1920, in *The Letters of Franklin K. Lane,* edited by Anne W. Lane and Louise H. Wall, Boston, 1922, pp. 337–338. See also *New York Post,* February 10, 1920, clipping in Gifford Pinchot Papers, Box 1948, Library of Congress.

[3] Lane to C. S. Jackson, December 29, 1919, in *Letters of Franklin K. Lane,* pp. 323–324; Lane to George W. Lane, September 11, 1919, *ibid.,* pp. 312–314, Lane to John Crawford Burns, December 29, 1919, *ibid.,* pp. 324–326.

would be something that would make for the best use of petroleum. . . ."

With beliefs like these Lane had been prepared to accept leasing legislation treating oil claimants more liberally than the
Pinchot group, or than Daniels, Gregory, or others. The details
had not concerned him greatly. One of the best things about his
job, he said, had been that he was concerned "only with big questions and not with details." [4]

As Lane himself commented, he had been "too anxious for
popularity." He had tried to take "a broad non-partisan view of
things," to get along with Theodore Roosevelt Republicans while
in Wilson's Cabinet, to appease the oil and business leaders, and
simultaneously to establish a sane conservation program. He
pleased almost no one except his coworkers in the Interior Department or those who were above the "battlefield," admiring his
breadth of vision and statesmanlike views. Oil men thought him
weak; he had not been able to control his own department.
Progressive Republicans frequently distrusted him as a pseudo-
progressive. His colleagues in the Cabinet apparently wished that
he had resigned long before. In Lane's words, he had had "hard
sledding."

On top of everything else, he was in dire financial need. As
early as November, 1919, when he had been offered two "fifty
thousand a year places, and another even more," he was thinking seriously of rehabilitating his fortunes in private industry. It
was E. L. Doheny's offer which he decided to accept.[5]

Just before his retirement in February, 1920, Lane brought up
the Honolulu Company's case. He appealed to President Wilson
once again to allow their claims to go to patent. The President
refused. In his opinion the "judgment of the General Receiver"
in California, adverse to the Honolulu Company, ought to stand.

---

[4] Lane to Manning, September 24, 1919, *ibid.*, pp. 315–316; Lane to George
W. Lane, November 28, 1919, *ibid.*, pp. 322–323.
[5] Lane to George W. Lane, *ibid.;* Lane to Hugo K. Asher, January 3, 1920,
*ibid.*, pp. 334–335. See also "Memorandum of an Interview with Mrs. Woodrow Wilson—January 4, 1926," Ray Stannard Baker Papers, Series I, Box
58, Library of Congress; Jonathan Daniels, *The End of Innocence*, Philadelphia, 1954, p. 324. The interpretation in Gerald T. White, *Formative
Years in the Far West: A History of Standard Oil Company of California
and Predecessors Through 1919*, New York, 1962, is also hard on Lane; see pp.
442, 450, and *passim*.

The matter, "fraught with so many dangers," must be handled with "utmost foresight," or it might lead to "serious scandals." With this presidential rebuke, but also with Wilson's "best wishes for the future," Lane ended his career in Washington.[6]

There is, of course, no evidence that Lane was dishonest or lacking in personal integrity. Rather, his judgment was poor, the final evidence of this being his acceptance of the job with Doheny. He also had shown too much his sympathy for California and the West. In spite of the positive achievements of his administration, the end result was reminiscent of what had happened to Ballinger and of what later happened to Fall. Each man in some degree was a victim of geography and the sectional striving of his own area.

## 3

Perhaps the most important fact about the new Secretary of the Interior, John Barton Payne, must be stated in the negative: he was not a westerner. Senators and other spokesmen from the West had, as usual, launched a campaign for a western man in the Interior Department. Going further, Senator Phelan wrote to Joseph Tumulty: "This Cabinet position is one that has been held long by California . . . and, of course, the State should be represented at the President's table." The refusal of Wilson to accept Clay Tallman (Nevada) or Alexander Vogelsang (California), or other holdovers from the Lane administration may suggest still further the distrust with which the President had come to regard his outgoing Secretary.[7]

The appointment of John Barton Payne was a compromise, satisfying neither the western extremists like Phelan, nor the

---

[6] Lane to Wilson, February 9, 1920, Wilson to Lane, February 11, 1920, Woodrow Wilson Papers, File II, Box 167, Library of Congress. See also Wilson to Lane, March 1, 1919, *ibid.*, File VII, Letterbook 56. For a recent appraisal of the oil dispute in the Wilson years see Arthur S. Link, *Wilson: The New Freedom*, Princeton, N.J., 1956, pp. 132–135. While showing the importance of the oil affair, this does not take sufficiently into account inconsistencies in Lane's attitude from 1913 to 1920 and the real issues that divided the disputants.

[7] Phelan to Tumulty, February 10, 1920, Wilson Papers, File VI, Box 49. See also John B. Kendrick to Woodrow Wilson, February 11, 1920, H. H. Schwartz to Joseph Tumulty, February 13, 1920, *ibid.*

Pinchot group and their allies. A native of Virginia, Payne had risen to prominence as a Chicago lawyer. In wartime Washington he had served with the Shipping Board and Railway Administration.

The power lodged in Secretary Payne, Secretary Daniels, and other administrative officers in 1920–21 was of unusual consequence. The mineral leasing act and the new federal water power act left large discretion in the hands of the Secretary of the Interior and his immediate subordinates. Leasing regulations must be established, suits over the oil lands must be compromised, precedents must be established in manifold ways.[8] There were, as usual, interdepartmental problems and disputes involving particularly the Interior, Navy, and Justice Departments. The United States Shipping Board was immediately interested in acquiring royalty oil from the public lands. Oil men and investors were interested in patents, leases, prospecting permits, and special advantageous arrangements with the government. Or in many instances they merely endeavored to understand the complicated new procedures governing public lands.

The Navy Department, through its naval oil reserves, was deeply involved in all of these matters. Its leaders sought a guaranteed supply for immediate and future requirements.

Commander Nathaniel Wright offered this warning to Secretary Daniels on March 1, less than a week after the leasing bill had passed: "Due to the fact that we have so divided the responsibility in connection with the Navy's future fuel supply, and that we have been so loathe to give the proper personnel for holding our own in this connection, the other Departments of the Government are likely to take the lead in oil reserve matters, and it is a matter of record that wherever such procedure has taken place in the past, the Navy has suffered."

Commander Wright recommended, among other things, that a naval officer should be placed in charge of oil matters in the Department with no other duties assigned and that the Department should accumulate information and make arrangements immediately for cooperation with other departments. He envisioned the pending naval appropriation bill as a means of add-

---

[8] See the descriptions in Harold D. Roberts, *Salt Creek Wyoming: The Story of a Great Oil Field*, Denver, Colo., 1956, pp. 137–143.

ing to the Department's power over the naval oil reserves and over the fuel situation generally.[9]

Significantly, Wright expressed deep concern over the hostility of oil men. The Navy had continued to demand oil at low prices and to commandeer supplies under terms of its emergency powers. But other departments of the government had taken little part in this policy. The Interior Department, said Wright, was "working largely with the oil men without regard to the price of oil or profits." Whether the Navy was right or wrong, there must be a change. It was "vitally necessary" to have the "GOVERNMENT and not the NAVY . . . adopt a fixed policy either of coercion or cooperation." For as the system now operated the Navy's tougher policy was hardly "defendable [sic] when looked at from an economic or commercial viewpoint." [10]

Thus the naval leaders appraised the domestic and international trends affecting them, and they debated their course. They had made enemies in the oil fight. In the courts and in Congress they had taken defeats along with victories, for even the leasing act, while recognizing the naval reserves, left them largely in control of the Interior Department, and private claimants continued to make inroads. Meanwhile naval forces had contributed mightily to winning the war in the Atlantic. They had transported 2,000,000 troops to Europe without a sinking. And amid the new international rivalries of 1919–20 they enjoyed the support of many demanding an American Navy second to none.[11] It was clear that the United States Navy must be assured of an oil supply.

Might this be an unparalleled opportunity to coordinate governmental activities relating to fuel oil and to assert clear-cut

[9] Wright, memorandum for the Secretary of the Navy, March 1, 1920, Navy Records, National Archives. See also recommendations of the Naval Fuel Oil Board, December 22, 1916, praised by Wright as being still valid, Josephus Daniels to Thomas S. Butler, March 5, 1920, Daniels to the Secretary of the Interior, March 5, 1920, Daniels to the Attorney General, March 5, 1920, ibid.

[10] Wright, memorandum for the Secretary of the Navy, March 18, 1920, ibid. See also Admiral Robert S. Griffin to the Secretary of the Navy, April 5, 1920, ibid.

[11] George T. Davis, A Navy Second to None, New York, 1940, chaps. ix–x; Annual Report of the Navy Department, 1918, Washington, 1918, pp. 1–5 and passim; Annual Report of the Navy Department, 1920, Washington, 1921, pp. 1–3, 7–8, 140–144, and passim.

control over the naval oil reserves? The naval leaders decided in the affirmative, and thereby a new chapter in the history of the petroleum reserves was inaugurated.

Secretary Daniels on March 5, 1920, wrote to Thomas S. Butler, chairman of the House Naval Affairs Committee, seeking enlarged power over the naval reserves. He described the problem of drainage and the necessity for the Navy and other departments to obtain supplies of oil. It had become imperative, he said, to provide machinery whereby the Navy could drill offset wells for the protection of its lands or "supply oil for the government's needs." "Crude oil," he continued, "whether from navy owned wells, royalties from naval reserves, or royalty oil purchased," should be exchangeable for refined oil. There should be the power to sell excess oil, to provide storage, and to engage in refining.

He then proposed an amendment to the naval appropriation act, giving the above and other powers to the Secretary of the Navy. A few weeks later an oil fuel office was established in the Navy Department with Commander H. A. Stuart as the head. Its purpose was to serve as a kind of "clearing house for the various activities and policies" of the Department.[12]

Daniels and other naval leaders, including Assistant Secretary Franklin D. Roosevelt, pressed for passage of the desired legislation. They also wanted new petroleum reserves in the Osage lands of Oklahoma, and they insisted that an investigation of the entire subject of fuel oil was warranted. However, they met a rebuff on the refining of oil, and were forced to accept the best terms they could get.

On June 1, with the amendment still in doubt, Daniels wrote to Carroll S. Page of Vermont, chairman of the Senate Naval Affairs Committee. He reviewed the question of fuel oil, its reputed scarcity, and the necessity of action. Over recent years, he declared, oil had become of "transcendent importance" to the

---

[12] Daniels to Butler, March 5, 1920, Navy Records; Secretary of the Navy, memorandum to divisions of the Department, April 30, 1920, *ibid.* See also Samuel McGowan, Navy Department, to the Bureau of Yards and Docks, March 25, 1920, *ibid.*; explanation of Commander H. A. Stuart in U.S. Congress, Senate, *Leases upon Naval Oil Reserves,* Hearings Before the Committee on Public Lands and Surveys Pursuant to S. Res. 282, S. Res. 294, and S. Res. 434, 67 Cong., and S. Res. 147, 68 Cong. 3 vols., Washington, 1924, pp. 782–790.

Navy: "As you may well imagine I have given the question of the future supply of fuel oil for the ships of the Navy grave and thorough consideration from the day I become Secretary of the Navy in 1913 to this hour. In fact nothing, except securing ships material and personnel has had so much of my attention." [13]

The Congress was impressed with these and similar arguments. On June 4, 1920, the fateful amendment was passed. For reasons of national defense, as they appeared to the Navy Department, and supported by arguments of progressives and conservationists as well, the Secretary of the Navy now assumed broad new authority over the petroleum reserves. He was "directed to take possession of all properties" in the reserves if not subject to pending applications for patent or to claims and applications for leases under the law of February 25, 1920; "to conserve, develop, use, and operate the same in his discretion, directly or by contract, lease or otherwise, and use, store, exchange, or sell the oil and gas products thereof . . . for the benefit of the United States. . . ." [14] There was no opposition, except that Senator Smoot succeeded in eliminating the power to refine the oil.

Here was the culmination of many years of naval and progressive agitation. Ironically, however, this capstone of "progressivism" was later to become a means of exploitation.

## 4

Meanwhile, as new administrative problems were quietly being met, the campaign of 1920 had gotten under way. Democratic leaders gathered in San Francisco, partly out of gratitude for California's decisive vote of 1916. But could the Democrats again carry California or the West?

In four short years of war and industrial mobilization the world had been so changed and even revolutionized that there were inevitable effects upon domestic politics. Petroleum almost epitomized what had happened. It alone had effected a kind of

---

[13] Daniels to Page, June 1, 1920, Navy Records. See also Daniels to Page, March 29, April 21, 1920, Franklin Roosevelt to Senator Claude Swanson, May 4, 1920, Daniels to Lemuel P. Padgett, May 21, 1920, *ibid.;* comments by Senator Walsh of Montana and Albert B. Fall in U.S. Congress, Senate, *Leases upon Naval Oil Reserves,* pp. 212–214.

[14] Quoted in *ibid.,* pp. 173–174. See also *Cong. Record,* 66 Cong., 2 Sess., pp. 6214–15 and *passim,* April 28, 1920.

revolution. Petroleum meant energy, power, money; it was no respecter of parties and ideals; petroleum could be thicker than blood. But also it was associated with national progress and patriotism and was therefore more formidable than it otherwise would have been. Among the diverse troubles of Democrats in 1920 were their own disagreements over petroleum policy, combined with opposition that they faced from resurgent capitalistic interests.

It was still true in 1920 that oil did not touch President Wilson, nor in a corrupt sense the members of his Cabinet, nor the Democratic presidential nominee. Nevertheless, the drift of things was unmistakable. At the head of the Justice Department, scrambling for his party's presidential nomination, was A. Mitchell Palmer. Among the delegates in San Francisco were oil men like E. L. Doheny and their friends, and congressional spokesmen such as Key Pittman. So far as oil men were concerned, however, the San Francisco convention did not promise much; Democrats had little chance to win. Governor James M. Cox, the nominee, was defeated before he began. Only those Democrats already in office—with favors to bestow until March, 1921—were worthy of much attention.

In spite of their weakness, Democrats made the usual motions of harmony. When the convention ended, for example, Secretary Daniels, Walsh of Montana, and Key Pittman journeyed together on the battleship *New Mexico* from San Francisco to Seattle. Amid so many troubles, with the worst yet to come in the campaign, it was a pleasant cruise. Secretary Payne joined the group later for a tour of Yellowstone Park.[15]

The most difficult task of Secretary Payne of the Interior Department was to resist political pressures and the blandishments of business interests. A well-meaning gentleman, seeking the path of moderation, he was quite capable of saying no to oil men. Yet his policy was rather liberal and sympathetic.

A case in point involved Senator Phelan, the Honolulu Company, and the senator's campaign for re-election. By mid-October, with the tide running strongly against the Democrats, Phelan among others was seriously in trouble. He wired Secretary Payne

---

[15] Walsh to Miles Taylor, July 13, 1920, Daniels to Walsh, August 7, 1920, Thomas J. Walsh Papers, Library of Congress.

suggesting that a lease to the Honolulu Company "would be at this time most effective." Secretary Payne was wary, promising only that he would deal with the matter "as promptly as possible." In December the leases were granted, but too late to do Phelan any good. He was defeated by Samuel M. Shortridge, a regular Republican, described as being intellectually a "duplicate of Senator Harding" with the exception that the "echoes in his mental corridors" dated from a decade further back.[16]

Oil men and lobbyists converged upon the Republican convention in Chicago, knowing full well that the new President and perhaps several of his Cabinet officers would be chosen there. This convention, William Allen White concluded, was more "completely dominated by sinister predatory economic forces" than any he had ever seen.[17] Nevertheless, when Warren G. Harding was nominated, White gave his support, as did Gifford Pinchot, Harry Slattery, and virtually all of the progressives left over from the "Bull Moose" campaign of 1912. It may be questioned whether politics and partisan emotion ever made greater dupes out of principled men than in the campaign of 1920. Even so, they were largely victims of circumstances.

Harry Sinclair, E. L. Doheny, and Jake Hamon of Oklahoma were the oil men most conspicuously seeking "deals" in Chicago. They were doubtless represented among the oil interests who approached General Leonard Wood, a main contender for the nomination, promising their support in return for three Cabinet posts. Wood rejected any such proposition. Oil men then concentrated their efforts on Harding and his manager Harry Daugherty, who were eager for support.[18]

Senator Walsh of Montana asserted later after his Teapot Dome inquiry that Harding was nominated "pursuant to a deal," according to which Andrew Mellon, Albert B. Fall, and Harry Daugherty were to receive Cabinet appointments.[19] There is evidence to support such a contention, although the full story

---

[16] Phelan to Payne, October 15, 1920, Payne to Phelan, October 18, 1920, Secretary's File, Department of the Interior, National Archives; Chester H. Rowell, "The Campaign in California," *New Republic*, XXIV (October 13, 1920), 164.

[17] Quoted in Bagby, "The 'Smoke-Filled Room,'" p. 670.

[18] *Ibid.*, pp. 658–671. This is a careful, convincing interpretation.

[19] Walsh to H. F. Alderfer, November 10, 1927, Walsh Papers. See also Walsh to Warren W. Price, April 1, 1924, *ibid.*

will never be known. It is abundantly clear that Jake Hamon, Sinclair, and other corruptionists were busily at work, cynically dispensing their money in the expectation of quick rewards. Hamon gained control of the Oklahoma delegation, using money freely. He hoped to control the Interior Department in return for large contributions to the Harding cause. But he ran into difficulty since Harry Sinclair and other oil men harbored the same ambition. Hamon later told one of his friends that Sinclair had "beat him to the goal," that Fall had been "bought like a steer." Sinclair, according to one of his employees, said that Harding's nomination had cost him $600,000. A somewhat more reputable Republican, George Harvey, of the *North American Review*, was asked why Harding was the choice of the convention. He will "go along," was the answer.[20]

It was a sordid affair. Harold Ickes, who, along with Robert M. La Follette and a few other progressive Republicans, refused to support the Republican nominee, summed it all up this way: "The Progressives revolted in 1912; they compromised in 1916 and they surrendered in 1920." [21] In another letter he made some excuses for his old compatriots: ". . . at the Convention they [the Old Guard] drove us into a corner, well knowing that we could do little else than the thing proposed to do, namely, swallow our medicine. . . ." [22]

## 5

The conduct of the Pinchot group in 1920 was supremely ironical. They who had fought so hard for conservation measures could at one stroke nullify much that had been accomplished. Of course they could not know the outcome of Harding's nomination, but they could suspect it. They were victims, on the one hand, of faith in the Republican party—even in such a Republican as Warren Harding—and, on the other, of an intense dislike of Woodrow Wilson and his "regime."

[20] Bagby, "The 'Smoke-Filled Room,'" pp. 664, 670–671; U.S. Congress, Senate, *Leases upon Naval Oil Reserves*, testimony especially of H. W. Ballard, pp. 3146–51, but also of Al Jennings, J. B. French, and *passim;* Morris R. Werner, "Hail! Hail! The Gang's All Here," in *Privileged Characters*, New York, 1935.
[21] Ickes to O. H. P. Shelley, October 12, 1920, Harold L. Ickes Papers, Chicago File, Box 2, Library of Congress.
[22] Ickes to Gustavus Pope, September 22, 1920, *ibid.*, Box 1.

Conservation leaders, like so many progressives of both parties, believed that the Wilson administration had broken down, had yielded to the reactionaries. They were scathingly critical. Pinchot and Slattery referred often to "Southern reactionaries" who must be removed from power. Henry C. Wallace of *Wallace's Farmer*, Governor Robert D. Carey of Wyoming, and many others expressed vigorously their belief that the Wilson administration was pro-Southern and unfair to the West. Next to Wilson himself, Albert S. Burleson and A. Mitchell Palmer were favorite targets. The conservationist group singled out Franklin K. Lane and his administration. Secretary Payne did not escape.[23]

But when the conservationists thought of A. Mitchell Palmer and his "surrender" of the Southern Pacific lands their rage knew no bounds. Pinchot wrote: "That Palmer was seriously considered for the nomination at San Francisco shows how low the Democrats have fallen. There may have been more unfaithful public servants than Mitchell Palmer but not many."

The accumulated resentments against Wilson, Lane, Palmer, and Burleson finally resulted in an emotional intensity and a hatred difficult for a later generation to understand. The relatively fair-minded George W. Norris could make this astounding statement about the President: "It may be that some things have been said in criticism of him that I would not approve, but I confess that of all the criticisms I have ever heard or read about him, I have no fault to find with any of them. . . ."[24]

In the light of the above passions it is easier to understand why the conservation group not only supported Harding but nurtured a hope that he could be converted to progressivism, that he could be made into a conservationist. Slattery expressed the view just after the convention that "Harding might be won over . . . to a constructive and advanced conservation stand." Pinchot agreed

[23] See, for example, Pinchot, quoted in *New York Times*, August 30, 1920, clipping in Pinchot Papers, Box 1860; Wallace to Ray Stannard Baker, November 3, 1919, Baker Papers, Series II, Box 97; Carey to Ickes, September 6, 1920, Ickes Papers, Chicago File, Box 1. See also Judge George W. Anderson to Ray Stannard Baker, October 19, 1920, Baker Papers, Series II, Box 98; William Kent to Baker, May 25, 1925, *ibid.*, Series IB, Box 41.
[24] "Copy of Letter for Republican Papers from Gifford Pinchot," October 2, 1920, Pinchot Papers, Box 1841; Norris in *Cong. Record*, 67 Cong., 1 Sess., pp. 539–540, April 21, 1921.

that they ought to try, but the more he saw of Harding "the sicker" he got. In August Slattery thought their "leaven" was working, and Pinchot also was encouraged. Harding, he believed, had "come through superbly on forestry." He added: "Harding referred to our friends the grabbers as hogs, and said he would call them so if it were not for its being campaign time. I don't think he will be another T. R. but I do believe he's much better in every way than I supposed. He's certainly going our way strong so far." [25]

The Pinchot-Republican line on conservation policy was to take credit for the Republicans for what had been done up to 1920. Thus Pinchot wrote to Theodore Roosevelt, Jr.: "We have won out as to coal, oil, water power, and have only been prevented from scoring a complete victory as to the public lands, by the inefficiency or worse, of two Democratic Secretaries of the Interior, who have taken the view which your Father despised, that they were not the guardians of the public interests except where the law specifically compelled them to be so. . . ." [26]

Meanwhile Harding was elected, and conservation leaders turned their thoughts to an all-important question: who would be the new Secretary of the Interior? Pinchot considered himself available. His friends Lenroot, James R. Garfield, and Thomas E. Campbell of Arizona were also highly recommended.

The Pinchot group actually thought for a time that they might control the selection. But western leaders of both political parties demanded a western Secretary of the Interior,[27] while oil men and business interests exercised an influence that is not entirely clear. It is clear that these interests and not the conservation group won out in the appointment of Albert B. Fall.

[25] Slattery to Pinchot, June 23, 1920, Pinchot to Slattery, June 27, Pinchot Papers, Box 1841; Slattery to Pinchot, August 14, 1920, Pinchot to Slattery, August 30, 31, 1920, *ibid.*

[26] Pinchot to Roosevelt, February 18, 1921, *ibid.*, Box 242. See also Slattery to Pinchot, June 5, 1920, *ibid.*, Box 1841; Republican National Committee, questionnaire on "Conservation of National Resources," summer, 1920, *ibid.*, Box 1860.

[27] A sheaf of papers with "Suggestions for Sec. of Interior, Dec. 11, 1920," *ibid.*, Box 1941; Senator William E. Borah to Governor Frank R. Gooding of Idaho, December 20, 1920, William E. Borah Papers, Box 208, Library of Congress; Borah to J. H. Richards, May 2, 1921, *ibid.*, Box 202; Senator Walsh of Montana to Fall, February 26, 1921, quoted in David H. Stratton, "Behind Teapot Dome: Some Personal Insights," *Business History Review,* XXXI (Winter, 1957), 390.

6

Administratively through the last months of the Wilson period, much was happening. The oil controversy seemingly was about to be terminated, but the hand of the politician, the oil man, or the "fixer" was sometimes visible. The commissioner of the General Land Office reported in June of 1921 that since the passage of the leasing act there had been an average of 722 applications per month for prospecting permits; 1,248 applications for relief had been received and 160 leases covering some 18,000 acres had been permitted. Constantly increasing business necessitated the temporary diversion of clerks from other duties, until a deficiency appropriation relieved the situation.

The commissioner commented optimistically upon the old problems now being liquidated: "Nearly all these old claims have been settled or are now in the process of settlement, the back royalty due the United States collected, the impoundments and escrows distributed, the suits dismissed, and possession of the land involved delivered to the lessees. The result has been the ultimate closing out of the great bulk of oil land controversies that have been demanding the attention of the office and field agents and of the Department of Justice and the Federal courts." [28]

Senator Key Pittman, dissatisfied with the initial administration of the new leasing law—which he felt was unduly harsh on claimants—kept up a fire of correspondence intended to bring about a more liberal interpretation. "Since the unfortunate days of Mr. Pinchot," he said, the government had sought "through idealistic and arbitrary regulations . . . to take the place of the successful prospector." Alexander Vogelsang of the Interior Department insisted that on the contrary, the leasing law was "liberal in the extreme in giving all good-faith claimants who have made any material expenditure on the ground, fair and reasonable opportunity to transmute such claims into permits and leases under the new law under far more practical working conditions than existed under the former laws. . . ."

Nevertheless, Pittman probably had a little success. He got the Department to relax slightly its interpretation of what con-

[28] Department of the Interior, *Report of the Commissioner of the General Land Office*, Washington, 1921, pp. 54–56.

stituted "diligence" in the prosecution of work, and he resolved to keep up the pressure on this and other points.[29]

An extremely difficult case for Secretary Payne, Vogelsang, Tallman, and others in the Interior Department was that of the Midwest Company. Section eighteen of the leasing act had provided that claimants, such as the Midwest Company, might relinquish their alleged rights to patents, receiving leases instead; but also they must pay back royalty in "an amount equal to the value at the time of production of one-eighth of all the oil or gas."

But how was this value at the time of production to be determined, particularly if Midwest had been able to keep crude prices down by monopoly control of the Salt Creek area? R. C. Bell, a special assistant to the Attorney General, argued that such a monopoly did exist and the government should exact far more from the Midwest Company than one-eighth of the prices actually paid or established on crude oil. Tallman argued to the contrary. He had no doubt that Midwest was "taking advantage of its contractual relations with affiliated and other oil producers, or transportation and pipe line rates and facilities . . . and of any other instrumentality . . . to hold down the price of crude." But such practices were not unusual in the United States. "Are not these the factors that fix the price of every service or article of trade and commerce?" he asked.

Secretary Payne did not take Tallman's advice. He learned from the Federal Trade Commission that their investigations showed a clear-cut monopoly situation in Wyoming: "The Commission is of the opinion that the differential of 75 cents [between Wyoming and Oklahoma] is entirely due to the lack of competition in the purchase of crude petroleum in the Wyoming fields." The Secretary then instructed Tallman to operate on the basis of the field price plus twelve cents a barrel up to January, 1918, and the field price plus twenty-five cents a barrel for the period thereafter.[30]

The question also arose as to current royalties in the rich Salt

---

[29] Pittman to Secretary Payne, June 12, 1920, Key Pittman Papers, Box 92, Library of Congress; Payne to Pittman, June 2, 1920, Vogelsang to William E. Mason, April 28, 1920 (a copy of which was sent to Pittman), *ibid.;* Payne to Pittman, June 23, 1920, *ibid.*

[30] Tallman, "Memorandum Re: Sum due the Government on account of past royalties for oil taken from Salt Creek Field, Wyoming," August 9, 1920, Secretary's File; Payne to the Federal Trade Commission, January 6, 1921,

Creek lands, where new leases were being granted. Tallman advised the Secretary that, while they had the authority to increase the royalties, they should not do so: "We want our leases to be in demand." E. C. Finney agreed. The law of averages should be considered. Salt Creek was rich, but the same companies had incurred losses in other exploration and would continue to do so. Another subordinate in the Department, while willing to go along, really disagreed. He had always thought royalties in that area were too low.[31]

Through interpretations such as these the Midwest Company and its allies proceeded under the new laws and regulations to establish themselves even more firmly in the Salt Creek area. It was rumored in 1919–20, and soon authenticated, that the Midwest Company had come under the control of the Standard Oil Company of Indiana. At the same time the Sinclair interests were entering the state. Tallman noted, in approving a preferential claim for a lease, that he was "informally advised" that this particular party was acting "as the agent for the Sinclair Consolidated Oil Company." He requested a "full showing" of what he called the Sinclair "trusteeship." However, Sinclair's operations continued to be cloaked in secrecy.[32]

So far as California lands were concerned, the most important departmental decisions involved the Honolulu case. The Honolulu Company never gave up in its demands, although its leader William Matson had died in 1917. In June of 1920 Secretary Payne, taking up where Franklin K. Lane had left off, but with more objectivity, handed down a decision on the Honolulu applications for patent in Naval Reserve No. 2: he denied them.

In the Navy Department and elsewhere there was rejoicing. Daniels declared: "This decision confirmed the long fight of the Navy Department to preserve this naval reserve, which was often threatened in litigation extending over years." Francis J. Kearful,

---

Huston Thompson, chairman of the FTC, to Payne, January 17, 1921, Payne to Tallman, January 22, 1921, *ibid.*

[31] Tallman, memorandum to Secretary Payne, November 4, 1920, with comment at the end by Finney, *ibid.;* CWM (Mahaffie), memorandum, November 5, 1920, *ibid.*

[32] Tallman to Payne, January 18, 1921, *ibid.* On the monopoly situation in Wyoming see Philip Wells to H. J. Trost, editor of the *Wall Street Journal,* January 5, 1921, Trost to Wells, January 11, 1921, Pinchot Papers, Box 1700; also Paul H. Giddens, *Standard Oil Company (Indiana): Oil Pioneer of the Middle West,* New York, 1955, pp. 155–158, 219–235.

now in Tampico, Mexico, was so elated he wrote the President a congratulatory letter. He felt that the President, former Attorney General Gregory, and he himself were now vindicated in this "last chapter" of the "desperate struggle to save the public oil lands for the Navy and the country." [33]

But the Honolulu interests were not beaten. Having finally lost in their applications for patents, they now sought leases. They were able to do so for all of their producing wells, or allegedly producing wells, inside of Buena Vista Hills. Naval leaders and Justice Department men were aware of the danger. They insisted that the Honolulu interests had not acted "honestly and in good faith" and that in many instances their wells were not producing wells within the meaning of the leasing act. Leases as well as patents should be denied.

Commander Stuart had little hope: "From the general attitude of Mr. Tallman I would hazard the guess that the oil companies will get about all they ask. . . ." Very nearly the worst predictions were fulfilled when on December 23, 1920, Secretary Payne upheld Tallman's decision giving a number of leases to the Honolulu Company.[34]

Secretary Daniels submitted a protest, but to no avail. Payne declared that there was an essential difference between requirements for a patent and a lease: "In a patent application, the bona fides and regularity of the acts of the original locators, as well as of their successors, must be considered. In the case of a lease, the inquiry is limited to the claimant and his actions and matters which he had reasonable grounds to know. I feel confident that, on further consideration, you will see that the cases are essentially different, and that the denial of a patent application does not necessarily preclude the granting of a lease." [35]

The Honolulu ruling was only one of many trials and disappointments for the Navy Department in the last months of the Wilson administration. Naval Reserve No. 2 and to a less extent No. 1 were critically threatened by private drilling. The South-

---

[33] *Annual Report of the Navy Department, 1920,* p. 142; Kearful to Woodrow Wilson, June 28, 1920, Records of the Department of Justice, National Archives.

[34] Commander Landis to Henry F. May, July 30, 1920, Secretary Daniels to Secretary Payne, August 7, 1920, H. A. Stuart to Landis, February 1, 1921, Navy Records.

[35] Payne to Daniels, January 27, 1921, *ibid.*

ern Pacific interests sold out their holdings to the newly formed Pacific Oil Company, which was expected to engage actively in drilling. Standard of California, the Pan-American Oil Company, and others were also active. There were problems of water infiltration in some areas, seeming to demand either government or private drilling to prevent further damage.

The Navy launched countermeasures intended to preserve its oil in the ground. It considered seriously the acquisition of private lands inside the reserve areas by exchanging, if possible, public lands outside. It made contracts with two private companies, one for the purpose of drilling five offset wells, the other for a lease of 120 acres where water infiltration was a serious problem. The Navy's reluctance to undertake drilling on its own is suggested by a statement of Commander Stuart's: "I am somewhat afraid of a government operation in the oil fields; we will no doubt encounter a great deal of opposition and I am not so sure that, everything considered, it would be any cheaper than a good lease proposition." [36]

A sudden surprise to naval men and to almost everyone in the government was the Section 36 case, "discovered" in February, 1921, and to become notorious in the Harding administration. This involved a school section in the heart of Naval Reserve No. 1 which had passed largely into the control of Standard of California. It was regarded by 1921 as one of the richest oil tracts in the state, with some nineteen Standard wells producing up to 3,500 barrels per day. Henry F. May commented that its intensive drilling would inevitably provoke competitive drilling in the adjacent Southern Pacific lands, thus draining the reserve. However, until February, 1921, he believed that little could be done about it: "The Section has always been supposed by this office, and so far as we knew by the Interior Department to be a school section to which the Standard Company had acquired good title."

Then the chief of the field division of the Land Office in San Francisco happened to be going through the "dead files" of his office. He discovered a letter from the commissioner in Washington, dated January 14, 1914, which had directed proceedings against Section 36. The basis was that the section was mineral

---

[36] H. A. Stuart to Landis, February 1, 1921, *ibid.* See also Stuart to Senator Walsh, April 9, 1924, in U.S. Congress, Senate, *Leases upon Naval Oil Reserves,* pp. 3258–60.

land and never should have passed to the state of California as school land, nor from the state to private interests.[37] In some strange way this letter had been misfiled and lost for six years. Neither the local agents, nor the commissioner in Washington, brought up the case again from 1914 to 1921. The efforts of May and other subordinates in the Department of Justice were futile— until the exposures in the Teapot Dome inquiry of 1924.

## 7

Thus the year 1920 produced a set of compromises on petroleum, some of which were secret and some public. The mineral leasing act of February had clearly represented a reconciliation of many interests, and questions of interpretation, administration, and influence still remained. The Navy act of June 4, 1920, brought almost to completion many of Daniels' hopes for genuine governmental and naval control of the reserves. There seemed little doubt that the Navy had won this round. In the campaign politics of 1920 occurred the worst compromises of the year. However, these arrangements were largely secret. The deals at the Blackstone Hotel in Chicago put Harding in the White House, and Fall was soon in the driver's seat where petroleum lands were concerned. Concurrently, Clay Tallman in the Interior Department, A. Mitchell Palmer in the Justice Department, or other Democrats were compromising Wilsonian policies in the notable cases of the Southern Pacific lands, the Honolulu lands, Section 36 in Naval Reserve No. 1, and the Midwest Company or related claims in Wyoming.

What happened in 1920 was the outcome of a long, bitterly contested argument. Neither side surrendered, but by fair means or foul the petroleum interests had acquired the upper hand.

---

[37] Henry F. May to the Attorney General, February 11, 1921, Navy Records. See also Leslie C. Garnett to the Secretary of the Navy, February 25, 1921, Daniels to the Attorney General, February 28, 1921, *ibid.;* testimony in U.S. Congress, Senate, *Leases upon Naval Oil Reserves,* pp. 1253 ff. and *passim.*

# The Origins of Teapot Dome

**CHAPTER XIII**

*. . . my experience here in inability to get action, has been very wear-*
*ing upon one who has been accustomed to dealing with business men in*
*a business way and achieving results.*
Senator Albert B. Fall, Washington, D.C., to the
*Albuquerque Evening Herald,* June 14, 1918

1

In 1921–22 the Harding administration sharply modified conservation policies associated with the Roosevelt-Taft-Wilson administrations. Some it reversed. If a single word may be employed
to explain what happened, it should be "reaction." The new
Secretary of the Interior, Albert B. Fall, the new Secretary of the
Navy, Edwin Denby, and others reacted against what they considered to be the unsuccessful programs of the recent past. Businessmen were reacting against the Progressive Era, or government interference with their lines of enterprise. Oil men were
reacting against specific government actions. Western men were
reacting against federal conservation programs and "Pinchotism."

Such a trend was by no means wholly new. A fight had raged
within the Wilson administration, and by 1919 the advocates of
a more liberal petroleum policy were beginning to win. Developments of the war period aided them considerably. Petroleum
was a precious commodity in the postwar world. Oil operators
who produced in the domestic fields, or who sought concessions
abroad, increasingly received the sympathetic attention of government officials. Then too, conservation programs had not al-

ways succeeded. To the extent that they failed, or seemed to, a case could be made for their abandonment.

The general trend of the times was reactionary. For example, former public officials moved almost en masse to positions with private business. The oil industry afforded many illustrations. Franklin K. Lane joined Doheny in California as a highly paid assistant, while another big name of the war period, Mark L. Requa, became vice-president of the Sinclair Consolidated Oil Company. Clay Tallman exchanged his position as commissioner of the Land Office for a post in the Midwest Oil Company. Lane's personal assistant in the Interior Department, Joseph J. Cotter, became a vice-president of Doheny's Pan-American Petroleum Transport Company. Van Manning, formerly head of the Bureau of Mines, became an industry spokesman with the Petroleum Institute. J. H. G. Wolf—for several years a trusted adviser to Commander Landis—went to the Honolulu Company. As revealed later in the Teapot Dome inquiry, William G. McAdoo was retained by Doheny for assistance with his Mexican petroleum problems. George Creel also joined the Doheny organization briefly and with another oil man attempted to persuade the Navy Department to open its reserves to private exploitation.

Most striking of all was the success with which E. L. Doheny and Harry Sinclair moved in high circles, adding prominent names to their employment lists. They paid for expert knowledge, but also for influence. They gladly hired both Democrats and Republicans, and they contributed to both parties in the campaign of 1920.[1]

But the backing for a reactionary program on the public lands was more apparent than real. Hard-won progressive victories of the past twenty years were not to be wiped out in a moment. There were too many in "the know," too many in and out of the government who had followed the oil question as closely as had Fall, for example. If his knowledge were used to circumvent the law, they could apply theirs no less effectively to expose or track

[1] See especially U.S. Congress, Senate, *Leases upon Naval Oil Reserves*, Hearings Before the Committee on Public Lands and Surveys Pursuant to S. Res. 282, S. Res. 294, and S. Res. 434, 67 Cong., and S. Res. 147, 68 Cong., 3 vols., Washington, 1924, pp. 436, 997–999, 1014–16, 1936–60, and *passim;* Mark Sullivan, "Public Men and Big Business," *World's Work*, XLVII (April, 1924), 607–613. The Senate hearings, cited above, are a gold mine of documents, testimony by the many witnesses, and questions or comments by the senators.

him down. Men of both parties could be expected to help. The bipartisan "alliance" in conservation matters had not disappeared.

## 2

In the controversies from Taft to Harding, the naval petroleum reserves achieved an importance far outreaching their size or monetary value. Ideologically and politically they were a kind of battleground. The story has been told in preceding chapters of a bitter conflict between the Navy Department on one side and the Interior Department on the other, each with many allies.

Originally the Interior Department had recommended strongly the withdrawal of public petroleum lands. It also called for the establishment of small tracts as naval petroleum reserves. Presumably these reserves would mean that the Navy could retain underground a proven supply of oil for future emergencies. Then it might gain the authority to undertake actual development of the ground and, on a small scale, the refining of its own petroleum products.

Josephus Daniels, Secretary of the Navy from 1913 to 1921, persisted in these plans. Antimonopolistic in his outlook, he accused oil companies of artificially maintaining prices. He wished to assure that, if necessary, the Navy should be able to obtain cheap oil by doing its own refining. In World War I Daniels refused to buy oil at the oil men's prices. Using his emergency powers, he requisitioned the necessary supplies, and he made a renewed effort to obtain statutory authority for the Navy to control its own reserves. In the statute of June, 1920, he seemed finally to have succeeded, although the provision for naval refining plants was lost.

By 1915 the Interior Department had modified its position on oil lands, and a jurisdictional dispute with the Navy soon was raging. In the famous Honolulu case, Clay Tallman and Franklin K. Lane gave their approval to extensive claims of the Honolulu Company inside Buena Vista Hills, or Naval Reserve No. 2. Daniels opposed such claims, winning the support, first, of the Justice Department and, second, of President Wilson. Time after time the Department of the Interior tried to gain presidential consent for Honolulu Company patents. It always failed.

But western senators, oil men, and others were sympathetic to the Interior Department position, denouncing what they referred to as usurpation of power by the Navy. Political affiliation meant little. Western senators almost to a man, including such Democrats as Thomas J. Walsh of Montana, James D. Phelan of California, Henry Ashurst of Arizona, Key Pittman of Nevada, and William H. King of Utah were critical of the manner in which Josephus Daniels and his Navy Department had allegedly overridden that agency properly charged with responsibility for the public lands, the Department of the Interior.

Slowly the tide began to turn against Daniels and his supporters. In truth, his efforts and those of the conservationists often had been violative of tradition, and often they had failed. Above all, Naval Reserve No. 2 had been lost. Daniels himself commented in 1919 (whether stating his actual beliefs or not) that the government's judicial defeat in the Southern Pacific case meant "the practical abandonment of the Naval Reserve Policy." By the end of 1920 Daniels observed that the pressure to open the naval reserves had been unceasing; it was now more serious than ever. The Secretary sounded defiant. Not only would he fight for his reserves, he called for the nationalization of coal, oil, and water. These were "God-created essentials" that ought to be "used for national needs."

George Otis Smith and others in the Interior Department observed that the situation now had changed, with reference to naval oil reserves. Smith had believed in 1912 in the possibility of a good, compact area for the Navy. He had been much influenced too, he said, by predictions of the Justice Department that they could win the suits against the Southern Pacific Railroad. But they had failed. Thus was "removed one of the strongest justifications for the creation" of Reserve No. 2. Furthermore, the relief sections of the act of 1920 had "riddled the remnant of the reserve" to such an extent that any discussions of it had to take on the nature of a "post-mortem." To a lesser extent Reserve No. 1 was also impaired by private holdings, particularly around Section 36, where the Standard Oil Company had begun intensive development.[2]

---

[2] Daniels to A. Mitchell Palmer, December 6, 1919, Navy Records, National Archives; Smith to E. C. Finney, first Assistant Secretary of the Interior, April 19, 1921, *ibid.;* extract of a speech by Josephus Daniels, "Fuel Oil for the Navy," *Journal of the American Society of Naval Engineers,* XXXIII (February, 1921), 60–63.

Could the Navy sustain any longer its petroleum policies under-taken on the basis of earlier conditions in the oil fields? Many said no. Resentments against the government, and especially the Navy, mounted to a dangerous height by 1920. Commander Nathaniel H. Wright and other naval leaders were deeply con-cerned, as well they might be.

The *Standard Oil Bulletin,* house organ for Standard of Cali-fornia, featured long and bitter attacks on the government's oil policy. An article of July, 1919, entitled "Crippling Industry at Public Expense," denounced the land withdrawals of 1909 and later court actions against alleged trespassers. In many "if not in most" of the actions before the Land Office and the courts, the findings had been in favor of oil men. The article cited particu-larly a case recently decided by District Judge Robert S. Bean, upholding the allegedly fraudulent McMurtry locations of 1909, which locations, or claims, had been opposed by the Navy and Justice Departments. It was high time, said the *Bulletin,* that "this insensate policy of obstruction be abandoned." A "prosperous industry" had been crippled "at enormous public expense."

Another article in August, 1919, was entitled, "The Navy's Oil Supply—a Protest." The Navy had continued to secure its oil, on requisition orders, at a price considerably under the market. But the *Bulletin* pointed out that marketing companies had now refused to continue with requisition agreements, and warned: "It is a serious matter when a great agency of the Government embarks on a policy of confiscation without hindrance by Con-gress or the Chief Executive. It is a blow at civil rights which must not go unchallenged. Against it the BULLETIN in common with the marketing companies and producers of the Pacific Coast raises a most solemn protest—a protest of nation-wide interest, and the grounds of which are of vital import to every citizen of the United States."

An article of September, 1919, condemned the government's "Litigious and Profitless Policy." The big Southern Pacific case had just been decided against the Justice Department, and using this as a starting point, the *Bulletin* broadened to a considera-tion of the government's "senseless" policy, dating back to 1909. It concluded that this had been altogether a "wretched" business, for which excuses could not be found.

By way of contrast, three years later the *Bulletin* was highly pleased with the Harding administration's policy "of encouraging business men to increase the national wealth, thereby promoting the national welfare." [3]

A chronic complaint running through the war and postwar years was government investigations of the oil industry. In December of 1919 the *Bulletin* observed that the oil industry was "again being investigated." The Federal Trade Commission and apparently the Justice Department were conducting their separate inquiries. This was uncalled for. Oil companies could "justly claim that their course throughout the recent war period was above criticism." Another oil editor, thinking of meddlesome politicians, could not control his indignation: "Big business," he said, "has done more for the people of this country in one minute than all the reformers combined have accomplished in years." [4]

Josephus Daniels, always a subject of controversy, frequently was treated with contempt. Thus one article in *The North American Review* was entitled caustically, "Seven Years of Daniels." Thomas A. O'Donnell, the California oil man and former aide to Requa, unleashed a bitter attack on Secretary Daniels in November, 1920. This was one of many addresses at the annual meeting of the American Petroleum Institute, held in Washington.

O'Donnell spoke with authority as president of the organization. The Navy Department, he charged, had "not been fair with the producers of the West." He continued: "We believe this to

---

[3] "Crippling Industry at Public Expense," *Standard Oil Bulletin,* VII (July, 1919), 1–2; "The Navy's Oil Supply—a Protest," *ibid.,* VII (August, 1919), 1–2; "A Litigious and Profitless Policy," *ibid.,* VII (September, 1919), 1–2; "The National Oil Policy," *ibid.,* IX (February, 1922), 1–2. As early as 1917 the petroleum industry had begun to object bitterly to Josephus Daniels and his attitude on prices and profits. "Secretary Daniels . . . goes on the assumption that no one's price is just but his own price, and he refuses to listen to any argument whatsoever from any of the business interests in justification of what the business men think is a fair price." "To Challenge Its Loyalty Unfair: Business, Which Must Pay for and Conduct the War, Gives No Cause for Such Remarks as Came from President," *National Petroleum News,* IX (July, 1917), 7.

[4] "Investigations," *Standard Oil Bulletin,* VII (December, 1919), 1–2; "A Surfeit of Investigations," *Oil and Gas Journal,* XXI (June 22, 1922), 10. See also William O. Maxwell, "Oil Men vs. Government Agents," *Oil Age,* XVI (May, 1920), 12–18; Robert A. Waller, "Business Reactions to the Teapot Dome Affair, 1922 to 1925," unpublished Master's thesis, University of Illinois, Urbana, 1958.

be due to the extreme prejudice of the head of that department. While an armistice has been signed with the Germans, no armistice has been offered to the oil producers by the Navy Department."

Oil men had been constantly subjected to public criticism and to investigations by the Senate, the Justice Department, the Federal Trade Commission, and the California Railroad Commission. Their petroleum supplies were seized by U.S. warships, he said, with a payment less than cost. They had been compelled in the courts to fight against various government charges.

At last these charges stood refuted. Oil men were cleared. What they needed and hoped for now was a "friendly fair and cooperative spirit" on the part of government; while oil men in turn must "give the public a square deal" and conduct themselves in a "conservative and proper manner," obeying the laws both in spirit and in letter.

At the same gathering Mark L. Requa, now with Harry Sinclair, spoke on "Conservation." (Sinclair was treasurer of this Petroleum Institute.) George Otis Smith, whose subject was a "World View of the Oil Supply," gave the expected arguments for an aggressive oil policy featured by cooperation between business and government.[5]

A few months later Thomas A. O'Donnell wrote to the Secretary of the Navy, Edwin Denby, suggesting that the California naval reserves be kept intact and developed as a whole by arrangement with private capital. He was personally willing to undertake the project.

To the new Secretary, O'Donnell indicated his opinion of the ex-Secretary: "A proper and substantial fuel supply for the

---

[5] Archibald Douglas Turnbull, "Seven Years of Daniels," *North American Review*, CCXII (November, 1920), 606–617; American Petroleum Institute, *Bulletin* (Washington, December 10, 1920), copy in Second Accession (petroleum), Box 44, Navy Records, and *passim* in *ibid.* Also *New York Times*, November 19, 1920. An ex-Secretary of the Navy had implied in 1915 that Daniels ought to be court-martialed, if possible. George v. L. Meyer, "Is Our Navy Going Right?" *Harper's Weekly*, LX (April 10, 1915), 346–347. Robert M. La Follette commented four years later on the "organized abuse" directed against Daniels since early in his naval career: "Few men in public life have ever endured the brutal assaults that he suffered at the hands of the great newspapers of the country published in the interest of private greed and at the hands of leading magazines of the country that were equally subservient." *Cong. Record*, 66 Cong., 1 Sess., p. 4750, September 3, 1919.

Navy has always seemed to me a subject of the utmost importance to all of us. The unfortunate controversies between the oil interests of the Pacific Coast and the former Secretary of the Navy Daniels, no doubt, brought about a lack of confidence on his part as to the motives prompting any advice that might be given by any of us on this coast engaged in the business." [6] It may be assumed that many, in and out of the government, "educated" Secretary Denby in petroleum matters. One of the best ways to do so was to set forth the errors of his Democratic predecessor.

## 3

Josephus Daniels thus came under attack, both frontal and oblique. Two leaders who reacted against him most strongly were Albert B. Fall and Edwin Denby.

Fall as senator and incoming Secretary of the Interior was keenly aware of the East-West struggle over disposition of western resources. He virtually personified, in fact, the western "pioneer." David H. Stratton, Fall's biographer, has said of him: "His belief in the unrestrained disposition of the public lands was as typically Western as his black, broad-brimmed Stetson hat and his love of fine horses." The New Mexico senator was full of indignation over eastern mismanagement of resources and federal control and interference. He knew the story of the naval petroleum reserves, of the Honolulu case, and of how officials of the Navy and Justice Departments had "usurped" the functions of the Interior Department. He knew all the rest: the land laws, the organization of the departments, and the means by which the Interior Department under his management could resume its rightful task of opening public lands to private exploitation. As for the naval petroleum reserves, they never should have existed in the first place. This was the typical attitude of western senators in 1920–21.[7]

---

[6] O'Donnell to Denby, April 18, 1921, Navy Records. See also Charles P. Fox of the *California Oil World* to Secretary Denby, March 25, 1921, C. Naramore to James N. Gillett, March 22, 1921, *ibid.*

[7] David H. Stratton, "Behind Teapot Dome: Some Personal Insights," *Business History Review,* XXXI (Winter, 1957), 386; Fall to Frank N. Page, May 31, 1916, Fall to *Albuquerque Evening Herald,* June 14, 1918, Albert B. Fall Papers, Huntington Library, San Marino, Calif. See also David H. Stratton, "New Mexican Machiavellian? The Story of Albert B. Fall," *Montana: The Magazine of Western History,* VII (October, 1957), 2–14; Burl

The election of 1920 seemed to give Fall his personal opportunity to set things right. A vigorous, egotistical leader, he would
bring an end to "Pinchotism" and the misguided programs of
Wilsonian leaders. Perhaps most important, he would settle the
argument over naval petroleum reserves. He would place them
back where they belonged—under control of the Interior Department. He would open them to private development. Moreover, if some of his business friends wished to favor him with
loans and gifts, he would be willing to accept.

In 1921, however, there was little reason to suspect Fall's integrity. He was often thought of as a special friend of Theodore
Roosevelt's, and he had placed the ex-President in nomination
for the presidency in the Republican convention of 1916. Fall
had courage, force, brains. He had risen through the rough and
tumble of New Mexico frontier politics to become a successful
lawyer, rancher, and businessman, member of the territorial
legislature, one of the first two senators from the new state in
1912, and finally Secretary of the Interior. As a forthright critic
of President Wilson's Mexican policy and a defender of western
economic interests against a federal bureaucracy, he seemed to
stand forth as a man of principle. No meek, compromising type
was Albert B. Fall. It is not difficult to understand the respect
in which he was held by Warren Harding, Theodore Roosevelt,
Jr., Herbert Hoover, the new Secretary of the Navy Edwin Denby,
and others.[8]

Fall was able to defend, on rational grounds, his belief in developing the public domain. He once replied to a critic rather
disarmingly, as he was capable of doing: "I'm surprised at you.
You've had a good education. You know something about history. Every generation from Adam and Eve down has lived
better than the generation before. I don't know how . . . [the
next generation will] do it—maybe they'll use the energy of the

---

Noggle, *Teapot Dome: Oil and Politics in the 1920's*, Baton Rouge, La.,
1962, pp. 8–14 and *passim*.

[8] Stratton, "New Mexican Machiavellian?" pp. 2–14; Fall to Theodore Roosevelt, August 3, September 21, 1916, and *passim*, Fall Papers; Diaries of
Theodore Roosevelt, Jr., March 23, 1922 (p. 219), July 29, 1922 (p. 350),
August 12, 1922 (p. 360), Papers of Theodore Roosevelt, Jr., Library of Congress. Fall had shown himself a political opportunist when he switched
from the Democratic to the Republican party in 1906.

sun or the sea waves—but . . . [they] will live better than we do. I stand for opening up every resource." [9]

The new head of the Navy Department, Edwin Denby, was to be quite susceptible to the influence of Secretary Fall. A conservative Republican from Detroit, he succeeded the "radical" Wilsonian, Josephus Daniels. Denby had been a gunner's mate in the Spanish-American War and a marine in World War I, and rose in the latter conflict from private to major. As a serviceman and marine officer, he could not escape the widespread feeling that Secretary Daniels was a mere newspaperman and politician, a landlubber who did not understand Navy traditions, who had exerted his influence in an extraordinary way.

Denby's Assistant Secretary, Theodore Roosevelt, Jr., had a low opinion of Daniels. He looked upon him as "a queer character, a combination of ignorance, kind-heartedness, and shifty opportunism." Roosevelt described to a friend the extremely "deplorable" conditions which Daniels had left in the Navy Department. It would take some time to straighten things out, he said. Disparagement of Daniels was to be found even among officers at the "oil desk" in the Bureau of Engineering, who had reason to know and respect him.[10]

How would Denby react to the widespread criticism of his

---

[9] Quoted in Stratton, "New Mexican Machiavellian?" p. 14. Fall was not uniformly an exploiter. He accepted the idea of national parks and was often their defender. See John Ise, *Our National Park Policy: A Critical History,* Baltimore, Md., 1961, p. 314.

[10] See Diaries of Theodore Roosevelt, Jr., December 6, 1921 (p. 70), and *passim,* Roosevelt to Nathan L. Miller, May 25, 1921, Papers of Theodore Roosevelt, Jr. Mrs. Edwin Denby later recalled what her friends had thought of Josephus Daniels: they seemed to believe that he lacked the knowledge or experience to be Secretary of the Navy, that he disliked to take advice from those qualified to give it, and that he had made many mistakes. Letter to the author, November 9, 1960; also author's interview with Mrs. Denby, October 31, 1959. Near the end of Daniels' administration Commander Stuart wrote to his fellow officer, Landis, in California: "Whatever else may be said of the present incumbent he has stood manfully by the Navy on the Reserve question." Later he wrote that in "this respect at least," so far as the reserves were concerned, they would regret the loss of Daniels. Stuart to Landis, February 1, 1921, Navy Records; Stuart to Landis, July 6, 1921, quoted in R. G. Tracie, senior petroleum engineer, Navy Department, "History of the Naval Petroleum Reserves," unpublished manuscript, compiled in 1937, copy in Josephus Daniels Papers, Box 264, Library of Congress. See also Alice Roosevelt Longworth, *Crowded Hours,* New York, 1933, p. 260; Jonathan Daniels, *The End of Innocence,* Philadelphia, 1954, p. 324 and *passim.*

predecessor? Would he defend him personally and uphold his policies? In connection with the public lands and naval petroleum reserves, would he pursue a course deeply resented in the West and opposed by his able colleague and friend from New Mexico, Secretary Fall?

Immediately upon taking office, Denby was confronted with the most intricate and complicated problems arising from the public lands. One can visualize him, ignorant of these matters, asking himself: should he, as Secretary of the Navy, really have to deal with western land problems?

There were others who frequently had asked such a question. In the Senate, for example, the Committees on Naval Affairs and Public Lands had waged a jurisdictional argument in 1918 similar to the argument at the same time between the Secretaries of the Navy and Interior. Had the naval reserves, like a naval yard or naval base, passed under the control of the Navy Department? Or were they still public lands, so that the Secretary of the Interior had jurisdiction? This question had not been wholly resolved by the new legislation of 1920.

At first Secretary Denby was cautious, and followed the path of his predecessor. For about a month he and his advisers said that the petroleum reserves must be kept intact; no change in policy was contemplated. Denby was relying upon the same officers in the Bureau of Engineering who had contributed so much to Daniels' policy: Admiral Griffin, Commander Stuart, and others.[11]

By May of 1921, however, Denby sharply altered the naval policy. From this time he believed in the desirability of leasing the naval reserves. He wished to turn the actual management over to the Interior Department, and to store the Navy's oil in tanks on seaboard, ready for use.

Almost in desperation now, Denby's officers in the Bureau of Engineering argued, explained, and protested. They tried to show the mistake that was being made. They pointed to the past and to the inevitable rivalry that had developed between the Navy and Interior Departments. The Navy must look out for its own interests. It must be willing to take "the risk of offending another government Department." In the long fight over western

---

[11] See Denby to J. W. Ragesdale, April 6, 1921, Navy Records.

oil lands, the Interior Department "almost always" had favored legislation "adversely affecting" the naval reserves. Most of all, when the Secretary was a western man, responsive to western interests, this could be expected. Commander Stuart thought of Franklin K. Lane and his record as Secretary of the Interior. He wrote that if one imagined Lane in control of the naval reserves he could see "the disastrous effect" of the present plan "on the Navy's future supply of fuel oil." [12]

These arguments fell on deaf ears. Not too surprisingly, Commander Stuart was soon detached for sea duty, and Admiral Griffin in Washington and Commander Landis in California were retired from active duty.

Assuming that Denby was honest and reasonably capable, as the evidence indicates, why did he reject the advice of his own officers? They were supposed to be experts on this oil question. Why did Denby fail to study and comprehend the problem? [13] To find the answers to such questions is not easy.

There is circumstantial evidence, however, that Denby was reacting against his naval advisers for his own good reasons. Why? Not only had they advised Daniels as Scretary of the Navy, they had advised Pinchot and his group. They had passed confidential information to La Follette and other "radicals" in the Congress. They had played politics in the handling of oil matters. They had intruded into areas where they did not belong, or so their critics said. They were vulnerable to conservative and reactionary attacks.

---

[12] Stuart to Denby, May 18, 1921, quoted in Tracie, "History of the Naval Petroleum Reserves." Also Griffin, memorandum for the Secretary of the Navy, May 27, 1921, Navy Records; testimony by Griffin and Stuart in U.S. Congress, Senate, *Leases upon Naval Oil Reserves*, pp. 347–348, 767–773, and *passim*.

[13] As to Denby's intelligence and general ability there can be little doubt, in spite of his weak performance testifying before the Public Lands Committee of the Senate in 1924. See comment by Senator William E. Borah, *Cong. Record*, 68 Cong., 1 Sess., p. 2073, February 8, 1924; also Amos Pinchot to Victor Watson, January 24, 1924, Amos Pinchot Papers, Box 47, Library of Congress. Phillip Harlowe Miller, "The Role of Secretary of the Navy, Edwin Denby, in the Teapot Dome Affair," unpublished undergraduate Honors thesis, University of Illinois, Urbana, 1957, pp. 3–5 and *passim*, finds Denby's early respectable career and his later troubles as Secretary of the Navy difficult to reconcile. Other intelligent men of good reputation were "taken in" by Fall's plans, including Theodore Roosevelt, Jr., Assistant Secretary of the Navy, and Foster Bain, head of the Bureau of Mines.

Denby was probably informed on the political role played by the Bureau of Engineering. If he was, his reversal of policy, and also his reluctance later to talk about it, becomes more readily understandable.[14] Denby, in any event, made his decision. He chose to follow the recommendations of Secretary Fall and of Admiral John K. Robison, an officer hostile toward the Daniels policies. Robison now became the new chief of the Bureau of Engineering.

Wishing to have harmony in the new administration, Denby accepted the idea of leasing the reserves. There were many arguments for doing so. First, there was the old problem of drainage. Unquestionably, Buena Vista Hills was almost destroyed. It could be asserted, though with less validity, that Elk Hills and Teapot Dome were quickly being drained by wells on the adjoining tracts. How much better, the logic ran, to get the oil out, to save it from drainage, and place it in conveniently located storage tanks. The use of tanks for additional storage above ground had been recommended previously, as in 1916 by the Naval Fuel Oil Board.

Second, it was possible to point to various leases already permitted under the new law of February, 1920. These included leases for producing wells inside the California naval reserves. Toward the end of his administration, Daniels had permitted an area lease of 120 acres in Buena Vista Hills. This was for defensive purposes only, but as Daniels had commented at the

---

[14] Slattery to Pinchot, June 21, 1921, Gifford Pinchot Papers, Box 242, Library of Congress. There are various references in the Slattery-Pinchot correspondence to a "confidential" source in the Navy Department. Also individual informants (officers) are referred to at times by their names. See Slattery to Pinchot, February 7, 1920, *ibid.*, Box 1841. In the Senate hearings of 1924 Commander Stuart suggests what may have been in Secretary Fall's mind, which would certainly have been communicated to Edwin Denby. Trying to explain Fall's hostile reaction toward him in 1921 and why he had been detached from Washington for sea duty, Stuart described vividly a meeting with Fall as the newly installed head of the Interior Department. Fall had butted into the conversation to state that "all the dissension and quarreling, or words to that effect, between the two departments [Navy and Interior] was going to end." He then discussed the Honolulu case, using strong language. "He was doing all the talking, practically. Of course, apparently he knew that I had been with Secretary Daniels and presumably had his views in the matter of the naval reserves, and it struck me that he was just making a declaration of principles." U.S. Congress, Senate, *Leases upon Naval Oil Reserves*, p. 777.

time, it might be employed later as a precedent for other leases.[15]

There was an assortment of arguments and excuses which, at least to some, sounded impressive. For example, strategy in the Pacific (vis-à-vis the Japanese threat) required storage tanks for fuel oil at Pearl Harbor. These tanks and facilities could not be financed out of normal appropriations, due to a budgetary stringency. However, they could be paid for in kind under the naval act of June, 1920. Royalty oil from the naval reserves could be exchanged for work and services provided.[16]

Such an interpretation was questionable, yet the phrasing of the act was a little ambiguous. Few people knew what its underlying purposes were supposed to be. Secretary Denby was more than willing to accept interpretations from the Interior Department and to follow its lead in petroleum affairs.

## 4

Fall must have felt a deep satisfaction in 1921 as he sat so firmly in his saddle—the new boss of the Interior Department. No longer would Justice and Navy tell Interior what to do in the handling of public lands. No longer would eastern politicians, government agents, and investigators interfere with the distribution of public lands, or prevent their development on lenient terms. Moreover, Fall employed in a rather overpowering way the direct approach. He was eager to talk face to face with great capitalists or the spokesmen for private interests. When Mark L. Requa wrote to the Assistant Secretary of the Interior, modestly seeking an interview with him or with Secretary Fall, the Secretary scrawled a brusque note: "Let Mr. Requa understand that he can come directly to me—this is a matter of *policy*."

By July, 1921, Commander Stuart observed that Secretary Denby was placing "entire confidence" in Secretary Fall. And in

---

[15] Commander Stuart to Senator Walsh, April 9, 1924, quoted in *ibid.*, pp. 3258–60; Stuart to Landis, February 1, 1921, Navy Records.
[16] An interesting version of this argument is to be found in an unpublished manuscript by Thomas T. Reed, formerly of the Bureau of Mines, "Newspaper Justice," New York, 1936, copy in possession of the author, pp. 116–127, 150–158. See also Fall to Warren G. Harding, June 3, 1922, quoted in U.S. Congress, Senate, *Leases upon Naval Oil Reserves*, pp. 27–53.

August he declared, "the Secretary of the Interior has practically
full sway in anything connected with the Reserves." [17]

Through 1921 and 1922 Secretary Fall proceeded rapidly with
his program. For most of his policies, so far as can be ascertained,
he did not receive payoffs, or loans of a persuasive nature; these
were unnecessary. He was more than willing to render a service
to the Honolulu Company or to other western interests with
whom he sympathized.

Commander Stuart reported in May of 1921: "Secretary Fall
has told me in so many words that he expects to reverse the decision of Secretary Payne in the Honolulu Oil Company case
and give the Company a lease on all their claims and that, but
for public opinion, he would give the Company an outright patent without any royalty accruing to the government." [18] Franklin
Lane also had wished to give patents to the Honolulu people
from 1915 to 1920. In November, 1921, Fall did the best he
could. In extraordinary fashion he conferred upon the company
leases to seventeen tracts within Naval Reserve No. 2, or a total
of 3,057 acres. Leases also were permitted in a number of other
cases within both of the California reserves. These covered
large areas, rather than producing wells, as the law seemed to
provide. Fall was lavish in his favors.

In his written decision in the Honolulu case, Fall gave more
than a hint of his motivation. William Matson and the Honolulu
Company, he said, had acted in "high good faith," and had taken
great risks, but they had been mistreated by the government and
compelled to undertake expensive litigation. Fall desired, if possible, to end this "apparently interminable controversy." The
Secretary also referred, with a resentment that was scarcely veiled,
to President Wilson's policy in the matter. There had been
executive interference. By a "most unique intervention of the
Chief Executive," the Honolulu Company had been denied the
patents that it really deserved.

In the Section 36 case involving Reserve No. 1 Secretary Fall

---

[17] Requa to E. C. Finney, July 10, 1922, and Fall's note on the bottom of this
letter, Secretary's File, Department of the Interior, National Archives; Commander Stuart to Landis, July 6, August 12, 1921, quoted in Tracie, "History
of the Naval Petroleum Reserves."
[18] Stuart to Secretary Denby, May 18, 1921, quoted in *ibid.*

summarily dismissed a proceeding against the Standard Oil
Company based on a charge of fraud, thus attempting to confirm
its title to one of the richest oil tracts in the United States. He
failed, and ultimately this title was returned to the federal government.[19]

On conservation policy in general, Secretary Fall challenged
Pinchot and all that he represented. He proposed to open the
resources of Alaska for quick development, and he attempted to
transfer control over the national forests from the Agriculture
Department to his own jurisdiction. In these efforts, however,
he was to fail completely, as Pinchot rallied his friends to oppose
the transfer and to exert their influence upon President Harding.[20]

There can be little doubt that Fall was reacting strongly
against "Pinchotism" and "Wilsonianism" from the moment he
assumed his office. The action which eventually landed him in
prison was his leasing of Teapot Dome and Elk Hills. Fall would
not have permitted these leases, unless he thought the political
and economic climate was right, or safe. Too, Fall was aware of
the intricacy of the oil question and its long history. There
seemed to be a previously existent, plausible excuse for every
move he contemplated (except the taking of money). To find

---

[19] U.S. Congress, Senate, *Leases upon Naval Oil Reserves*, pp. 1248–79, 3448–
54, and *passim;* Department of the Interior, *Decisions of the Department
of the Interior in Cases Relating to the Public Lands,* vol. 48, Washington,
1922, pp. 303–313; Secretary of the Navy to the Inspector of the naval petroleum reserves, March 26, 1940, Navy Records; *New York Times,* March
26, 28, 1940. Section 36, being located in Elk Hills, had exercised a considerable influence over government policy for the entire reserve. That is,
while controlled by Standard Oil, it tended to drain the surrounding reserve and was used as an excuse for the lease to Doheny. One illegal holding
thereby became a means to a much larger illegal holding. See Senator Walsh
in *Cong. Record,* 68 Cong., 1 Sess., p. 1536, January 28, 1924.

[20] See especially Burl Noggle, "The Origins of the Teapot Dome Investigation," *Mississippi Valley Historical Review,* XLIV (September, 1957), 237–
266; also David H. Stratton, "Behind Teapot Dome: Some Personal Insights,"
*Business History Review,* XXXI (Winter, 1957), 385–402; Pinchot to his
sister "Nettie," Cannes, France, January 25, 1924, Pinchot Papers, Box 249;
Fall to Nicholas J. Sinnott, March 4, 1922, Richard A. Ballinger to Fall,
March 15, 1922, Fall to Ballinger, March 23, 1922, Fall Papers. Fall had
been in financial trouble for some years. His personal problems help to explain why he took certain "loans," but they do not adequately explain his
broad changes of policy. See Fall to Will P. Lapoint, May 13, 1912, Fall to
Alfred Barstow, January 15, 1923, *ibid.*

him out would be difficult. It is tempting to believe that Fall was primarily a victim of history, for, shrewd as he was, he misinterpreted the recent past: he failed to appreciate the continuing strength of the conservation movement and his susceptibility to a counterattack.

# Conclusion: The Irony of Teapot Dome

CHAPTER XIV

---

*The continued and rapid growth in the use of petroleum products has made questionable the need for maintenance of the relatively small naval petroleum reserves as a significant defense measure, since it would appear that the nationwide, even worldwide, petroleum industry must be relied upon to provide efficiently for our petroleum requirements in both peace and war.*

From President Eisenhower's Budget Message, January, 1959

---

If Teapot Dome developed into the greatest scandal of United States history, it also became the most ironic. The ironies and paradoxes are not without significance, and they are better understood in the long perspective of the oil fight. The name itself was ironic, for the historic dispute over public lands had related mostly to the rich fields of California. Nevertheless, a limestone rock in central Wyoming, shaped somewhat like a teapot, gave its name to the oil dome underneath and eventually became the designation for the major scandal of the 1920's. "Teapot Dome" encompassed the California leases and other questionable arrangements, and its implications of notoriety spread far and wide. As one writer said: "Teapot Dome is an alluring and provocative name. It has a mysterious sound and comes trippingly from the tongue." [1] As a term of scandal and opprobrium, it could not be surpassed. Yet time would show that this reserve was not very rich. Intrinsically, Elk Hills in California was far more important.

---

[1] Paul Y. Anderson in *Labor* (Washington, D.C.), January 26, 1924, clipping in Walsh Scrapbook, Thomas J. Walsh Papers, Library of Congress.

Whatever else is said about it, Teapot Dome must rank as a case of flagrant corruption, involving top officials of the government, leaders of the petroleum industry, newspaper publishers, and others in public life. Important politicians were adjudged, at the least, as guilty by association. There was much that was sordid, and sobering, to students of American life. Yet the scandal had its lighter and brighter aspects.[2]

Secretary Albert B. Fall, while not to be described as a villain in a melodrama, certainly was the prime mover in this affair. It seemed, for a time, that Fall was merely following an audacious course in which no corruption was involved and that, in a sense, he was beating the progressives at their own game. One of the beliefs, and hopes, of the progressives and conservationists had been strong leadership, with liberal discretion left to executive officers such as the Secretary of the Interior. Fall proved himself a strong leader—but with reactionary views. The new Secretary took every advantage of loopholes in the leasing law of February, 1920, and the naval act that had passed in June. These were the measures that progressives had fought so hard to get, or to improve, and for which they had high hopes.

In May of 1921, along with Secretary Denby, Fall effected the transfer of the petroleum reserves to his jurisdiction, accomplished by an executive order of the President. Next he entered upon negotiations with E. L. Doheny for offset wells in Reserve No. 1 (Elk Hills) and for the construction of storage tanks on the seaboard; these would be paid for with the Navy's oil. Fall and the California oil man finally arranged for the lease of Elk Hills in its entirety. Concurrently, Fall discussed with Harry Sinclair the lease of Teapot Dome, which was consummated early in 1922.

Whether deliberately or not, Fall exploited one of the heroic names of the Progressive Era—that of Roosevelt. His friendship with Theodore Roosevelt (now dead) contributed to his influence in the Navy Department, where Theodore Roosevelt, Jr., in

---

[2] Burl Noggle, *Teapot Dome: Oil and Politics in the 1920's,* Baton Rouge, La., 1962, is well written and scholarly. Morris R. Werner and John Starr, *Teapot Dome,* New York, 1959, fails to incorporate manuscript sources (such as the papers of Senator Walsh) and also neglects the work of recent historians; though interesting, it is often unreliable. John Ise, *The United States Oil Policy,* New Haven, Conn., 1926, continues to be a valuable study.

1921 became the Assistant Secretary. Young Roosevelt would hear no wrong about his father's old friend. At this same time it happened that another Roosevelt son, Archie, was in the employ of Harry Sinclair.[3]

Secretary Fall had been regarded in Washington as a forthright, blunt, brash westerner. Teapot Dome shattered his reputation for frankness, since his oil deals were largely secret, and he did his utmost to keep them secret. The lease of Elk Hills and of Teapot Dome occurred without competitive bidding. Moreover, contracts and records of the proceedings were transferred from the Land Office to the Bureau of Mines, and Secretary Fall wrote: "These contracts form part of the confidential records of the Navy Department and are not for public inspection." [4]

Under the veil of secrecy, some amazing transactions occurred. There were those who must be paid to maintain silence and to acquiesce in what was going on. The old matter of rival claimants rose up to plague Secretary Fall and Harry Sinclair. No truly valid claims existed in Teapot Dome, but by asserting their shadowy "claims," several parties threatened to expose the exclusive leasing privilege that had been given to Sinclair. Before this sordid business was over, Sinclair had to pay out more than a million dollars in "hush" money.

Even more amazing, Secretary Fall in one case employed armed force to maintain his policy. A certain oil company had entered upon Teapot Dome and begun operations. The time-honored method of bringing such operations to a halt, if they were illegal, was to appeal to the courts. Fall, instead, called upon the Navy for a detachment of marines. They were obtained, sent to Teapot Dome, and with a show of their weapons had no difficulty in stopping the drilling operations. Sinclair's lease, for the time being, was safe.[5]

---

[3] Noggle, *Teapot Dome*, p. 19; J. Leonard Bates, "Senator Walsh of Montana, 1918–1924," unpublished Ph.D. dissertation, University of North Carolina, Chapel Hill, 1952, pp. 304–305, 313–314, and *passim;* U.S. Congress, Senate, *Leases upon Naval Oil Reserves,* Hearings Before the Committee on Public Lands and Surveys Pursuant to S. Res. 282, S. Res. 294, and S. Res. 434, 67 Cong., and S. Res., 147, 68 Cong., 3 vols., Washington, 1924, pp. 175–309, 391–405, and *passim;* Diaries of Theodore Roosevelt, Jr., January 30, 1922 (pp. 167–168), March 23, 1922 (p. 219), Papers of Theodore Roosevelt, Jr., Library of Congress.

[4] Fall to William Spry, commissioner of the Land Office, January 22, 1923, Secretary's File, Department of the Interior, National Archives.

[5] See especially the testimony of Frederick G. Bonfils in U.S. Congress, Senate,

If Fall had not taken money, such tactics of desperation would not have been required, and probably he could have continued with his leasing campaign. This is the keenest irony of all. Fall could not be indicted for moving the naval reserves into his jurisdiction; for leasing the reserves to "save" them from drainage; for exchanging royalty oil from the naval reserves for tanks in which to store the oil; or for other technical aspects of his new policy. As he doubtless anticipated, experts disagreed, as they always had. When the oil leases first came under intensive investigation (in the fall of 1923), the results were inconclusive. Only when Fall's financial affairs came under surveillance did his defenses collapse. He had accepted $100,000 from E. L. Doheny, delivered in a little black bag; and he had accepted from Harry Sinclair payments and loans totaling about $300,000.[6]

By going too far, Fall played into the hands of Gifford Pinchot and his other critics and enemies. His exposure was perhaps inevitable. Independent oil men, critics in the Navy Department, enemies in New Mexico politics, and outraged conservation leaders subjected his policies to the closest scrutiny. Independents in Wyoming were suspicious of the Midwest Company and its close relations with the Standard Oil Company of Indiana and with Sinclair. Their political spokesman was Senator John B. Kendrick of Wyoming, who had a thorough knowledge of the oil story. Ironically, the country was flooded with surpluses of petroleum in 1921–22, after the long period of wartime shortage. Fall was hard-pressed to justify his measures for intensified development at such a time of overdevelopment.[7]

---

*Leases upon Naval Oil Reserves*, pp. 1973–2058; testimony of George K. Shuler, ex-captain in the Marine Corps, in *ibid.*, pp. 1054–60. Commander Wright, testifying in a House hearing in 1918, had commented upon the prevalence of blackmail in the oil fields. Sinclair's later problem was by no means an isolated instance. U.S. Congress, House, *Oil Leasing Lands*, Hearings Before the Committee on Public Lands on H.R. 3232, to "Authorize Exploration for and Disposition of Coal, Phosophate, Oil, Gas, Potassium or Sodium," and S. 2812, to "Encourage and Promote Mining of Coal, Phosphate, Oil, Gas, and Sodium on the Public Domain," 65 Cong., 2 Sess., Washington, 1918, pp. 1088–89.

[6] Testimony of Doheny in U.S. Congress, Senate, *Leases upon Naval Oil Reserves*, pp. 1771–1823, and *passim* for other testimony and important documents; David H. Stratton, "Behind Teapot Dome: Some Personal Insights," *Business History Review*, XXXI (Winter, 1957), 385–402.

[7] See Senator John B. Kendrick to Joseph O'Mahoney, June 21, 1922, John B. Kendrick Papers, University of Wyoming, Laramie. On Fall's problem with overproduction see Frederick G. Bonfils of the *Denver Post* to Fall

Rumors, ugly rumors, filled the air in 1921 and after. They seemed almost too much to believe. But Fall's cavalier handling of something like the Honolulu case was of symbolical importance to those who knew the bitter struggle which had occurred over this matter for so many years. And the transfer of naval petroleum reserves out of the Navy Department meant the reversal of a policy to which many individuals had given a good part of their lives. It was simply intolerable to them. Josephus Daniels wrote: "After having given eight years to preventing the spoiling of these reserves, I cannot write about it without using asbestos." [8]

Senator La Follette and the Pinchot group spearheaded the investigation. Without them, it is entirely possible that Fall might have avoided detection. Philip Wells, Harry Slattery, Pinchot, and La Follette and his staff maintained a continuous interest in the operations of the Interior Department. Wells, for example, early in 1921 was trying to understand how the Midwest Company had obtained a monopoly of the Salt Creek field, through government leases, in apparent violation of anti-monopoly provisions in the leasing act. Then, in June of 1921, he prodded the Interior Department about its newly acquired control over the naval reserves. He wanted an explanation. Slattery in the meantime was busily checking his confidential sources in Washington and reporting his findings to Pinchot.

In June, 1921, Slattery wrote a remarkable letter on the oil situation. Fall's doom was virtually sealed, considering the fact that Slattery, La Follette, and others had so often demonstrated that they were "watchdogs" of conservation. "Dear Mr. Pinchot," Slattery wrote:

> I had a talk this morning with Senator La Follette and his son, at his request, re the Naval Oil Reserve. You will remember Denby got the President to transfer the reserves to Fall. . . . Yesterday Fall reopened the Honolulu Case, which Barton Payne had turned down just before leaving office. This means that the Honolulu case will probably go through. La Follette has information from the Navy Department (confidential) that the President's transfer is illegal under the law. He is

---

(telegram), June 14, 1921, Fall (telegram) to Bonfils, June 15, 1921, and Fall to the Petroleum World Publishing Company, Los Angeles, July 20, 1922, Secretary's File. This and similar correspondence reveals how Fall was trying to rationalize his actions and to "cover up."

[8] Daniels to Dr. Randolph W. Hill, June 1, 1922, Josephus Daniels Papers,

getting it looked up. After talking it over, he plans to either by resolution or by action of a committee ask for the facts, including correspondence, etc. . . .[9]

It remained only for La Follette to press ahead with his plans and to find the necessary support. He checked into the latest moves by Fall, he evaluated tips from various sources, he enlisted the support of Democratic senators and others. In April, 1922, the Senate passed his resolutions providing for a comprehensive investigation. This was conducted by the Public Lands Committee.

In 1923 Senator Walsh of Montana, with La Follette's backing, assumed charge of the inquiry and went on to the sensational disclosures of 1924. Names formerly unfamiliar to the general public, such as Teapot Dome, Elk Hills, Buena Vista Hills, the Honolulu Company, and Section 36 suddenly became front-page news. A flood of witnesses appeared before the committee. Many were the same men, from governmental departments or from private life, who had figured prominently in the long dispute over oil lands. On the committee itself Senators Reed Smoot, Irvine L. Lenroot, and Walsh were notable for their long familiarity with the subject.

Walsh and Lenroot also illustrated the reversal of roles that sometimes occurred. The junior senator from Wisconsin, formerly an ally of the Pinchot group, now became an apologist for policies of the Harding-Coolidge administrations. Walsh, often identified in the past with the western bloc in the Senate, now emerged as the chief protector of the naval reserves, and was highly effective in building up the evidence and opening new lines of inquiry.

In 1924 it became apparent that Senate investigators were rendering a genuine service to the nation. But, paradoxically, there was bitter opposition to the investigation and widespread

---

Box 594, Library of Congress. See also Admiral Griffin to Daniels, December 9, 1923, *ibid.*
[9] Slattery to Pinchot, June 21, 1921, Gifford Pinchot Papers, Box 242, Library of Congress; Wells to H. J. Trost, January 5, 1921, E. C. Finney, first Assistant Secretary of the Interior, to Wells, June 7, 1921, *ibid.*, Box 1700. John Ise, then doing research for his *United States Oil Policy,* was one of the first to suspect Secretary Fall. He noted what appeared to be "an excessive zeal on the part of the Interior Department in the granting of leases on the Government oil lands." Ise to Gifford Pinchot, April 27, 1921, *ibid.*, Box 238.

apathy in places where applause might have been expected. Senator Walsh complained that high officers of the Navy had little interest in his attempt to save the petroleum reserves. Eventually Josephus Daniels, Admiral Griffin, Commander Stuart, and others did come to his aid; but, even so, it seemed that the department of the government that should have been most concerned was only slightly concerned. Why? Always there had been many who doubted the efficacy or the necessity of naval petroleum reserves. Probably at no time were more than a few high-ranking officers deeply interested in this question.[10]

Amid the excitement of Teapot Dome the old arguments were not forgotten; that is, arguments over the intrinsic merits of the oil reserves, and over related questions of government and private action. In some ways, time and fate seemed to conspire with the oil men. They had maintained that naval reserves were of doubtful importance, that free enterprise in the development of resources must continue, and that the oil industry would provide whatever was required by the Navy or the government. Blessed by new discoveries in 1921–23 and thereafter, oil men did provide. Also, the idea that "large-unit" production was necessary and most efficient gained increasing support.

According to a view prevalent in the business community, the Teapot Dome investigators were "muckrakers" of the 1920's, voices out of the past. They paid little heed to grand achievements of the petroleum industry. Rather, they ranted and raved about the misdeeds of a few and exaggerated out of all possible importance two little tracts called naval petroleum reserves. Other businessmen were by no means so hostile, recognizing that a scandal had occurred.[11]

---

[10] Walsh to Josephus Daniels, Raleigh, N.C., October 8, 1923, Walsh Papers; author's interview with Admiral J. O. Richardson (ret.), March 27, 1961. In 1929 a federal jury found Fall guilty of accepting a bribe, but those who gave him the money escaped conviction. For contempt of the Senate and tampering with a jury Harry Sinclair did receive a short sentence.

[11] See Robert A. Waller, "Business and the Initiation of the Teapot Dome Investigation," *Business History Review*, XXXVI (Autumn, 1962), 334–353, for an analysis of tendencies and divergencies in business opinion. As the origins of Teapot Dome would suggest, independents in the oil industry were most critical of the Fall leases and therefore most sympathetic toward the Senate investigation. Mark L. Requa, by 1925, seemed to be trying hard to prove that the real criminals were officials like Josephus Daniels, who had interfered with and misunderstood the petroleum industry and by their

From a later vantage point, it seems apparent that both sides were "right" in the long dispute over naval reserves. Almost inevitably the federal government in the twentieth century assumed a larger responsibility for its own public lands, broadened its supervision or control of private business as affecting the public interest, and engaged in limited competition with business. The creation of naval reserves was a part of this trend. Petroleum experts of 1908 and 1909, soberly predicting shortages in the near future, had pointed the way to executive action. As it happened, their predictions were much too pessimistic, so in that respect the naval petroleum reserves were based upon a wrong idea. Nevertheless, those in the government who originated or fought for conservation policies were ahead of their times, and they merited most of the praise received.

Men like La Follette, Daniels, Pinchot, Walsh, and Slattery performed a relatively disinterested public service. If at times they seemed fanatical, they faced opponents who were no less fanatical; those, for example, who had flatly denied the government's right to establish the reserves. They also showed in the case of Teapot Dome that their "fanatical" charges of corruption were true.

Always the oil question had been mixed with politics. However, nothing so big as Teapot Dome had occurred before, and Democrats believed in the spring of 1924 that they could win the presidency with this issue. But everything seemed to go wrong for them. Harding had died in August, 1923, and Calvin Coolidge moved into the White House. "Puritan Cal" handled himself with political finesse and was able to perch on the upswing of the business cycle. When the Democrats attacked, charging flagrant corruption, the Republicans counterattacked. Republicans also cleaned house sufficiently to protect themselves.[12]

The Democratic failure is partly explained by the origins of

"blind obstinancy" had "largely lost" the naval reserves. Mark L. Requa, *The Relation of Government to Industry*, New York, 1925, pp. 119–120. For a mid-century defense of the continued maintenance of the petroleum reserves see Matthew V. Carson, Jr. (Commander, U.S. Navy), "The Case for the Naval Petroleum Reserves," *United States Naval Institute Proceedings*, LXXIX (March, 1953), 267–271.

[12] J. Leonard Bates, "The Teapot Dome Scandal and the Election of 1924," *American Historical Review*, LX (January, 1955), 303–322; Noggle, *Teapot Dome*, pp. 152–176 and *passim*, for the story in greater detail.

Teapot Dome. Conservation was a bipartisan policy. It first had flourished in the era of Theodore Roosevelt. Then, under Taft, came major withdrawals of petroleum land. Taft's administration also added the naval reserves in California, and Woodrow Wilson added Teapot Dome. Opposition to the new policies came primarily from the West. Even Senator Walsh had favored at one point leases within the petroleum reserves, and many western Democrats (like Key Pittman of Nevada) had a point of view that closely resembled Albert B. Fall's.

The major parties were divided. Neither, as a political organization, had a good record on petroleum. They carried "the smell of petroleum, both crude and refined," according to one newspaper.[13] Ideologically they had differed but little on this question. Each had yielded to special interests, although Republicans became conspicuously susceptible to criticism in the Harding years.

Meanwhile, bipartisan defenders of the naval reserves went on with their task. Senator La Follette and the Pinchot group (progressive Republicans) joined with Senators Kendrick, Walsh, other Democrats, and with assorted government leaders and private citizens, to launch and bring to a successful conclusion the oil investigations.

---

[13] *Springfield* (Massachusetts) *Republican,* February 3, 1924.

# Bibliography of Manuscripts and Works Cited

## I. Manuscripts

### A. Personal Papers

Baker, Ray Stannard. Papers, Library of Congress.

Borah, William E. Papers, Library of Congress.

Burleson, Albert S. Papers, Library of Congress.

Daniels, Josephus. Papers, Library of Congress.

Fall, Albert B. Papers, Huntington Library, San Marino, Calif.

Gregory, Thomas W. Papers, Library of Congress.

House, Edward M. Diary, Yale University Library, New Haven, Conn.

Ickes, Harold L. Papers, Library of Congress.

Johnson, Hiram. Papers, Bancroft Library, University of California, Berkeley.

Kendrick, John B. Papers, University of Wyoming Library, Laramie.

Norris, George W. Papers, Library of Congress.

Pinchot, Amos. Papers, Library of Congress.

Pinchot, Gifford. Papers, Library of Congress.

Pittman, Key. Papers, Library of Congress.

Roosevelt, Theodore, Jr. Papers and Diaries, Library of Congress.

Rowell, Chester. Papers, Bancroft Library, University of California, Berkeley.

Slattery, Harry A. Papers, Duke University Library, Durham, N.C.

Walsh, Thomas J. Papers, Library of Congress.

White, William Allen. Papers, Library of Congress.

Wilson, Woodrow. Papers, Library of Congress.

### B. National Archives

Department of the Interior. Correspondence of the Secretary of the Interior and Records of the General Land Office, 1909–24.

Department of Justice. Correspondence of the Attorney General and Public Land Division, 1913–25.

Department of the Navy. Correspondence of the Secretary of the Navy and of Officers in the Bureau of Engineering, 1913–40.

C. AUTHOR'S INTERVIEWS

Mrs. Edwin Denby, October 31, 1959.
Admiral J. O. Richardson (ret.), March 27, 1961.

II. PUBLIC DOCUMENTS

A. EXECUTIVE DEPARTMENTS

Department of the Interior. *Annual Reports.* Washington, 1913–18.
———. *The Classification of the Public Lands,* by George Otis Smith
and others. Bulletin 537, United States Geological Survey. Wash-
ington, 1913.
———. *Decisions of the Department of the Interior in Cases Relating
to the Public Lands,* vol. 48 (February 1, 1921–April 30, 1922).
Washington, 1922.
———. *Petroleum Withdrawals and Restorations Affecting the Public
Domain,* by Max W. Ball. Bulletin 623, United States Geological
Survey. Washington, 1917.
———. *Report of the Commissioner of the General Land Office.* Wash-
ington, 1915; 1921.
Department of Justice. *Annual Reports of the Attorney General of the
United States.* Washington, 1912–19.
———, Attorney General. *Withdrawn Oil Lands of the United States,*
Supplement to the Annual Report for the Fiscal Year 1915 Em-
bodying a Report upon the Litigation, House Document 593,
64 Cong., 1 Sess. Washington, 1916.
Department of the Navy. *Annual Reports.* Washington, 1902–21.
United States Federal Trade Commission. *Report on the Price of Gaso-
line in 1915.* Washington, 1917.
United States Fuel Administration. *Final Report of the United States
Fuel Administrator, 1917–1919,* by Harry A. Garfield; *Report of
the Oil Division, 1917–1919,* by Mark L. Requa. Washington,
1921.

B. UNITED STATES CONGRESS (GENERAL)

*Congressional Record,* 61–68 Cong. (1910–24).
*United States Statutes at Large,* XXXVI, Part I (1911), 1015.

C. UNITED STATES CONGRESS (SENATE AND HOUSE COMMITTEES)

HEARINGS, UNITED STATES HOUSE OF REPRESENTATIVES

*Oil-Land Withdrawals and the Protection of Locators of Oil Lands,*
Hearings Before the Committee on Public Lands on H.R. 24070,
61 Cong., 2 Sess. Washington, 1910.
*Water-Power Bill,* Hearings Before the Committee on Public Lands
on H.R. 14893, 63 Cong., 2 Sess. Washington, 1914.
*Oil Leasing Lands,* Hearings Before the Committee on Public Lands
on H.R. 3232 and S. 2812, 65 Cong., 2 Sess. Washington, 1918.

HEARINGS, UNITED STATES SENATE

*Water-Power Bill,* Hearings Before the Committee on Public Lands on H.R. 16673, 63 Cong., 3 Sess. Washington, 1914.

*Leasing of Oil Lands,* Hearings Before the Committee on Public Lands on H.R. 406, 64 Cong., 1 Sess. Washington, 1916.

*Oil-Land Leasing Bill,* Hearings Before the Committee on Naval Affairs on "So-called Relief Provisions of the Leasing Bill Relative to the California Naval Petroleum Reserve," 64 Cong., 2 Sess. Washington, 1917.

*Leasing of Oil Lands,* Hearings Before the Committee on Public Lands on S. 45, 65 Cong., 1 Sess. Washington, 1917.

*Leases upon Naval Oil Reserves,* Hearings Before the Committee on Public Lands and Surveys Pursuant to S. Res. 282, S. Res. 294, and S. Res. 434, 67 Cong., and S. Res. 147, 68 Cong. 3 vols. Washington, 1924.

HEARINGS, JOINT COMMITTEES

*General Leasing Bill,* Proceedings of the Special Joint Conference of the Committees on Public Lands and Representatives of the Departments of Justice, Navy, and Interior, on H.R. 406, 64 Cong., 2 Sess. Washington, 1917.

REPORTS, UNITED STATES HOUSE OF REPRESENTATIVES

*Locators of Oil and Gas on the Public Domain,* House Report 519, 63 Cong., 2 Sess. (6559). Washington, 1914.

*Exploration for and Disposition of Coal, Oil, Gas, etc.,* 2 pts., House Report 668, 63 Cong., 2 Sess. (6559). Washington, 1914.

*Oil or Gas Lands,* House Report 695, 63 Cong., 2 Sess. (6559). Washington, 1914.

REPORTS, UNITED STATES SENATE

*Exploration for and Disposition of Coal, Phosphate, Oil, Gas, etc.,* Senate Report 319, pt. 2, 64 Cong., 1 Sess. (6898). Washington, 1916.

*Reserve Oil Supply for United States Navy,* Senate Report 481, 61 Cong., 1 Sess. (5583). Washington, 1910.

DOCUMENTS, UNITED STATES SENATE

*Mining and Metallurgical Society of America,* Senate Document 233, 64 Cong., 1 Sess., vol. 41 (6951). Washington, 1916.

D. FEDERAL COURT CASES

Supreme Court of the United States. *Burke v. Southern Pacific Railroad Company,* 58 Law. Ed., 234 U.S. 1527 (1914).

———. *U.S. v. Midwest Oil Company et al.,* 59 Law. Ed., 236 U.S. 673 (1915).

———. *U.S., Appt., v. Southern Pacific Company et al.,* 64 Law. Ed., 251 U.S. 97 (Elk Hills, 1919).

Circuit Court of Appeals, Ninth Circuit. *Southern Pac. Co. et al. v. United States,* 249 Fed. Rep. 785 (1918).

District Court, N.D. California, S.D. *United States* v. *Southern Pac. Co.,* 260 Fed. Rep. 511 (1919).

E. MISCELLANEOUS

*Oil Land Leasing Act of 1920 with Amendments and Other Laws Relating to Mineral Lands,* compiled by Elmer A. Lewis. Washington, 1952.

F. STATE OF CALIFORNIA

McLaughlin, R. P., and Waring, C. A. *Petroleum Industry of California.* Bulletin 69, California State Mining Bureau. Sacramento, 1914.
Secretary of State. *Statement of Vote.* Sacramento, 1916.


III. NEWSPAPERS

*Curb News* (New York), October 22, 1917.
*Helena* (Montana) *Independent,* February 17, 1924.
*New York Times,* January 7, November 10, 1916; April 28, 1918; December 6, 1919; November 19, 1920; March 26, 28, 1940.
*San Francisco Chronicle,* November 10, 1916; March 1, 2, 3, 1919.
*Springfield* (Massachusetts) *Republican,* February 3, 1924.


IV. CONTEMPORARY LITERATURE

Arnold, Ralph. "The California Oil Industry," *The Journal of Geography,* IX (June, 1911), 270–272.
Baird, Joseph H. "Key Pittman: Frontier Statesman," *American Mercury,* L (July, 1940), 206–319.
"The Baker-Lane Controversy," *The Outlook,* CXVI (July 11, 1917), 385.
"Bedford on War Organization of the Petroleum Industry," *The Oil Age,* XIV (April, 1918), 14–15.
"Big Merger Progresses," *National Petroleum News,* Oil Producer's Section, VII (May, 1915), 23.
"Business and the War," *Army and Navy Journal,* LV (September 29, 1917), 155.
"Business's Big Bit," *Standard Oil Bulletin,* V (July, 1917), 1.
"C. A. Canfield Dead," *The Oil Age,* VIII (August 22, 1913), 1.
Colby, William E. "The New Public Land Policy with Special Reference to Oil Lands," *California Law Review,* III (May, 1915), 269–291.
"Coming Age To Be One of Petroleum, Says Clark," *National Petroleum News,* X (April 3, 1918), 16.
"Commission Must Not Disturb Requa's Control," *National Petroleum News,* X (May 15, 1918), 11.
"Conservation," *Standard Oil Bulletin,* III (July, 1915), 1–2.

Creel, George. "Daniel of the Gold Fields," *Collier's*, XCVII (April 25, 1936), 25.

————. "The Oil Story," *Pearson's Magazine*, XXXVI (September, 1916), 197–202.

"Crippling Industry at Public Expense," *Standard Oil Bulletin*, VII (July, 1919), 1–2.

Daniels, Josephus. "Fuel Oil for the Navy," *Journal of the American Society of Naval Engineers*, XXXIII (February, 1921), 60–63.

Day, David T. "Fuel Oils: Their Origin, Production and Treatment," *United States Naval Institute Proceedings*, XL (January–February, 1914), 79–102.

Dunn, Arthur Wallace. "An Interested Westerner," *Sunset*, XXXII (May, 1914), 1095–97.

————. "The New Attorney General," *The American Review of Reviews*, LIX (April, 1919), 374–375.

Editorials, *The Independent*, XIC (July 7, 1917), 13–14; (August 25, 1917), 274; (September 1, 1917), 312; (September 8, 1917), 384.

Erwin, Will. "Franklin K. Lane, the Story of a Presidential Impossibility," *Collier's*, LVI (February 26, 1916), 12–13, 30, 32–33, 36.

"Fights Requa on Pipe Line Ruling," *National Petroleum News*, X (April 10, 1918), 38.

"For a Common-Sense Policy," *Standard Oil Bulletin*, V (March, 1918), 1–2.

Gilman, C. H. "Important Decision," *Oil and Gas Journal*, XIV (January 13, 1916), 60.

"Government Oil Land Suits," *The Oil Age*, VI (July 26, 1912), 8.

"Governor in Committee Reports Findings," *The Oil Age*, XIII (July, 1917), 10–14.

"A Great Public Servant," *The Outlook*, CXXIV (February 18, 1920), 268.

Hale, Sydney A. "The Coal Problem of Today," *World's Work*, XXXVI (July, 1918), 318–328.

Hall, Wilbur. "How Doheny Did It," *Sunset*, XIL (July, 1918), 21–23.

Hay, James, Jr. "The Fighting Commissioner," *Cosmopolitan*, L (March, 1911), 569–570.

Hendrick, Burton J. "The American Home Secretary," *World's Work*, XXVI (August, 1913), 396–405.

Hungerford, Edward. "A. C. Bedford," *System*, XXXIII (July, 1917), 48–49.

"In the Driftway," *Nation*, CVII (December 14, 1918), 730.

"Introducing New U.S. Oil Controller," *National Petroleum News*, X (January 16, 1918), 11.

"Investigations," *Standard Oil Bulletin*, VII (December, 1919), 1–2.

La Follette, Robert M. "Husting's Death Is Loss to People," *La Follette's Magazine*, IX (November, 1917), 1.

Lane, Franklin K. "Land Is Land: An Ancient Fallacy Exposed," *The Independent*, LXXVIII (April 6, 1914), 18–21.

———. "Red Tape in Alaska," *The Outlook*, CIX (January 20, 1915), 135–140.

———. "Some Results of This War," *Harper's Weekly*, LX (April 3, 1915), 318.

"Lane Says Relief Is Due California Operator," *National Petroleum News*, VII (December, 1915), 93.

"Lane, the White Hope of the Wilson Cabinet," *Current Opinion*, LV (September, 1913), 163–164.

"Leasing System for Mineral Lands," *The Oil Age*, V (February 2, 1912), 9.

Lenroot, Irvine L. "The War Loyalty of Wisconsin," *Forum*, LIX (June, 1918), 695–702.

"Lenroot and La Follette: A Contrast," *The Outlook*, CXV (April 18, 1917), 691.

"A Litigious and Profitless Policy," *Standard Oil Bulletin*, VII (September, 1919), 1–2.

Low, A. Maurice. "The South in the Saddle," *Harper's Weekly*, LVII (February 8, 1913), 20.

"Makes New Appeal on Pipe Line Order," *National Petroleum News*, X (May 29, 1918), 7.

"Marketers May Refuse Oil from Government Land," *The Oil Age*, VII (April 25, 1913), 1–2.

Maxwell, William O. "Oil Men vs. Government Agents," *The Oil Age*, XVI (May, 1920), 12–18.

McGregor (A. J. McKelway). "Unlocking the Far West," *Harper's Weekly*, LVIII (April 4, 1914), 15.

Meyer, George v. L. "Is Our Navy Going Right?" *Harper's Weekly*, LX (April 10, 1915), 346–347.

Middleton, James. "A New West: The Attempts to Open Up the Natural Treasures of the Western States—Utilization and Conservation vs. Monopolistic Greed—the Department of the Interior," *World's Work*, XXXI (April, 1916), 669–680.

"Mr. A. C. Bedford on Thrift and Investing," *World's Work*, XXXVI (June, 1918), 133.

"The National Oil Policy," *Standard Oil Bulletin*, IX (February, 1922), 1–2.

"Naval Board to Investigate Oil Supply," *The Oil Age*, XII (June, 1916), 14.

"The Navy and Its Oil Supply," *Standard Oil Bulletin*, VIII (August, 1920), 1–2.

"Navy May Become an Oil Operator," *National Petroleum News*, X (January 30, 1918), 13.

"The Navy's Oil Supply—a Protest," *Standard Oil Bulletin*, VII (August, 1919), 1–2.

"No Naval Reserve Lands," *The Oil Age*, VI (November 22, 1912), 8–9.

"Notes from the Capital—Franklin Knight Lane," *Nation*, CII (January 20, 1916), 70.

"Oil Committee Deserves Trade's Solid Backing," *National Petroleum News*, IX (July, 1917), 9.

"The Oil Industry Association," *Standard Oil Bulletin*, III (November, 1915), 1–2.

"Oil Industry Faces Government Regulation," *National Petroleum News*, IX (July, 1917), 8.

"Oil Land Bill Not Yet out of Committee," *The Oil Age*, XIV (April, 1918), 1.

"Oil Land Legislation Taken Up," *The Oil Age*, XIII (December, 1917), 1.

"Oil Leasing Bill Will Not Be Vetoed," *The Oil and Gas Journal*, XIV (June 1, 1916), 28.

"Organization for Conservation," *Oil and Gas Journal*, IX (August 25, 1910), 8.

Peabody, E. H. "Developments in Oil Burning," *Transactions of the Society of Naval Architects and Marine Engineers*, XX (proceedings of the twentieth annual meeting of the Society, 1912), 245–283.

———. "Recent Developments in Oil Fuel Burning," *International Marine Engineering*, XVIII (February, 1913), 60–64.

Pinchot, Gifford. "How Conservation Began," *Agricultural History*, XI (October, 1937), 255–265.

"A Plea for Peace," *Standard Oil Bulletin*, II (April, 1915), 1–2, 16.

"The President and the Public Lands," *The Outlook*, CIX (March 24, 1915), 657.

"Produce More Oil," *Standard Oil Bulletin*, VI (May, 1918), 1–2.

"Promoting a Crisis," *Standard Oil Bulletin*, V (May, 1917), 1–2.

"Requa Adds Another Californian to Staff," *National Petroleum News*, X (April 17, 1918), 12.

Richardson, J. O. "Naval Petroleum Reserves No. 1 and No. 2," *United States Naval Institute Proceedings*, XLII (January–February, 1916), 93–123.

Rowell, Chester H. "The Campaign in California," *The New Republic*, XXIV (October 13, 1920), 164–166.

"Seek Development of Coast Reserve," *National Petroleum News*, X (May 8, 1918), 38.

"Senator Phelan's Amendment," *Oil and Gas Journal*, XIV (February 10, 1916), 26–27.

Sherman, E. A. "The Supreme Court of the United States and Conservation Policies," *Journal of Forestry*, XIX (December, 1921), 928–930.

Smith, George Otis. "Where the World Gets Its Oil," *National Geographic Magazine*, XXXVII (February, 1920), 181–202.

"Southern Pacific Loses Elk Hills Land," *The Oil Age,* XV (December, 1919), 1.

"Southern Pacific Wins," *The Oil Age,* XV (September, 1919), 12–14.

"Southern Pacific Wins First Round," *The Oil Age,* IX (June 26, 1914), 8–9.

"Standard Oil Company's Position as Result of Oil Land Litigation," *Standard Oil Bulletin,* I (October, 1913), 1–2.

"Successful Oil Burning Steamer Test," *Army and Navy Journal,* XXXIX (May 31, 1902), 983.

Sullivan, Mark. "Public Men and Big Business," *World's Work,* XLVII (April, 1924), 607–613.

"A Surfeit of Investigations," *Oil and Gas Journal,* XXI (June 22, 1922), 10.

"Thomas W. Gregory," *Newsweek,* I (March 4, 1933), 19.

"Title to Mining Lands," *Salt Lake Mining Review,* XVI (August 15, 1914), 16–17.

"To Challenge Its Loyalty Unfair: Business, Which Must Pay for and Conduct the War, Gives No Cause for Such Remarks as Came from President," *National Petroleum News,* IX (July, 1917), 7.

"Trade Commission Charges Profiteering by Oil Trade," *National Petroleum News,* X (May 1, 1918), 1.

"Trend Towards Further Regulation," *National Petroleum News,* X (May 22, 1918), 5–7.

Turnbull, Archibald Douglas. "Seven Years of Daniels," *The North American Review,* CCXII (November, 1920), 606–617.

"Waking Up to Facts," *Standard Oil Bulletin,* II (March, 1915), 1–2.

Welliver, Judson C. "The Triumph of the South," *Munsey's Magazine,* XLIX (August, 1913), 731–743.

"What Is a Fair Price for Coal," *Survey,* XXXVII (December 2, 1916), 247–249.

Willsie, Honoré. "Mr. Lane and the Public Domain," *Harper's Weekly,* LVIII (in 4 pts.): "The New Word in Washington" (August 23, 1913), 6–8; " 'The New Freedom' in Washington" (August 30, 1913), 6–8; "Young America in Washington" (September 6, 1913), 6–8; "A Renaissance in Washington" (September 13, 1913), 6–8.

"Wilson Holds Fate of Oil Trade," *National Petroleum News,* X (May 8, 1918), 5.

Woehlke, Walter V. "Grabbing the West's Liquid Fuel," *Technical World Magazine,* XVII (June, 1912), 372–383.

———. "Legalizing Land Burglary," *Sunset,* XXXIII (July, 1914), 159–160.

———. "Petroleum and the Placer Claim," *The Outlook,* XCVI (December 24, 1910), 951–960.

V. Memoirs, Reminiscences, Autobiographies,
and Published Letters

Atherton, Gertrude. *California: An Intimate History*. New York: Harper and Brothers, 1927.
——. *My San Francisco: A Wayward Biography*. New York: Bobbs-Merrill, 1946.
Butt, Archie. *Taft and Roosevelt: The Intimate Letters of Archie Butt, Military Aide*. 2 vols. Garden City, N.Y.: Doubleday, Doran and Company, 1930.
Connelly, W. L. *The Oil Business as I Saw It: Half a Century with Sinclair*. Norman: University of Oklahoma Press, 1954.
Daniels, Josephus. *Editor in Politics*. Chapel Hill: University of North Carolina Press, 1941.
——. *The Wilson Era: Years of Peace, 1910–1917*. Chapel Hill: University of North Carolina Press, 1944.
——. *The Wilson Era: Years of War and After, 1917–1923*. Chapel Hill: University of North Carolina Press, 1946.
Lane, Franklin K. *The American Spirit: Addresses in Wartime*. New York: Frederick A. Stokes Company, 1918.
——. *The Letters of Franklin K. Lane*, edited by Anne W. Lane and Louise H. Wall. Boston: Houghton Mifflin Company, 1922.
Longworth, Alice Roosevelt. *Crowded Hours*. New York: Charles Scribner's Sons, 1933.
McAdoo, William G. *Crowded Years*. Boston: Houghton Mifflin Company, 1931.
Roosevelt, Theodore. *An Autobiography*. New York: Charles Scribner's Sons, 1926.
Steffens, Joseph Lincoln. *The Autobiography of Lincoln Steffens*. New York: Harcourt, Brace and Company, 1931.


VI. Secondary Accounts

A. Books

Barron, Clarence W. *The Mexican Problem*. Boston: Houghton Mifflin Company, 1917.
Blum, John M. *Joe Tumulty and the Wilson Era*. Boston: Houghton Mifflin Company, 1951.
Camp, William Martin. *San Francisco: Port of Gold*. Garden City, N.Y.: Doubleday and Company, 1947.
Cleland, Robert Glass, and Hardy, Osgood. *March of Industry*. San Francisco: Powell Publishing Company, 1929.
Daggett, Stuart. *Chapters on the History of the Southern Pacific*. New York: Ronald Press Company, 1922.
Daniels, Jonathan. *The End of Innocence*. Philadelphia: Lippincott, 1954.

Davis, George T. *A Navy Second to None.* New York: Harcourt, Brace and Company, 1940.

Debo, Angie. *And Still the Waters Run.* Princeton, N.J.: Princeton University Press, 1940.

Forbes, Bertie C. *Men Who Are Making the West.* New York: B. C. Forbes Publishing Company, 1923.

Gabriel, Ralph H. *The Course of American Democratic Thought.* 2nd ed. New York: Ronald Press Company, 1956.

Giddens, Paul H. *Standard Oil Company (Indiana): Oil Pioneer of the Middle West.* New York: Appleton-Century-Crofts, 1955.

Gruening, Ernest. *The State of Alaska.* New York: Random House, 1954.

Hays, Samuel P. *Conservation and the Gospel of Efficiency: The Progressive Conservation Movement, 1890–1920.* Cambridge, Mass.: Harvard University Press, 1959.

Hoffman, Lewis Edwin. *Oil and Gas Leasing on the Public Domain.* Denver, Colo.: F. H. Gower, 1951.

Ise, John. *Our National Park Policy: A Critical History.* Published for Resources for the Future, Inc. Baltimore, Md.: The Johns Hopkins Press, 1961.

———. *The United States Oil Policy.* New Haven, Conn.: Yale University Press, 1926.

Kerwin, Jerome G. *Federal Water Power Legislation.* New York: Columbia University Press, 1926.

La Follette, Belle C. and Fola. *Robert M. La Follette.* 2 vols. New York: Macmillan, 1953.

Lesher, C. E. *Prices of Coal and Coke.* Washington: Government Printing Office, 1919.

Link, Arthur S. *Wilson: The New Freedom.* Princeton, N.J.: Princeton University Press, 1956.

Maxwell, Robert S. *La Follette and the Rise of the Progressives in Wisconsin.* Madison: State Historical Society of Wisconsin, 1956.

McGeary, M. Nelson. *Gifford Pinchot: Forester-Politician.* Princeton. N.J.: Princeton University Press, 1960.

Mowry, George E. *The California Progressives.* Berkeley: University of California Press, 1951.

Noggle, Burl. *Teapot Dome: Oil and Politics in the 1920's.* Baton Rouge: Louisiana State University Press, 1962.

Pinchot, Amos R. E. *History of the Progressive Party, 1912–1916,* edited by Helene M. Hooker. New York: New York University Press, 1958.

Pinchot, Gifford. *Breaking New Ground.* New York: Harcourt, Brace and Company, 1947.

Requa, Mark L. *The Relation of Government to Industry.* New York: Macmillan, 1925.

Richardson, Elmo R. *The Politics of Conservation: Crusades and Con-*

*troversies, 1897–1913,* University of California Publications in History, vol. 70. Berkeley: University of California Press, 1962.

Rister, Carl C. *Oil! Titan of the Southwest.* Norman: University of Oklahoma Press, 1949.

Robbins, Roy M. *Our Landed Heritage.* Princeton, N.J.: Princeton University Press, 1942.

Roberts, Harold D. *Salt Creek Wyoming: The Story of a Great Oil Field.* Denver, Colo.: W. H. Kistler Stationery Company, 1956.

*Roosevelt and Daniels,* edited by Carroll Kilpatrick. Chapel Hill: University of North Carolina Press, 1952.

Stewart, Kenneth, and Tebbel, John. *Makers of Modern Journalism.* New York: Prentice-Hall, 1952.

Van Hise, Charles R. *The Conservation of Natural Resources.* New York: Macmillan, 1913.

Werner, Morris R. *Privileged Characters.* New York: R. W. McBride and Company, 1935.

———, and Starr, John. *Teapot Dome.* New York: The Viking Press, 1959.

White, Gerald T. *Formative Years in the Far West: A History of Standard Oil Company of California and Predecessors Through 1919.* New York: Appleton-Century-Crofts, 1962.

Zimmermann, Erich W. *Conservation in the Production of Petroleum: A Study in Industrial Control.* New Haven, Conn.: Yale University Press, 1957.

B. ARTICLES

Bagby, Wesley B. "The 'Smoke-Filled Room' and the Nomination of Warren G. Harding," *The Mississippi Valley Historical Review* (Cedar Rapids, Iowa), XLI (March, 1955), 658–671.

———. "Woodrow Wilson, a Third Term, and the Solemn Referendum," *The American Historical Review* (Washington), LX (April, 1955), 567–575.

Bates, J. Leonard. "Fulfilling American Democracy: The Conservation Movement, 1907–1921," *The Mississippi Valley Historical Review,* XLIV (June, 1957), 29–57.

———. "The Midwest Decision, 1915: A Landmark in Conservation History," *Pacific Northwest Quarterly* (Seattle), LI (January, 1960), 26–34.

———. "The Teapot Dome Scandal and the Election of 1924," *The American Historical Review,* LX (January, 1955), 303–322.

Carson, Matthew V., Jr. "The Case for the Naval Petroleum Reserves," *United States Naval Institute Proceedings,* LXXIX (March, 1953), 267–271.

Cronon, E. David. "Josephus Daniels as a Reluctant Candidate," *The North Carolina Historical Review* (Raleigh), XXXIII (October, 1956), 457–482.

DeNovo, John A. "Petroleum and the United States Navy Before

World War I," *The Mississippi Valley Historical Review,* XLI (March, 1955), 641–656.

Fausold, Martin L. "Gifford Pinchot and the Decline of Pennsylvania Progressivism," *Pennsylvania History* (Gettysburg), XXV (January, 1958), 25–38.

Link, Arthur S. "The Wilson Movement in North Carolina," *The North Carolina Historical Review,* XXIII (October, 1946), 483–494.

Livermore, Seward W. "The Sectional Issue in the 1918 Congressional Elections," *The Mississippi Valley Historical Review,* XXXV (June, 1948), 29–60.

McGee, W J. "The Conservation of Natural Resources," The Mississippi Valley Historical Association, *Proceedings for the Year 1909–1910* (Cedar Rapids, Iowa), III (1911), 361–379.

Noggle, Burl. "The Origins of the Teapot Dome Investigation," *The Mississippi Valley Historical Review,* XLIV (September, 1957), 237–266.

Rakestraw, Lawrence. "The West, States' Rights, and Conservation: A Study of Six Public Land Conferences," *Pacific Northwest Quarterly,* XLVIII (July, 1957), 89–99.

Stratton, David H. "Behind Teapot Dome: Some Personal Insights," *The Business History Review* (Boston), XXXI (Winter, 1957), 385–402.

———. "New Mexican Machiavellian? The Story of Albert B. Fall," *Montana: The Magazine of Western History* (Helena), VII (October, 1957), 2–14.

Waller, Robert A. "Business and the Initiation of the Teapot Dome Investigation," *The Business History Review,* XXXVI (Autumn, 1962), 334–353.

Warth, Robert D. "The Palmer Raids," *The South Atlantic Quarterly* (Durham, N.C.), XLVIII (January, 1949), 1–23.

## VII. Unpublished Studies and Accounts

Bagby, Wesley M. "Progressivism's Debacle: The Election of 1920." Unpublished Ph.D. dissertation, Columbia University, New York, 1954.

Bates, J. Leonard. "Senator Walsh of Montana, 1918–1924." Unpublished Ph.D. dissertation, University of North Carolina, Chapel Hill, 1952.

Fisher, Walter L. "Autobiography." Manuscript copy, presented by his son, Walter T. Fisher, Chicago, in possession of the author.

Hennings, Robert Edward. "James D. Phelan and the Wilson Progressives of California." Unpublished Ph.D. dissertation, University of California, Berkeley, 1961.

Miller, Phillip Harlowe. "The Role of Secretary of the Navy, Edwin

Denby, in the Teapot Dome Affair." Unpublished undergraduate Honors thesis, University of Illinois, Urbana, 1957.

Pinkett, Harold T. "Gifford Pinchot and the Early Conservation Movement in the United States." Unpublished Ph.D. dissertation, American University, Washington, D.C., 1953.

Reed, Thomas T. "Newspaper Justice." Unpublished manuscript, New York, 1936, copy in possession of the author.

Stratton, David H. "Albert B. Fall and the Teapot Dome Affair." Unpublished Ph.D. dissertation, University of Colorado, Boulder, 1955.

Tracie, R. G. "History of the Naval Petroleum Reserves." Unpublished manuscript, compiled in 1937, copy in Josephus Daniels Papers, Box 264, Library of Congress.

Waller, Robert A. "Business Reactions to the Teapot Dome Affair, 1922 to 1925." Unpublished Master's thesis, University of Illinois, Urbana, 1958.

Wiens, Henry W. "The Career of Franklin K. Lane in California Politics." Unpublished Master's thesis, University of California, Berkeley, 1936.

# Index

fers bill, 53; opposes Midwest decision, 60

Clark, Sheldon: on oil men in World War I, 97

Claimants: seek congressional aid, 62; excessive demands, 63; and Phelan bill, 85–87; and Swanson plan, 122–124; and wartime strategy, 124; attacked by Gregory, 196–197; under leasing law, 213–216 *passim;* blackmail Sinclair, 238; routed by marines, 238; mentioned, 98. *See also* Oil lobbyists; Oil men; Relief

Coal crisis, 101–103

Coal operators: meeting of, 101–102

Cobb, Frank, 95

Commandeering: considered for increased production, 107; and Navy plans, 135–136; considered for West Coast, 143; compromise attempt, 144–145; and Salt Creek field, 145–149, 173; planned, 150. *See also* Government operation; Navy Department

Commandeering bill, 132, 135, 139; debated, 139–140; criticized, 138–139, 141

Committee on Coal Production, 103

Compromise: early failure to achieve, 85, 114; efforts in 1917, 121–124; new antagonisms of wartime, 124–125; legislative failure of 1918–19, 144–145; new influences, 181, 182; laws of 1920, 198–199, 206–207; and compromise on broader front, 218. *See also* Claimants; Daniels, Josephus

Connelly, W. L.: quoted on scramble for oil, 14

Conservation: as bipartisan policy, 2, 10–11, 244; as coordinated movement, 2–10; as democratic movement, 3–4; Republican origins, 4; lawyers in movement,

4–5; and conservatism, 7; and southerners, 7; defined by *Standard Oil Bulletin,* 8; in Ballinger-Pinchot affair, 8; and election of 1912, 9; influence of Wisconsinites, 9–10; under Wilson summarized, 10–11; and oil claimants, 28; importance in 1916, 79; under Lane, 80–83; and new spirit abroad, 146; and Senate debate, 164; party records on, 183; in Congress, 194–195; and leasing law of 1920, 198. *See also* Lane, Franklin K.; Oil land policy; Pinchot, Gifford; Wilson, Woodrow

Conservationists: as progressives, 3; aims, 3–4; cleavages, 7–10; weakened by deaths, 134; as supporters of Harding, 210–212; guard against "reaction," 220–221; as violative of tradition, 222; strength, 234–235; as pessimists on oil supply, 243; public service of, 243; as "fanatics," 243. *See also* "Pinchot group"; West

Consolidated Midway Oil Company, 42

Consolidated suit: Southern Pacific wins, 174–175; chances of appeal, 175–176; appeal expected, 176. *See also* Southern Pacific cases

Continental Oil Company, 137n

Coolidge, Calvin: political finesse, 243

Corruption. *See* Bribery

Cotter, Joseph J.: joins Pan-American Petroleum Company, 220

Council of National Defense, 98, 99, 103

Cox, James M.: doomed to defeat, 208

Cox, Thomas: joins Oil Division, 106

Creel, George: possible influence on Wilson, 159n; joins Doheny